T0282072

A Man Returns

The Journey of a Seawolf

BEN "SMITTY" SMITH

A Man Returns: The Journey of a Seawolf
Copyright © 2023 by Benjamin "Smitty" Smith

Published by: HigherLife Publishing & Marketing
PO Box 623307
Oviedo, FL 32762
AHigherLife.com

ISBN 978-1-958211-35-9 (paperback)
ISBN 978-1-958211-94-6 (ebook)

LCCN 2023917134

BIO-023000 BIOGRAPHY & AUTOBIOGRAPHY / Adventurers & Explorers
BIO-008000 BIOGRAPHY & AUTOBIOGRAPHY / Military
BIO-034000 BIOGRAPHY & AUTOBIOGRAPHY / Aviation & Nautical

Printed in the United States of America

10 9 8 7 6 5 4 3 2 1

IN MEMORY OF JOY E. SMITH

I'm writing this book in memory of my mother. She always wanted me to write my story, but there was never time nor desire. My mom passed away in 2006. She was a published poet and wrote children's stories. My mom loved the Seawolves. She said we were knights in shining armor. I credit her for being able to write this book. She saved all my letters and anything related to the Seawolves. Without her contribution, this book would not have been possible. She felt like our story should be told. She was a big *Reader's Digest* fan and had a subscription forever. She wrote suggesting they do a story on the Seawolves. She did not hear back from them. She wrote them again, a stronger letter this time. She finally heard back: they would not be writing a Seawolf story. She was heartbroken, and promptly canceled her subscription, demanding a refund for the remaining year. After that, she would no longer purchase any of their products.

I returned home the summer of 1969 for a thirty-day leave. While I was home, my mom wrote a poem titled "A Man Returns." I thought it only appropriate that I name this book after that poem.

A Man Returns

by Joy E. Smith (1931-2006)

The tired lines around the eyes,

tell the true story behind the smiles.

The restless pacing of the floor,

shows the terrible marks of war.

A Man Returns

A man returns to the ones he loves

    and kneels and prays to his God above,

Thanks be to Him for life and limb,

    but with laden heart he remembers his friends

Who will never again walk the earth green

    Or smell the rain so cool and clean.

With gas pedal pressed to the floor,

    He tries to erase it forever more,

But there is no escaping this terrible pain.

    No longer the world will be the same.

The depths of hell: a boy falls in

    and a man returns with mankind's sins.

ACKNOWLEDGMENTS

I would like to thank a few people who helped make this book possible: my wife, Rachelle, my daughter, Michelle Hagerty, and my good friend, Bill Magerlein. A special thank you to my daughter-in-law, Casie Knospe, for being a major contributor.

Thank you all so much,

Smitty

SEAWOLVES

1968, Rung Sat Special Zone, South Vietnam, deep in the Mekong Delta region

As the pilot rolled the Huey over on its side, the only thing keeping me in the helo was inertia. I was looking straight down the barrel of my .50 cal at two sampans loaded with Viet Cong (VC) and supplies. They were headed straight toward the shore. I squeezed down on the butterfly trigger. All hell broke loose. A shower of incoming rounds severed the mount on the .50 cal, almost taking me out the door.

1967, Memphis, Tennessee, November

I came to Memphis straight out of boot camp to attend Avionics school: six months of grueling classroom work, studying aviation radar and navigation electronics. Needless to say, I was ready to get out of the classroom and do something. I always say, better to be lucky than good—and my luck has always carried me through. Speaking of luck, at muster one morning, I saw in the Plan of the Day (POD) that the Navy was forming a Special Forces helicopter attack squadron. It was all volunteer and they were signing guys up. You know what they say: never volunteer. Still, it looked right up my alley. Being a patriot, I was ready to do my part. I'd be graduating in a few days, so the timing was perfect. That afternoon I hot-trotted over to the building where they were having signups to get the total picture. My friends told me I was on my own. None of them even wanted to come and see what it was all about. All they kept saying was, "You're going to get yourself killed." The guy at the desk answered some of my questions, but told me to hold off until I saw the video about the Seawolves and listened to the presentation. Then they would have a question-and-answer segment and signups. A few days later, I and a few other guys attended the presentation. I was hooked and signed on the dotted line. I was on my way to becoming a Seawolf. Goodbye, avionics training, and hello, gunnery training and a lot more.

Before they could cut my orders to report to the Seawolves, I had to pass a list of requirements. First, I had to see a psychiatrist. He asked all kinds of crazy questions, but what it boiled down to, I think, was whether I had a death wish and was kill crazy or not. He told me the same thing the Seawolf guy told me: the life expectancy of a helicopter door gunner in Vietnam was not very good. It didn't matter. I was old school: communism had to be stopped, and at the time, I really believed we needed to help the Vietnamese people, and at the same time provide twenty-four-hour coverage for our troops and maybe even save a few lives in the process. The psychiatrist was no problem.

Next, I reported to the hospital where I spent the entire day getting checked from stem to stern. If you were color blind or did not have depth perception, you could not fly. You also had to pass a security clearance. I passed all that with flying colors and was ready for the next test—water survival. They called it swim quals, but I swear they tried to kill me. I'm okay in the water but it's not one of my strong points. I passed with no problems except for drinking half of the pool. Then it was back to the psychiatrist for one more go-round. Again, there was no problem.

They said it would be a few days for processing and that turned into two weeks. I had originally planned on being home for Thanksgiving during this time, so I was a little disappointed, as was my family. But as it turned out, Hotdog! I got orders for the Seawolves. This was a brand-new outfit, and they told us that they didn't have all the bugs worked out yet. As I was to find out, things did get a little screwy at times, but it always worked out.

I was to take a seven-day leave, then report to Seawolf training camp in Little Creek, Virginia. I broke the news to my girlfriend in Millington, just outside of Memphis. It was emotional. She had been hoping I would get stationed somewhere in the U.S. and I didn't tell her that I volunteered for Nam. We said our goodbyes and promised each other that we would write and stay in touch. We did for several months and then the letters and the phone calls got fewer and fewer.

Flying standby, which I always did, I caught a flight out of Memphis to Pittsburgh and then on to Scranton's Avoca airport in Pennsylvania. My father would not pick me up, which was no surprise. My mom doesn't drive, so she had to get a friend to take her and a couple of my siblings to the airport to pick me up. It was nice to see everyone again. My father wanted to know what the hell I was doing at home. He said, "I thought you were in the Navy." It was very cold, and snow was everywhere. Even so, it was nice.

They had a Christmas tree set up, and we celebrated Thanksgiving and Christmas together. I would still be in training and would not be coming home for the holidays. The week went by fast. I did not tell my mom that I volunteered for Nam or anything about the Seawolves. I told her about my military life insurance policy. She said she didn't want to hear about that and got very emotional. I felt that it was something that I needed to bring up and now was the only time I could. I told her I would be repairing avionics gear at a safe base in Nam and that I would be fine. She made me swear that I would write often. I had a good friend drive my mom and a couple of my sisters and me to the airport.

A Man Returns

Flying standby again, I had no trouble catching a plane to Norfolk, Virginia. Upon landing, I caught a bus to Little Creek. Let the fun begin.

The bus dropped me at the gate, and guards directed me to the building that housed the Seawolves. After a long trek with a heavy seabag, I finally found the building. There were a few guys from Memphis, and we hooked up right away. I found an empty bunk and was about to unpack my seabag when one of the guys told me I might want to hold off on that because tomorrow we were getting issued olive drab uniforms and jungle boots. This would be the last time I would wear Navy blue for the next two years.

We were treated very well everywhere we went. The chow hall was great. I know a lot of guys complain about the food, but I had no problem with it. Everything was max slack except for the training. That was a whole different story.

Our classes started on Monday, December 11, 1967, at 7 a.m. We also had physical training (PT) every day which consisted primarily of running and calisthenics, which we normally did before class. On our first day of physical training, we met our drill instructor. He had us line up, then with a clipboard in hand, he walked down the line taking names. He was having trouble with the spelling of most names, so he had everyone spell them for him. When he got to me, I told him, "I better spell it for you. S-M-I-T-H." He looked at it for a minute and said, "You and I are going to become good buddies. I'm going to see to it personally that you get the most out of each exercise." I had to go through another medical examination to make sure my body was fit enough to go through all the punishment that lay ahead.

It was rainy and cold almost every day but mostly while we were in class. We started those with an introduction to counterinsurgency followed by Vietnam orientation along with a movie about the country, what to expect, the people, their customs, and their language. The next couple days we studied Viet Cong movements and forces and more on counterinsurgency.

I got to go to the dentist, and I had a few minor problems that could be taken care of later.

On December 14, we started the good stuff I'd been waiting for. First up: the M14 and M16. We learned everything about these guns, including taking them apart and putting them back together. Later in our training, we would get to fire them too.

They introduced us to survival: building shelters, fire, traps, and how to conceal ourselves. Later in the training, we would get to do all of this in the field. We were tested regularly before we moved on to the next course.

We had a weekend off, so a couple of us caught a ride to the Norfolk Naval Station to look around. We ended up at the EM club for a few drinks. We met a sailor who was stationed on a submarine there. I told him that I had originally wanted to become a submariner on a nuclear sub, but had changed my mind when I found out that I had to sign up for six years. I didn't really want to do that without knowing whether I even liked the Navy. Instead, I had chosen avionics and the flying navy.

He invited us for a tour of his sub. How cool that was! We checked it out from stem to stern. After the tour, I was glad of the choice I had made. The sub was very tight quarters. I could have gone conventional subs with a four-year enlistment, but had decided against it.

On Sunday, we took in the big city of Norfolk. Not as big as I thought it would be. I had heard that Norfolk was not military friendly and that they had signs in their yards that read, "Sailors and dogs keep off the grass." I didn't see any of those signs, but you would think with such a large military presence there, that that wouldn't be the case.

A Man Returns

December 18–20

Back to school, and what a week. We spent a lot of time in the field. We learned about (and got to fire) the M79 grenade launcher and the 60 mm and 80 mm mortars. We learned to take apart (and put back together) .30 and .50 caliber machine guns. We also spent time on the range learning to fire all these weapons. We spent more time on the M60 machine gun than all the rest. It would be the weapon we used most of the time. We learned to take it apart and put it back together *blindfolded.* We had a class on maintaining and cleaning all these weapons. We also learned about first aid, health, and hygiene in the field.

The Operational Training Squadron (VOT) put on a full-blown ambush fire power demonstration for us. So impressive. It was quite different to watching it on TV. It reverberated right through you and the smoke was unbelievable. I like the smell of gunpowder, which is a good thing because I would be smelling a lot of it.

We had a water survival course—nothing in the water, all classrooms. Later I would take a deep-water survival course where, I swear, they tried to drown you. But that's a different story.

We had a Survival Evasion Resistance Escape (SERE) briefing and got to see what was expected of us in the coming weeks. We were also issued our SERE equipment. I can only remember a few of the items we received: poncho, flint, backpack, 36" x 36" piece of parachute, metal canteen, compass, a length of parachute cord, and if you smoked, a pack of cigarettes. We were also able to take a canteen of water and either a pack of gum or a roll of Life Savers. And last but not least, the very important flashlight.

There were fifty-eight of us taking the training and we were divided into nine- and ten-man elements. Each element was given a colored armband to wear. I was in the yellow element. The senior man in each element was the element leader.

They reminded us that this was an all-volunteer outfit and that anytime you wanted during this training, you could wash out. We finished up the week with a weapons review and examination.

December 21–22

We learned about all the different mines and booby traps the Viet Cong were using. What to look for and ways to avoid them.

We learned what kinds of plants we could eat, fishing techniques, and different kinds of animal traps and a whole bunch more.

We went over the Geneva Convention and the military code of conduct.

We learned how to read grid maps and how to navigate by compass—first in the classroom, and then in the field.

We finished up with our final class on the principles of escape and evasion followed by a final examination.

December 23

Holiday leave began. A bunch of us were not going anywhere. Money was tight. Because we were on Temporary Duty (TDY) we hadn't been paid, and they couldn't tell us when we would. I spent the holiday sightseeing, taking in a couple movies, and just hanging out. I did spend some time absorbing everything we'd learned so far. This Seawolf outfit was going to be one hell of an adventure. Thinking about my family, I called my mom.

The only thing I remember about New Year's Eve was that we were invited to a party. The next thing I remembered I was throwing up in the back of a bus. Everyone was moving forward, and the bus driver was yelling at me to get off the bus.

A Man Returns

January 2

I didn't feel so good, and the most grueling part of our training started now.

At 7 a.m., we picked up all our gear, boarded a bus, and headed to the SERE training area where all the fun would begin.

Each element was dropped off in different areas of the forest. First thing on the agenda: find a suitable campsite area and get our shelters built. It was freezing cold, and every now and again, we had sleet and snowflakes coming down. I found out right away that I was with a bunch of city boys, and they were having a hard time of it. I built a standard lean-to with the opening facing away from the wind. I covered the ground with pine boughs and enough leaves to snuggle in. I then surveyed the area around us. We had a small stream not too far away for water and it had minnows in it. I got a fire going with my flint and knife and heated up a canteen of water. I had a Life Saver and drank a cup of warm water to help deal with the cold and damp. Everyone was working hard to get a shelter built and a fire going before dark. An instructor came by just before nightfall and evaluated each of our campsites. We all turned in early, and it seemed like we had just gotten to sleep when we were abruptly awakened by one of our instructors. We were going on a two-mile compass hike through the forest. It was midnight and just above freezing. I don't remember much about the hike except that it was miserable, and I was glad to get back to my shelter.

I woke up early to a dead rabbit hanging from a tree in the middle of camp: very nice. Most of the guys had never skinned an animal, let alone cooked one over an open fire. I had found some wild onions and roasted them to go along with my piece of rabbit. Another Life Saver for dessert. Today was filled with different tasks. We set different kinds of animal traps and did a hide-and-seek thing. Those are the only two I can remember from that evening.

Later, I used my piece of parachute canopy to catch minnows using rocks, flipping the canopy material. Some I ate raw, but they were better toasted on the end of a stick over a fire. I had some more wild onions with them. I was glad I had eaten something because that evening, they came into our camp to let us know we were going on another night patrol. This time without an instructor.

Nightfall came quickly with no moon. To make things worse, it was sleeting. On this patrol, we were going to have to find a small building three miles away. A hot cup of coffee would be waiting for us.

Enemy patrols would be looking for us, so we had to travel stealthily—no lights.

Conditions were bad, not to mention that we were tired and hungry. It was pitch black with heavy sleet at times. The forest was sometimes very thick except for the areas that were really torn up. We found out later that it was a tank training area. The tanks had created small ponds of water everywhere that we had to wade through.

I was second man back from the element leader and I could see he was having issues with navigating and was getting a little panicky. I offered to help, and he jumped at the chance to take a backseat.

It was slow going. Twice we had to hunker down to avoid patrols and capture. We found the building without getting captured and were the first element to get there. All I can say about the coffee is that it was full of grounds, but it was hot. Several of the other elements were captured.

After all the other elements got there, we hiked back to camp via a dirt road, thank goodness. We were all spent. It was 5 a.m. and I went out like a light.

A Man Returns

Gunshots at 0530. Several instructors were firing off automatic weapons. We were told to get up and leave everything. We were going on a patrol. We headed out through the forest; it was still dark. One of the instructors was leading and another bringing up the rear. We hiked until we came upon a clearing, and to our surprise, there were other elements. No time for reunions. We were told to get into two lines and that we would be going down a trail at the other end of the clearing. "Let's get moving!" I was freezing, not to mention dead tired, terribly hungry, and dying of thirst.

We found the trail and proceeded down it. We had been walking for about a half hour and it was just getting light when all hell broke loose. Men dressed like Viet Cong came running out of the trees firing machine guns and explosions were going off everywhere. I don't know how many men there were, but there were a bunch of them. We were told to get down on our stomachs, now! Some of the guys were already getting knocked to the ground. Then they started walking on us and pushing our faces into the ground. They were slapping and kicking us and pulling our hair while sitting on our backs. All the while, they kept screaming at us and firing their guns. The air was thick with smoke and my ears were ringing from the machine-gun fire next to my head. After everyone had been badly beaten up, they made us stand, form two lines, and wrap our right arm around the guy's neck in front of us. We took off down the trail like this, locked together. All the while we marched, they kept harassing us. Knocking us down. Their favorite was slapping you across your ice-cold face and ears. It stung just a bit.

We knew where we were headed: the prisoner of war camp. We had heard nothing but bad things about this place. There it was looming in the fog ahead. Barbed wire everywhere, it looked like the real thing. Off to one side was a small building, and sitting next to it, of all things, an ambulance. I had good and bad feelings about it being there. They had Viet Cong flags flying over the camp. We were told to stop and face the side of the trail at attention. They ran up and down our ranks, screaming at us, asking stupid questions. Punching, slapping, kicking, making us do push-ups, pulling our hair while we did them. They had us strip down naked, and it was fucking freezing. They passed sacks around to each of us. The sack had a number on it. Inside the sack was a round wooden disc with a number on it, same as the sack. The disc had a hole with a string through it. We were to tie the disc around our neck with the string and put all our belongings in the sack. The number was our new name, and it must always face out so that it could be easily seen. The disc did not want to face out so that gave them a good reason to fuck with us. I think we all got nailed on that one.

They finally let us put our clothes back on. Then it was down on our hands and knees to the prison camp. Again, the screaming and the beatings continued until we reached the prison camp gate. Inside the compound, we had to go to a squat position with one hand on our head.

With the other hand, we picked up pine needles of which there were plenty to go around. One needle at a time, we placed them on top of a pile in the middle of the compound. All the while we were doing this, they were screaming at us and kicking us over and beating us and making us do stupid things.

Numbers were called. If your number was called, you had to drop to your hands and knees and crawl over to a gate where there was a guard. He put a piece of paper in your mouth, and you crawled through the gate. The guard closed the gate and you were gone. Sometime later we would see them crawling back through the gate. Nobody knew where you went. You didn't find out until your number was called. We could not talk or look at anyone. If you were caught looking at a guard, they usually double-teamed you. They played

A Man Returns

Vietnamese music. Very loud at times. My number was finally called. I crawled to the gate on my hands and knees. The guard stuck a piece of paper in my mouth. I crawled through the gate and down the trail to a small plywood building. There was another guard standing in the doorway, and he was huge. He took up the whole doorway. He told me in a very nice way to get off my hands and knees and walk upright like a man. I did so. He told me to come in and have a seat. I could not believe he wasn't screaming at me. I still had the piece of paper in my mouth, and he told me to give it to him, which I did. He read it and crumpled it and put it in his pocket. He then offered me a sugar cube which I took. He made a little small talk and then started asking personal questions. I told him I couldn't answer those questions, and gave him my name, rank, and serial number.

He got instantly pissed off. Then I mentioned the Geneva Convention and that was it. He reached out and grabbed me by the front of my jacket. He lifted me in the air and bounced me off the plywood ceiling, then off three walls back, back to the ceiling, and then to my chair. He repeated the questioning and again, I started with the Geneva Convention. He grabbed me again and once again we did the bounce thing—ceiling and three walls, but this time, instead of my chair, he threw me out the door. I picked myself up and he quickly knocked me back down and told me to get on my hands and knees. He stuck another piece of paper in my mouth, told me to bark like a dog, and follow the trail to the next guard. It was a way—about five hundred yards. When I reached the guard, he told me to stand up and give him the paper. He looked at it and just like the other guard, he crumpled it and put it in his pocket. Behind the guard were two more guards, both yelling obscenities at me. There were also three wooden boxes of different sizes: small, medium, and large, you might say. Each was sitting at a separate small table. They all had hinged tops with a large clasp and padlock. It was decided I was a medium, and before I knew it, the three guards had me in the air and were cramming me into the medium box using the lid to finish the last of the stuffing. I heard the clasp catch and the padlock click. It was hard to breathe. I had to control my breathing.

Holy shit, if you were claustrophobic, you would be in real trouble. The guard yelled at me, and every time someone banged on the box, I had to scream out my name, rank, and service number. They banged on the box quite frequently. I don't know how long I was in there. In between the blows to the box, I used the downtime to sleep. Finally, they opened the box and let me out. I had to crawl back to the same gate I had come through. Back to picking up pine needles. They had three new graves dug inside the compound. I don't know what you had to do to get to personally check them out and I hoped I didn't find out. Every now and then, they threw someone into one of them and had them lie face down. Then they had prisoners throw dirt on them until they were covered—except for their faces. They would also have you strip down and stand in front of a tree, leaning onto it with your arms and hands until you couldn't hold yourself up any longer. Then, with a little help from a couple of guards, they would get you back into position with a couple good slaps. Then they would wait for you to fall again.

We endured all kinds of punishment, of which I can only remember a few. And it went on into the night. We were all very hungry, thirsty, and worn out. We had been thrown around and beat up so much that it was hard to think straight. It started to seem almost real. One morning, it was just starting to get light when all hell broke loose. Helicopters came flying in, men rappelling out of them. Explosions and automatic weapon fire went off everywhere. Troops were coming through the gate and over the wall. I saw two guys take down the Viet Cong flags and raise an American flag. About that time, everything started settling down. We had been rescued. I don't think there was a dry eye in the place. We were all cheering and going crazy. They brought in C-rations, drinks, and blankets. We devoured everything. A camel never tasted so good. We all loaded up in buses and headed back to the base for hot showers and clean clothes. We were checked out by the doc and got a couple more shots. Then off to the chow hall.

We stuffed our faces with C-rations and found that we couldn't eat anymore. Then it was time to hit the rack and we all pretty much passed out.

The next day, we all met in the auditorium for a debriefing and evaluation. It was a good meeting. We found out that six guys had quit during the training and one guy had a broken nose. Overall, we did pretty well. We had heard a lot of bad stories about SERE, and most of them were true. We received our personal evaluation sheet and I had done pretty well. I was so ready to get on with the rest of my training. We did the checkout thing and got our orders to Fort Benning in Columbus, Georgia. Fort Benning is an Army base, and we all knew this was going to be a little different. We had no idea what to expect. We knew we were getting our Helicopter Door Gunner training there and I was stoked. I couldn't wait to get in the air.

January 1968

When I arrived at Fort Benning, the front desk knew exactly who I was and where I was going. They called for a truck to pick me up. What a deal. I already liked this Army base. He dropped me at a barracks next to the 101st Airborne training area. We had fun later harassing those guys. It turned out that John Wayne and the whole Hollywood gang had all just left. They had been filming *The Green Berets*. They said the place had been crazy while they were there.

Red clay and pine trees everywhere. The wind sounded sweet blowing through those long needles.

The school was three weeks long and we would be in the field most of the time. We didn't have to get up early. We had our own truck and driver, and he took us wherever we needed to go.

There were only fourteen gunners here and I didn't know where the rest of them went. My two buddies from SERE training were here, so that's good.

I was still broke, so I told them that I hadn't been paid in a while. They gave me twenty dollars and told me I would be paid at the end of the three weeks' training. It would take that long to get the paperwork to the Navy and back.

Everyone treated us great. Our uniforms and flight suits didn't have markings on them, so no one could know who we were. We even got special treatment in the chow hall. We were issued flight gear, helmet, gloves, flight suit, and aviation brown boots. We even got a nice flight jacket. I was a lot farther south now but it was still chilly here, especially hanging out of a helicopter doing 100 mph.

The pilots for the Seawolves were also here getting checked out on the UH-1B (the Huey). We spent a couple days loading their gunships with 7.62 ammo for the M60 flex guns and putting rockets together and loading them in the tubes. The pilots were getting their gunnery training. The copilot fired the four M60 flex guns and the pilot fired the rockets. We practiced hot turnarounds where they don't shut the chopper down. We got it down to three minutes.

We were already checked off on the M60, so our training started right in the field. They started us out in the prone position with the bipod mounted on the barrel. We shot up old oil drums, refrigerators, jeeps, trucks—all kinds of stuff. Next, we fired from the standing position without the bipod. We fired thousands of rounds. The training I had been waiting for finally came. We didn't go up right away though. They had us sit in the gunner seat while the helicopter was turning, and we fired out the door. In Nam, we would be the only gunman who handheld our M60! That gave us the freedom to shoot wherever we needed. The Army and the Marines fired from a mount or bungee cord. The gunners that were training us were awesome. They had all done one to two tours in Nam and knew what they were doing.

Our first time up we didn't get to fire a round. They wanted to see if we would get sick. I sat in the gunner seat hanging out the door. A five-foot gunner's belt kept us from falling to the ground. It was better than any carnival ride. Going 130 mph ten feet off the deck, pulling up over treetops and dropping back to the deck. The pilot would fly up about 3,000 feet and then he would cut the engine and we would auto rotate almost to the ground before the pilot would pull power. You would think the rotor blades were going to break off with all that stress and loud popping noises. On one occasion, the pilot got a little too zealous and didn't pull the stick soon enough and we hit the ground hard. We were all okay, but the skids on the chopper sprung. This kind of flying was not for everyone, and we lost a few more guys.

The day finally came, and we got to shoot out of a flying helicopter. We started with firing straight out the door at various targets along a ridge. Not as easy as it sounds. Because of the speed of the helicopter and every fifth round being a tracer round, you could see your rounds making a big curve to the ground. With practice, we learned to walk our rounds right up to the target. The more we practiced, the faster we could get on the target. We finally worked our way up to doing actual attack rocket runs. What a rush! The pilot rolled straight in on a target, and you were hanging out the door freehanding the M60 at over 100 mph. You not only had the weight of the gun and the pressure from the wind, but you had the M60 pulling a belt of ammo out of the box. The two M60s located on the pylons on each side were chattering away at over a thousand rounds a minute and the pilot was punching off rockets right under your feet. You were fighting the wind and the g-forces trying to stay on target and not shoot the helicopter. Not to mention trying not to fall out of the aircraft.

After several days of this and a lot of beer, we graduated to night runs. A whole new ballgame, and this was what most of our flying would be: at night in the rain and fog, when Charlie (the Viet Cong) did most of his moving.

It was eerie and everything became magnified at night; it was like another sense kicked in: watching the tracers streak through the night and the rockets blasting off under your feet, leaving a trail of sparks, some bouncing off you. Making you think you'll catch on fire. My helmet had a full face shield to protect from the wind, bugs, sparks, and anything else that came my way. We got to pop and deploy different kinds of parachute flares. What a trip flying around, above, and through them. Trying to lay down accurate fire and not be blinded by the light was a little tricky.

One day we were all taking a break and one of the pilots said to me, "Would you like to go for a ride in the pilot's seat?" He didn't have to ask me twice. I headed to the chopper. As I sat there in the copilot's seat watching him do the startup, I wondered for a moment how different things might have been if I had gone to college. I could be the one sitting in the pilot's seat. As we were taking off, he began giving me a crash course flight lesson. When we got to 3,000 feet, he leveled off, and said, "You got it." I sure did—a handful of diving chopper starting to shake like crazy. In a panic-stricken voice, I told him he needed to take it back. In a very calm voice, he talked me through the rudder pedals, the stick, and the collective. Everything must move together. The trick, he told me, was *not to do it*. He said you just had to think about doing it and the chopper was so sensitive, it just did it. By darn, I got it leveled off without the chopper vibrating apart and I even got to do some different maneuvers. All in all, it was a great thirty minutes and I felt pretty good about it. He told me that you never knew when you'd have to take one of those seats if either the copilot or pilot were shot. The rest of the day, we practiced firing from the helicopter and rearming. We also got to throw smoke out of the helo, learning how to mark targets.

We were about to finish up our training and take a short leave when we got cut new orders. No leave. I was going to Fort Gordon in Augusta, Georgia. Another Army base. I'd be there for two to three weeks, learning more about the chopper and its electronic systems. We were all splitting up. Everyone was going for more training in their specific field. My friends, Tony Marciano and Stuart Seal, were both electronic, so they were going to Fort Gordon too.

We turned in all our flight gear, including the nice flight jackets the Army had loaned us. Then we finally got a paycheck. In fact, it was more than we expected. Hey, we were broke, and if Uncle Sam wanted to pay us, so be it. This would later come back and bite us on the ass.

That night, we had a big beer bust party to celebrate another phase completed. The next morning, we checked out and went looking for some of the guys that trained us. We found most of them and thanked them for sharing their experiences with us and the training.

We had a few days before we had to be at Fort Gordon. Tony had already taken off to parts unknown and Stu had a great idea. He said, "Let's go to my house in Thibodaux, Louisiana!" My home was in Pennsylvania, too far to go with only a few days off. We caught a bus, and we were on our way to Thibodaux. Stu's mom and dad took me in like I was their long-lost son. His mom and dad were French Cajun, and they had that cool accent. Man, did they put out a feast every day we were there. All Cajun cooking, of course, and I don't think there was anything that I didn't like.

We did so much in four days, it seemed like I was there for a month. Besides all the family stuff—the get-togethers and the eating and drinking—we did manage to hit Bourbon Street in New Orleans for two nights. Stu gave me a tour of the French Quarter and I got to meet more of his family.

We took a trip into the bayou in his uncle's pirogue to visit friends. All the houses were on stilts and rough looking. He took me on a trip way out in the swamp to see all kinds of animals and birds. I'd never been around Spanish moss before and there was plenty. I would imagine that at night it might be a little scary, but I think it's beautiful. I saw my first gator in the wild. It was a small one.

We stopped way out in the middle of nowhere and he pulled up to this little piece of land, saying, "Let's get out and stretch our legs before we head back." I jumped out to pull the boat up, and at the same time, he gunned it in reverse, slammed it forward, and was gone. Yikes! I listened as the motor faded into the distance. Wow! What silence. I was standing on this three-foot by ten-foot piece of water-logged swamp grass. Nothing but cypress trees, Spanish moss, swamp grass, and water. I knew he'd be back, but there is always that one little spot in your mind that calls out, *He might forget where he dropped you.* We had been pounding down a lot of beers. Then, in the distance, I could faintly hear salvation—my rescue boat. By the time he picked me up, I was into a good laugh, and so was he.

I had a date two of the nights we were there. Both very nice French girls with that cute accent. One of them was Stu's cousin and we spent the night at her place.

Stu's folks had a big get-together our last night. It was great. So many nice people and so much food. We ate too much, drank too much, and stayed up way too late.

A Man Returns

February 1968

We checked in at Fort Gordon without a problem and again, every-one treated us very nice. We were dead tired. The bus trip was terrible. We were hoping to get some shut-eye on the bus, but that didn't hap-pen. Everyone was looking at us when we got there, wondering what sailors were doing on an Army base.

Augusta, Georgia, wasn't a happening place. It was a nice looking town but there was nothing to do. We pretty much stayed on base and frequented the Enlisted Men's (EM) Club. School was easy but a little boring after the schools we had just gone through.

Another change of orders came and we were *not* going to Nam after this school. We were to take thirty days leave after this school. Yes! After that, I was to report to Ream Field Naval Air Station at Imperial Beach, California. More training, hand-to-hand combat, and the like. Alright, California! And the base is near the beach and only seven miles from Tijuana, Mexico. Better and better.

They said we might not get to Nam until May.

California! Maybe I would get the chance to hook up with my best friend from home, Cpl. Lance Jenny. His family was my second family. He was a radio operator in the Marine Corps getting some final training before he went to Nam.

Finally checkout day came and I was ready for a thirty-day leave.

The last thing on our checkout sheet was picking up our pay-checks, and did we get a bad surprise. That overpayment came back to bite us. That was quick. The government doesn't mess around when it comes to money. We did get a small check. They called it subsistence pay: a couple dollars a day just to keep you breathing. Holy shit, we were going on a thirty-day leave with almost nothing. It might be the last time we saw our friends and family, and that would be hard to do without any money. Fortunately, I was able to borrow a couple dollars here and there to get by. I hated that. I don't like not having a couple dollars in my pocket. Not rich, but not needy.

The thirty days went by too fast. Most of my friends were gone. Most of them were in the service. I had to get wild and crazy by myself. I hooked up with a couple of girls while I was home. Maybe they felt sorry for me because I was going to Nam. When I left home for active duty, I gave my sister my most treasured possession: my 1960 Chevy Impala, Roman red with a red-and-white checkered interior. A whole lot of memories were in the back seat of that car. I had twelve months left to pay for it. I told my sister she could have the car if she would take over the payments and she agreed. I would be able to drive it when I came home for leave. Well, she didn't make the payments and I was pissed. My father and I didn't get along, but he didn't get along with anybody anyway. However, in one of his weaker moments, he signed for the car for me. Unbelievable. My mother went into shock (only kidding). Now he was making the payments. My sister really did throw me under the bus on that one. Thank goodness, I did get to drive it while I was home though—and check out the back seat a few more times.

February and March, 1968

I don't remember much about my thirty days of leave. I do remember a lot of people treated me like they were never going to see me again.

I didn't tell my mom that I had volunteered for Nam and that I was going to be a door gunner. She would eventually find out, but she was already stressing out badly, so I didn't want to lay that on her too.

My leave time was up. It was time to say goodbye to everyone and head for California. I stopped in at my second dad and mom's place to say goodbye. I also wanted to let them know that I was going to try and hook up with Lance. Did they want me to take anything to him?

When I got ready to leave, Beverly took me over to her china cabinet where she kept all her treasures. In one corner of the cabinet, she showed me a collection of things I left there over the years. She told me that stuff was a part of me and that when she held it in her hands, she felt like we were close. She told me that while I was in Nam, she'd be holding the stuff a lot more often.

Hugs and kisses from Beverly, and Jake extended his hand for a shake and palmed a twenty-dollar bill in my hand. He had heard I was broke. (Love you, Jake and Bev!)

All the goodbyes were sad, but I was so happy to leave the cold weather behind.

California, here I come. Another adventure. I got to drive the Impala one last time to get to the Scranton-Wilkes Barre Avoca airport. Next stop, San Francisco, then Los Angeles, and a bus ride to Imperial Beach.

Sunshine, palm trees, the Pacific Ocean, and bikini-clad babes, here I come.

March 1968

We got checked in and I didn't like the attitude of anybody there. I wanted to go back to the Army bases where we were treated well.

Next, the beach. We caught a bus near the front gate and headed out to find one. Wow! The Pacific Ocean, very rocky beach, but gorgeous, and the weather was terrific. Not as many bikinis as we would have liked. We would be checking out more beaches.

What a rude awakening: military life, muster, watches, and saluting. We only had to do this for a few days until they figured out what to do with us. At first, we had to try and look busy all day. Finally, they got their act together and we started tactic classes, exercises every day, and hand-to-hand training.

Tijuana was off-limits to military personnel, but we didn't really care and went the first three nights we were there. After that, we were broke. Once you crossed that border the whole world changed.

What a difference in everything. Every taxi driver had a "seester" they wanted you to meet. Everyone on the street was trying to sell you something. We were told not to eat anything with meat in it because it could be rat or dog meat. Playing cards with the naked ladies was a popular item. I did buy a poncho. The shows were something else—girls doing it with dogs and donkeys. If you threw a coin or bill on your table or floor, the girls would pick them up with their pussies. At one place, a girl was going around, taking a long-necked beer bottle off your table and sticking it up her pussy until it disappeared. Then she'd pull it back out and set it back down in front of you. Everyone would start clapping and chanting for you to drink up. All the bars were crazy. We also got to see one of their wild and crazy parades with everyone dressed in costumes.

They say Americans disappear in Tijuana, never to be seen again. That's why it's off-limits. We traveled four of us together, so we felt pretty safe. We even tried some street food despite the warning.

Back in California, I checked into the dentist. I'd never been to a dentist, and he told me there was some work that needed to be done. He told me that he could get it all done before I left for Nam.

The San Diego Zoo was a great place. I went two days in a row and took lots of pictures. It was free to the military, which was very nice, seeing that Tijuana broke us.

I finally got a hold of Lance at Camp Pendleton and he could only get off one day. We met up in San Diego and did the town. I don't remember anything. I don't remember how I got back to the base. I know that we had a good time because we knew we might not see each other again. So, that time was very special.

They changed our orders again. At first they told us we would be here for about ten weeks. After we got here, they said it would be five weeks. Now it looked like just over two weeks. I was to leave April 4 on a Thursday at 5 p.m. from Travis Air Force Base.

The dentist I had was great. He was as good as his word. He worked me in, and I spent two days in the chair with my mouth jacked open and tools sticking out of it. He got everything taken care of. One less thing I'd have to worry about.

April 1968

Tuesday, April 2, was checkout day. We said all of our goodbyes and wondered if we would see each other again in Nam.

Early Thursday morning, April 4, we boarded a bus for Travis Air Force Base. What a mad house. Thousands of guys all dressed alike, some coming and some going. It was a huge place. Someone gave us directions and we headed for one of the lines. I had sent my mom a letter on April 1 letting her know that I was leaving earlier than planned, when I was leaving, and where from. She got the letter on April 4. I was sitting with some of the Seawolves shooting the breeze when my name came over the PA system, which had been blaring almost constantly. I about fell out. I was to report to the nearest in-formation desk. I couldn't believe it. What could they possibly want with me? I got to the information desk and told the guy who I was. He told me to pick up that phone over there. I picked it up, and couldn't tell who it was at first. There was nothing but crying. It was my mom. I couldn't believe it. She was having a tough time talking because she was crying so much. I got her calmed down and we had a nice goodbye conversation: you know, the "don't worry, I'll be okay, see you in April" kind. I carried that phone call in my heart for the rest of my life. I hated to think how much that phone call cost her.

Later, when I came home on leave, she told me how much trouble she had to go through to get to that information desk. She said it was almost a losing battle, but her German stubbornness got her through. After that, I waited.

We finally got through all the paperwork and climbed on board. It was a regular commercial airliner. I had heard that a lot of guys had to go by ship. From Travis, we flew to Anchorage, Alaska, then to Japan, and finally to our final destination, Saigon's Tan Son Nhut Air Base. I was very glad and thankful that we landed in the daytime. Things seem friendlier in the sunlight. Stepping off the plane, I remember being hit square in the face with a heatwave. It was 100 degrees, and even hotter on the tarmac. It was the dry season (another good thing) and sand was everywhere. Even in the air. I would soon get used to all of it. Coming out of an ice-cold airplane with all the booze I drank turned me into an instant sweatball. My hats off to all the stewardesses on board for putting up with us on such a long flight. They kept smiling and bringing us drinks.

This place was just as crazy as Travis Air Force Base had been: men everywhere. One big difference though was the choppers everywhere and the fighter jets taking off. I could hear explosions in the distance. I stood in a very long line, thinking, *I can hear the war all around me.* We got checked in and did the money exchange thing: greenbacks for piasters. We would later be issued military pay certificate (MPC) to be used as money on base. You were not allowed to use greenbacks or MPC off base. We all called the MPC monopoly money because of all the different colors. This was all in an effort to keep these monies off the black market. Everyone did it anyway so the government would have a conversion day or C-day. You would wake up one morning and all the bases would be locked down. Very hush-hush. No one was supposed to know about it. You had so many hours to exchange your MPC certificates for new ones. This left all the merchants, racketeers, black market folks, and whores with worthless MPC. Needless to say, that would really piss everyone off and there were accounts of retaliation because of it. When C-day first happened to me, I was on flight duty and our whole fire team was flying scrambles and almost didn't get our MPC converted.

Another thing the government did to try and curb some of the black-market dealings was to issue everyone ration cards. These were for purchasing everything from beer and cigarettes to watches, cameras, TVs, and so on.

I finally found myself on an old school bus painted, of course, battleship gray with chicken wire covering the windows. We found out that the chicken wire was to keep the Viet Cong from throwing hand grenades into the bus.

I cannot even begin to describe the sights and sounds of Saigon: people trying to carry on everyday life with barricades, barbed wire, and military everywhere. We were dropped off at the Annapolis Hotel. It was a two-story concrete structure that didn't look anything like Vietnamese architecture. Most of the buildings I saw on my way from the airport looked French. The first thing I noticed upon entering this building was the ceiling fans. They were turning so slowly that I wondered if they did any good. I know I couldn't feel them. After checking in at the desk, a cold beer and a shower was next on my agenda. The showers were cold only, and with very little water pressure, you almost got wet. I wondered if there would be showers where I was going.

I was too wound up to be tired. That was a good thing because right from the git-go, another Seawolf and I drew machine gun watch on the roof for four hours. It seems the VC had been targeting this building and anywhere else Americans were staying. Welcome to the war. Here I was, just arrived, and already surrounded by sandbags at one end of the roof with my buddy on the other. We both had .30

caliber machine guns with bipods. I know it sounds crazy, but after all that training, I was hoping something would happen. Sitting there in the dark, I could see explosions and tracers in the distances. The Tet Offensive had just begun and there were still lots of areas close by that were held by the Viet Cong. My four hours went pretty fast and all was pretty quiet. My relief was a welcome sight—time to get some shut-eye.

I remember not being scared. I was ready. My first taste of Vietnamese beer was Ba Muoi Ba, and it was good—cold and wet. Something gave the beer a nasty taste, but you got used to it after a while. It was (erroneously) said that the beer contained formaldehyde which stayed mainly in the bottom of the can, so we would not drink the last couple of swallows. When I got back to the States, I found myself doing that for quite a while before I finally broke the habit.

Saigon was wrapped in pillboxes, concrete barricades, sandbags, and barbed wire. There were open sewage ditches everywhere, kids running around naked peeing and pooping in the ditches and the side of the roads. The smells coming from the street vendor food and the restaurant doors were not appetizing. Fermented fish: now that's a real treat for your nostrils. It turned my stomach upside down. No one drank the water anywhere here. Most everyone drank Coke or beer.

April 6

The same gray bus picked us up and took us back to Tan Son Nhut Air Base and dropped us off. We were told to wait in a certain area. A plane on its way to Vũng Tau would pick us up. There was a pile of us. Mostly Army, a couple of Australians, a handful of Patrol Boat River (PBR) people, and a few Seawolves. Vũng Tau was a resort town with hotels and sandy beaches on the South China Sea. It also had an Army base and that's where Seawolf and PBR headquarters were located. We were burning up on the tarmac when the plane finally showed up.

Awesome! It was a Caribou! It taxied right up to us, stopped, and the whole back end opened to form a ramp. You could drive a vehicle into this thing. A guy in the back of the plane was hollering for us to load up. Everyone headed in that direction. I was kind of in front. The first thing I noticed was that there were no seats. Crewman told us to form lines on the painted yellow lines on the deck and park our asses on them. We had to ditch our gear forward first, and finally, we all got seated. We were all nuts-to-butts packed in. We passed a cargo strap down each row, which was connected to the bulkhead on each side, and tightened up. You slipped both arms over the strap and that gave you something to hang onto. Especially on takeoff, this kept all of us from piling up in the back of the plane. Vũng Tau was only about seventy-five miles south-southeast of Saigon so it was a short trip, thank goodness.

Vũng Tau is a peninsula and our headquarters were at the very southern tip. It was a French resort town and is now used for in-country rest and recuperation.

Two large mountains shadow Vũng Tau and on the shorter of the two is a huge statue of Jesus.

The Australians also shared a piece of the Army base. Well, I found out real quick that an Aussie hat was a real prize. I saw more than one fight break out over someone stealing one.

Our base was nothing like the resort town. It was sand, sand, and more sand. The only place that didn't have sand was the Perforated Steel Planking (PSP) airfield. You could fry an egg on it just about any time of the day.

We saw hundreds of barrels of Agent Orange being onloaded and off-loaded. Little did we know at the time, the grief and suffering that Agent Orange would bestow upon us later.

Thank you, Uncle Sam, one more time. We got directions to the Seawolf building, checked in, and were shown our barracks. The barracks consisted of a wood building with a metal roof. The sides were like louvered doors with screen covering the open area. It gave some ventilation. There was an electric wire that ran down the middle with a couple lightbulbs hanging from it. Some of the guys were already complaining, but I was thinking this was a lot better than a tent or worse, a foxhole. At each end of the building was a sandbagged bunker used for mortar attacks. The latrine and showers were about a half a block away. We spent the rest of the day checking out the base and locating everything. We also got our fatigues and flight boots.

April 9

I was so pissed. I found out that I was not going to a detachment for four weeks, subject to change. The first two weeks I'd be in plane captain school learning all about prevention maintenance (PM) and general upkeep of the aircraft. I got night shift, 7 p.m. to 7 a.m. It was cooler at night and that would give me a chance to go to the beach during the day. I did and it was gorgeous. Vũng Tàu, being a resort town, was very nice. The war had just about did them in though; the only people I saw were military. On my first trip to the beach, my buddies and I were in the surf enjoying a nice cool down when suddenly, a wave dumped a load of jellyfish on us. Yikes! Instant burn and stinging. We rubbed ourselves with sand and it helped a little, but we still burned.

On my third trip to the beach, we were blasted out of the water by a megaphone from one of the guard towers telling us to get out of the water. There were tiger sharks in the surf. We watched as two of the guards launched a small boat into the surf, carrying an M14 rifle. We could see the shark in the surf, and it was huge. It was busy chasing schools of fish and did not see the boat heading toward it. At about twenty-five yards, one of the men opened fire. You could see the water exploding all around it. Then the shark was gone, and everything seemed to get quiet. Suddenly someone yelled, pointing straight out. The shark had reappeared almost in the same place, just a little farther out. The guys in the boat took off after it, firing as they went. Again, the shark disappeared under the waves. The shark surfaced again, but this would be its final time. They pumped a few more rounds into it and it lay still. They tied it around the tail and towed it to shore. Wow! The shark was gorgeous. It was my first time looking at a shark up close. It was twelve feet long and I got a good look at the business end of that bad boy.

They told us that our second two weeks would be more schooling. God damn! I was tired of going to school. I was ready for a

Bunker complex after airstrike

detachment—to do what I'd been training to do. I finished plane captain school, and we had the next day off. We headed to the beach and had a great day enjoying cold beer, sun, and surf.

The next day, my buddy and I had just gotten back from breakfast and were waiting to find out what we were doing next. In the door came a runner from the office telling us to get our things together. We're to catch a chopper in two hours. We were headed to detachment six in Đồng Tâm.

We packed our seabags and checked out at the office. We were to wait for a chopper at the maintenance hangar. It wasn't a very long wait. The chopper was there in the hangar getting a few final things wrapped up. It was a Seawolf gunship, and they were taking it to Đồng Tâm to trade out a chopper. When it was finally ready, they took it for a spin around the base and then stopped by for us. I was on my way. I remember being so excited. I hoped that I might know some of the guys.

Đồng Tâm was northwest of Vũng Tau located near Mỹ Tho on the Mỹ Tho River. As we came in, I noticed that the base was fairly large. It had a small hospital and a thousand-foot runway. The Army's 9th Infantry Division was stationed there along with a detachment of PBRs. They had dug a huge harbor going out to the Mekong River which the PBR called home.

Đồng Tâm had a bad reputation for getting mortared. It lived up to its reputation my first night there. They dropped three mortars in. I was dead to the world, and the next thing I knew, I was being pulled from my bunk and there was a siren going off. I got my feet under me and followed the rest of the guys out the end of our barracks and piled up in the bunker. We would be mortared several more times before I left Đồng Tâm. The casualties from these mortar attacks were usually Vietnamese civilians.

The 9th Infantry had an artillery installation there. Holy shit, day and night, artillery going off. They told me I'd get used to it.

There was a small hospital about two blocks away, and again, day and night, medivac choppers went in and out. If that wasn't enough, there were the B-52 strikes constantly dropping five-hundred- and one-thousand-pound bombs. We could feel the ground tremble from the explosions.

The chopper ride into Đồng Tâm was awesome. We flew at 1,500 feet over nothing but water, jungle, and rice paddies. I saw the huge craters where the B-52s had hit their mark and areas where Agent Orange had done its job—not a leaf on a tree. You could also see the remains of a huge bunker and tunnel system that the defoliant had exposed and air strikes had demolished. They told me I would be in Đồng Tâm until May 6 and then back to Vũng Tau for a couple more weeks of school. For now, I was ground pounding and not happy about it. That meant I might not fly for another month. That was crazy. These guys were busy coming and going on missions and scrambles and we were steadily humping ammo and rockets for them, waiting for our day.

On Friday, they got scrambled out to an Army of the Republic of Vietnam (ARVN) outpost under attack. It took several hot turn-arounds before they got things under control. They found out today that they killed forty-five and wounded fifteen. They took a couple rounds but nothing serious.

April 24

I was still in Đồng Tâm and got my first mail, a card and letter from my mom. It felt good. It was terribly hot and dry. You wore and ate sand all day long. I was getting a great tan. I received my black beret today. The tradition was that I would celebrate my first kill by cutting the silk loop on the back of the beret followed by a lot of beers.

April 30

My mom sent me a care package, and in that package were a handful of live daffodils. I couldn't believe it. She felt like I needed a little touch of home, she said.

My buddies Stu and Tony were still in Vũng Tàu, and it took a heavy mortar attack the night before. I hoped they were okay. Several Americans and Vietnamese were killed and wounded.

May 3

The Seawolf office sent a Wolfgram to your folks back home every month. They tried to mention everyone and give families an idea of what we did each month. Most of it was on the light side. I was going to be in this month's issue, and I couldn't wait till my family read about us. (My mom saved all the Wolfgrams so I was able to draw a lot of information from them to write this book.)

Finally, my transfer came. My buddy, James Robinson, and I were headed back to Vũng Tàu. One more week of gunnery training and a week of plane captain school. I went to school in the evening so that left my days free. We'd been hitting the beach pretty regularly.

So far this Vietnam thing had been quite an adventure, but I was ready to do what I'd been training for.

Robby and I finished our schooling and were both headed to Nhà Bè, Det 2. We couldn't be more excited. Nhà Bè was located about twelve miles south of Saigon at the junction of the Soài Rạp and Lòng Tàu Rivers.

A Man Returns

I was a little disappointed about not going back to Đồng Tam because of the friendships I'd formed. Then again, I wouldn't miss the artillery going off at all hours.

Nhà Bè was a small base with only a small helo runway two hundred feet long. It had four revetments, two of which were for the Seawolves. The revetments were located on the sides of the runway and made of fifty-five-gallon drums held together by long steel rods welded to them. The barrels were filled with sand and had sandbags on top of them. This offered some protection on two sides. We stored rockets and ammo within the revetments. They didn't offer much protection against mortar attacks. Like Đồng Tâm, Nhà Bè had its share of mortar attacks day and night.

Just off the runway was the Seawolf ready room. It was completely covered in layers of sandbags. The Seabees had just finished our barracks. They were pretty nice compared to some of the other dets. We had an officer's club, an enlisted men's club, and a great chow hall. I say great because I went from 165 pounds to 184 pounds while I was there. Located on the main shipping channel from the South China

Fire Team Ready Room

Sea to Saigon, Nhà Bè got plenty of good groceries. All the ships knew we were the ones to call if they came under a VC attack—and we got plenty of those calls. PBR and mine sweeps were also based here and we got plenty of calls from those guys too. We shared our barracks from time to time with SEAL Teams One and Two. They were another reason the Seawolves were established. Their operations were mainly at night and often in bad weather. There was nobody to cover their insertions and extractions at the time, let alone bail them out if things went south. Besides covering all these guys, the Seawolves covered all friendly operations in the T-10 area and the Rung Sat Special Zone. These two areas were believed to hold thousands of enemy troops along with complete bunker and tunnel systems. The area was a triple canopy jungle too thick for troops to penetrate. In the months to come I would get plenty of action out of those two areas.

Before 1967, the VC pretty much had control of the entire Mekong Delta. They had plenty of time to build hundreds of tunnels and bunkers. They also built up stockpiles of food and weapons. We flew regular patrols, usually two during the day and one at night. We called them H and I missions: harassment and interdiction. We could put in strikes on areas that (through different intelligence sources) were thought to have VC activity. Sometimes we got lucky and saw secondary explosions. If that happened we would sometimes, depending on the situation, call for an airstrike from a carrier offshore as well. Time allowing, we would often drop a strike on the area. The first time I saw the F-4 Phantom IIs drop their loads, it blew me away. It was such a rush. The sound went right through me. I saw them drop napalm several times and that's a whole different experience. They outlawed napalm later because it was inhumane.

A battleship, the USS New Jersey, had just been recently recommissioned, and sat just offshore from the delta in the South China Sea.

A Man Returns

We had the pleasure of seeing just what her sixteen shells could do against targets we found. It could send a 2,600-pound, armor-piercing shell twenty-three miles and be right on target.

Our gunships, the UH-1B, were obtained from the Army. They were phasing out the B and moving up to the UH-1C. Those birds already had a lot of hours on them and some of them were in pretty bad shape. My hats off and a special thanks to our maintenance crews who kept us supplied with flyable birds. Just getting parts from the Army must have been a real pain in the ass on its own. They had a single jet engine that was underpowered for the load we carried. The birds on the Landing Ship, Tank (LST), could not carry a full load of fuel or ammo as the land-based birds did. As it was, when they launched off the LST, they would sometimes drop and barely skim the water before getting enough lift to get airborne. In the afternoon, when the sun was the hottest and the air was the thinnest, it could be very dangerous.

Our gunships at Nhà Bè carried twin M60 machine guns and seven tube rocket launchers mounted on pylons on each side of the aircraft. In 1970, they changed out the M60 for the mini guns. The 2.75 mm rockets came in two parts, the finned propulsion body and the warhead, depending on the operation and/or pilot preference. The majority of the time we used the HE (High Explosive) head. We also had the WP (Willie Peter) white phosphorus head. The real bad-ass head that could eat up some jungle and penetrate helmets was the flechette warhead. It was filled with 2,400 steel darts that exploded just above the ground. I can't imagine what that must have sounded like coming at you through the jungle. The M60s were fed by a flex chute connected to ammo trays between the gunners. They each carried approximately 1,500 rounds.

The pilot fired the rockets. He used the drop-down sight that swung down in front of him to aim them. Some pilots just used a grease mark on the windshield. They could choose how many rockets they wanted to fire at one time. It was a real process sighting the rocket pods. The copilot fired the pylon-mounted M60. He could move the guns using a lever connected to servos. They had stops on them to keep them from shooting the aircraft or the rotor blades.

The left door gunner on each bird fired an M60 machine gun with 2,000 rounds of 7.62 ammo in a box between his legs. We were the only gunship gunners that handheld our M60. We did this for flexibility, so we were able to be anywhere necessary. We had to be in complete control of the gun at all times or we'd end up shooting the rotors, the aircraft, or worse. Some gunners added a pistol strapped on with a stainless steel clamp about halfway down the gun. We also wired a steel rod to the gun extended out past the barrel. We did this to prevent us from accidentally bringing the gun inside or upon taking a hit. We also carried a spare M60 and three or four spare barrels kept in a rack in front of you just behind the pilot's seat. We could change a barrel in seconds by flipping a lever up and pulling it out with an asbestos glove or pad. Once you stuck in another barrel, flipped the lever back down, and cocked the gun, you were ready to fire again. In a firefight, the barrels got so hot they glowed cherry red, and you could actually see the bullets going through the barrel. During the Tet Offensive in 1968, the Seawolves burned out 275 barrels. We had to borrow more from the Marines in Da Nang which they special delivered in an H46.

We had to hold the machine gun on its side and fire with our little finger to keep the brass and links from catching the air stream back to the tail rotor and damaging it. Holding the gun in this manner sometimes caused the ammo belt to get hung up. Some gunners attached a soup can to the side of the gun so the ammo belt would slide over the can and into the receiver.

A Man Returns

On our detachment, the trail bird crew chief/gunner fired twin .30 caliber machine guns with 2,000 rounds of ammo. On the lead bird, the crew chief/gunner fired a .50 caliber machine gun with about 1,000 rounds of ammo. The ammo came in one hundred round boxes which were placed in a bracket alongside the gun and held down with a bungee cord. We carried several different kinds of .50 cal ammo: incendiary, armor piercing, armor piercing incendiary, and the regular ball round. My favorite was the incendiary.

All the gunners also carried a .45 or .38 caliber pistol either off the shoulder or on the hip. I carried mine on the hip because I didn't like the feel of it under my armor chest plate. The pilots also carried handguns along with the M16 they hung on the back of their seats.

On the aircraft, we also carried an M79 grenade launcher with a couple belts of ammo. On the floor, we had a steel box that carried regular grenades. Hung across the back bulkhead were two steel cables upon which were hung a variety of colored smokes, mainly used to mark targets. In a time of celebration, we used an asbestos glove and streamed smoke out both sides of the aircraft.

Several incendiary grenades also hung on the cable. We used them to blow up and set fire to enemy hooches. (A hooch was an enemy hut.) If we got shot down and were in danger of being overtaken, we would set off several of these grenades in the aircraft to prevent the enemy from getting anything usable. On that same cable were tear gas canisters that we called Charlie Sierras. They were used primarily to force people from restricted areas. We did that a lot in the T-10 zone.

We carried pop flares and MK24 parachute flares too. We didn't use them a whole lot because they also lit us up. They did come in handy at times though, especially when outposts were being overrun.

The pilots sat in a bulletproof seat but their legs were exposed from the knee down. To protect their front, most pilots used the breastplate from the ceramic vest. This was especially useful on rocket runs when bullets came through the windshield. In the event a pilot was hit, there was a tilt lever on the seat that enabled the seat to be tilted back so the pilot could be pulled off. Then the crew chief would climb into the seat and tilt himself forward and be ready to take the controls just in case something happened to the other pilot. The gunner would take care of the pilot and we would head to the closest medical facility.

Most crew chiefs got stick time for this reason. I got to fly in the copilot's seat on several occasions and got some stick time. It was quite the rush. Most of the pilots were pretty good about letting you get some time in the seat.

The gunners sat in an aluminum-legged canvas seat up against the bulkhead and at the edge of the door. Most of the gunners wired a back plate from one of our bulletproof vests under the seat for obvious reasons. We were attached to the five-foot nylon belt just in case we fell out the door. That would be okay as long as the pilot wasn't firing rockets or the copilot firing the M60. Nothing like getting a rocket shot up your ass.

Our gunships had no side doors. They weren't necessary and we didn't need the extra weight. Most of the pilots kept their doors.

We carried a pair of starlight binoculars to look for sampans in the canals at night. They were hard to use due to the vibration of the aircraft. We didn't wear the standard green jungle boot for a couple of reasons. The boot was made mainly of nylon and in the event of a fire, it could melt around your foot. The second reason was that typically in the Navy, all aviation Navy personnel wore a brown leather boot, hence the terms "Brown Shoe Navy" and "Black Shoe Navy." All of us wore the standard olive flight suit and that was all for most of us except for maybe a good dowsing of body powder. In the aircraft, we first put on a Mae West orange water survival vest, named after the buxom actress because of how it looked when inflated. Over that, we put on the ceramic bulletproof vest made up of one-inch thick ceramic back plate and front plate, held together with Velcro straps. It was very heavy, and some gunners elected not to wear the back plate. On top of all that, you wore a flak jacket. The jacket worked really well at keeping all the deadly ceramic shards from exploding everywhere if you got hit. We also wore gloves and a visored helmet connected to an intercom system.

We had two gunships at each detachment. All the gunships were set up pretty much the same way except for the right door gunner/ crew chief. Instead of the traditional M60 machine gun, some had .50 caliber and twin .30 caliber machine guns mounted in the doorway. To cover a larger area and still have a reasonable response time, we had seven detachments located throughout the delta. Two more detachments were added later. I believe they were added due to the increase in VC activity coming in along the Cambodian border.

Det 1 was located on the LST Harnett County anchored in the middle of the Bassac River. Det 2 was land-based at Nhà Bè. Det 3

Nhà Bè Det 2

was also land-based at Vinh Long. Det 4 was located on the LST Garrett County and was anchored in the Cổ Chiên River. Det 5 was also on the river on the LST Hunterdon County anchored in the Hàm Luông River. Det 6 was land-based in Đồng Tâm, and Det 7 was land-based in Binh Thuy Air Base.

Đồng Tâm was alright, but I really liked Nhà Bè. There was so much more to do. I was glad I didn't get an LST. I always say, better to be lucky than good. I was beyond excited for my first mission in the gunner's seat. After all the weeks of training, here I was ready to put it all to good use.

In the ready room before our patrol, our team leader went over a map showing where we were headed and gave us a quick rundown on where the friendlies were in the area. I had been studying the maps, so I would know where all the outposts were in our fly area.

I was assigned to the trail bird as the left door gunner firing the M60 machine gun. The crew chief on the bird fires the twin .30s.

My responsibility as the left gunner before we took off was to arm the seven rockets on my side of the chopper by setting the spring-loaded contacts onto the center of the rockets. (Nothing like climbing out on the pylons and hanging upside down to set the contacts after you're airborne because you forgot to set them before takeoff.) Also, I checked both pylon-mounted M60s to be sure the ammo belts were in the receivers, inserted the barrels, and locked down. Then I got on all my gear, jumped in, and radio-checked my intercom to be sure it was working. The crew chief unwrapped the rotor tie-down from the stinger and brought the rotor blades around in front of the aircraft. The pilot fired up the jet engine and I watched the rpm gauge start to rise. The crew chief held the rotor blade until he felt pressure and then released it and jumped in. When the rpm reached 6,000, the pilot pulled the aircraft up to about five feet and did a hover check. Then he keyed his mic and said, "Clear!" The crew chief answered

Author on twin .30 caliber

back, "Clear." We swung out of the revetment and down the helo pad out over the river and were on our way. Wow! It was a rush every time.

This first time out was just a routine patrol: checking out an area that previously had VC activity. We flew down the shipping channel just a few feet above the water and about two hundred yards from the riverbank. We did this quite often, trying to draw fire. One of the Charlie's favorite things to do was set up along the riverbank and lob mortars at passing ships. The riverbank was on my side, so I kept a sharp eye out. My hands were sweating and I was as tense as a wound-up rubber band. We flew on the Rung Sat Special Zone without incident.

Our Flight Team Leader (FTL) decided to put a strike in the area where the possible VC activity was reported. I was so ready. I leaned out of the aircraft and the wind hit me at over 100 mph. I watched the lead bird head down and start his rocket run, and then it was our turn to follow him down. I saw the lead bird light up as all its machine guns opened fire. Then the pilot fired the rockets and I could see them exploding in the jungle.

My crew chief opened up with the twin .30s and I followed suit and opened up with my M60, putting fire under the lead bird to cover his break. Then the copilot opened up with the pylon-mounted M60.

Author in gunners seat holding the M60

A Man Returns

As the lead bird made his break, our pilot punched off several rockets showering me with sparks. They went up my flight suit, burning my legs. It was unbelievably loud. Your face got black from all the gunpowder. As we made our break, the Gs were pulling down on me, making it hard to hold the M60 up. The rotor blades popped so loud, I thought they might break off any minute! With all this going on, I still had to hang out the chopper and put down fire, covering the break. The lead bird was now coming around with that gunner firing under us to cover our break. We climbed back up several hundred feet and did the same thing all over again. While we were climbing, I kicked all the brass out of the aircraft. We flew low and slow back over the area we just pounded to see if we could see anything, but there was nothing to see.

On the way back we got a call from a couple of PBRs. They had a junk ahead of them tied off to the riverbank and wanted to know if we could give them cover while they investigated. They were just ahead of us, so we told them we would do a low and slow fly-by and they said okay. It only took a few minutes and we were there. We didn't see anything suspicious. The PBR pulled alongside, took a look, and everything looked okay. They thanked us and we were on our way.

Upon landing, the crew chief and I removed the barrels from the flex guns and the contacts from the remaining rockets. This prevented any accidental firing. When the rotor blade stopped turning, the crew chief hooked the blade and pulled it around to the tail of the aircraft and tied it to the stinger to keep it from flopping around. The stinger was the tail rotor guard. It kept the tail rotor from accidently hitting the ground. While we were rearming, the fuel truck pulled up with JP-4 jet fuel. While I'm on the subject of fuel, one of the things we did on a more-than-regular basis was check the bottom of the fuel tank using a flashlight. The fuel opening was large enough for a grenade to fit through. The VC were known to pull the pin on a grenade, wrap it with tape, and drop it in the fuel tank. The fuel ate away the tape and *kaboom!* The chopper went up in a ball of flames.

After we were fueled and rearmed, we did a post-flight on the aircraft, checking for any damage like bullet holes and we also checked the fluid levels. I cleaned out any shell casings and links that I hadn't kicked out on the way back. After we were all done, we met in the ready room for a debriefing. Besides talking about the mission we just came back from, we got a rundown on what was going on in the area: where the friendlies were, where airstrikes were happening, where any artillery was being laid down in our area, and where suspected VC action was. We also found out if there were any special operations going on and what up-and-coming operations might be coming our way.

Studying our area of operation on the map was very important. During the day, it was not bad, but at night in the pouring rain, it became a real challenge. Crews flew twenty-four hours on and twenty-four hours off with sixteen men at each detachment. If someone took ill or was injured, someone from the off-duty crew would have to take their place. That was never a problem. There was always someone there ready to take your place.

When on duty, we all slept in the ready room, and most of us slept fully dressed. If we got scrambled or there was a mortar attack, we could have the chopper in the air in minutes. We passed the time watching movies and playing cards, darts, and ping pong. Everyone had stereo gear to keep them busy recording music. We had a club at Nhà Bè and it stayed pretty busy. Beers were ten cents a can.

We took turns filling the water jugs. We filled them from a water buffalo, a water tank outside our barracks. We used the water mainly for coffee, Tang, and Kool-Aid. We also took turns stocking the beer and cold drinks, and they were on the honor system. Mail call was also on a rotating basis.

My second mission, which took place on my first day on flight duty, was one of my most memorable. We were flying a search-and-destroy mission trying to draw fire or flush out any VC in the area of the Rung Sat Special Zone. We were following a canal at about 400 feet above the water. The lead bird was well ahead of us, flying low trying to draw VC fire. We were listening to some good rock and roll when our radio came alive. It was our flight team leader calling. He said he had VC in a sampan loaded with supplies headed to shore. This was a free-fire zone and we didn't have to call it in. I was ordered to take them. The leader said, "He's only going to have one chance. They are almost to the shore." "Roger that," my pilot answered. "Smith, you copy that?" I keyed my ICS button, "Yes, sir." By this time, we could see them, and my pilot was rolling in on them. We closed the distance pretty quickly. I was shaking from the adrenaline rush. As I brought the M60 up to my shoulder, I saw muzzle flashes. They had opened on us. I squeezed down on the trigger with my little finger and 550 rounds a minute poured out of my gun, tearing up the water just behind the sampan. As I walked the rounds up to the sampan, they both dove overboard. My rounds cut through them, and they went limp in the water. I continued firing on them and the sampan until we made our break. My ICS lit up with everyone cheering and congratulating me on my first kills. This is what I had been training for all these months and the answer to the question I'd had in the back of my mind: *How would I feel after killing someone?* It felt good. I was relieved that I now knew I would be able to do my job, the job that I was being paid to do. The job that I believed in. The lead bird came around and their crew chief on the .50 cal sunk the sampan. As we came back around to join the lead bird, I could see the two VC floating down the canal.

The trip back to base was quiet, but I knew there was going to be a party. I had come straight in on a target and taken care of business on my first try, and I knew that would lock me in with the rest of the gunners. We all depended on each other to do our jobs, and I was off to a good start. I didn't realize it at the time but the image of those two VC floating down the river would stay with me for the rest of my life.

The off-duty crew was waiting when we came in and I got congratulations from everyone. The next evening I was off duty, and we had the traditional ceremony of cutting the loop on the back of your black beret party that signified you had gotten your first confirmed kill. We partied at the club. SEAL Team One was there and they joined us. They would be there for three weeks of operations as they rotated around constantly to different detachments and bases. While there, they bunked in our same barracks and it was pretty cool seeing the different weapons they carried and watch them get painted up and geared up for a mission. Nothing like getting drunk with these guys and listening to the stories fly.

Mortars were still coming in every once in a while, keeping everyone on their toes. The mortars only managed to kill and wound a few Vietnamese civilians and destroy a few structures. Everyone was getting plenty of flight time scrambles off and on mostly at night, and then plenty of operations and search-and-destroy missions during the day. We'd taken a few hits here and there, but so far only one aircraft had to be hauled out by Chinook to Vũng Tau.

It was Mother's Day and I sent my mom fifty dollars. I knew she could use it. Her eyes were in bad shape and the doctor she was going to told her she would eventually go blind. A friend of hers talked her into seeing a different eye doctor and found out she had been getting the wrong treatments. Now her eyes were doing much better.

A Man Returns

I'd made it through my gunnery trial period and was now a full-fledged part of this detachment. The lead bird's door gunner's time was almost up and they were sending him to Vũng Tau for a couple weeks and then home. I got lucky (better to be lucky than good) and they gave me his position which I really liked. I liked my new pilot. He was a hot rod, a maverick, and here to get the job done. Only a few years older than me, he had a cobra painted on the back of his helmet, so we called him Daddy Cobra. It turned out that his brother was flying Cobras in the Army. Later on I would become his crew chief and we would do some crazy stuff.

I took the military requirement test for Third Class Petty Officer and passed it. They told me I could either take the field promotion for Third Class Petty Officer or take the test and receive a field promotion to Second Class Petty Officer when I returned to the States. I elected to take the test now, since things were still pretty fresh as I'd gone to school last summer. The test was in August.

We all just got a pay raise! I got ten dollars more a month. When I go over two years, I'll get a fifty dollar raise, and if I make third class, I'll get an additional seventy dollars per month plus an additional fifty dollars more in hazardous duty pay. I'd be raking it in.

I had asked my mom if she could send me some of my favorite record albums and she did! They arrived in fine shape. What a trip playing my records in Vietnam. How crazy was that. I played them on my buddy's player. I sent my father a Father's Day card. I doubted he'd open it though. I don't think my father has ever celebrated a holiday in his life.

At that time, we had a lot of guys leaving and a lot of new guys coming in. It looked like I wasn't the new guy on the block any longer. We had a Navy combat camera crew there for a few days. They had been flying with us and taking a lot of pictures and videos and doing interviews. They were filming a documentary and visiting all the detachments.

Maintaining our weapons in this environment was a real challenge. We were in the monsoon season, so we had the rain along with the sand. We usually cleaned our weapons on our off-duty days. We had two fifty-five-gallon drum halves filled with JP-4 jet fuel with a wooden table in between. Our fuel truck guys kept them full for us.

You had to take off your rings and watch when you're cleaning your weapons because the JP-4 would blister your skin under the jewelry. I lost my North Pocono High School class ring in the sand, cleaning my weapons. My buddies and I searched and searched for it, but could not find it. Every once in a while I would think about it and do some more searching. I'm still pissed. After cleaning and replacing any worn parts, we test fired them in the river, usually firing at debris floating down the river.

One of the guys picked up a puppy. This was his third. His first one disappeared and the second was run over by the fuel truck. He named it Key. So we had a new mascot. Maybe this one would be around a while.

I thought I picked up something from one of the gals in town. That's always scary, but it turned out to be a kidney infection. Never thought I'd be happy about a kidney infection.

Before coming to Vietnam, the Navy made sure we attended several lectures and videos on the different kinds of venereal disease (VD) we could contract in Vietnam. It was enough to make all of us swear that we would have no sexual contact while in country. And if that wasn't enough of a deterrent, before you could go home you had to be checked out at sick bay. If you had a venereal disease, they sent you to the Naval Hospital at Subic Bay in the Philippines instead of sending you home. You stayed there until you were clean enough to go home unless you had one of the incurable diseases. Then I don't know what happened to you.

Instead of going into town to get laid, you could be a short-timers, and settle for a blow job. It was a lot safer. There was a VD avoidance chart floating around. If you followed the chart, it would lower your chances of getting a venereal disease. It said this:

- 5% If you looked at the pussy first and it appeared clean.
- 5% If you pissed after having sex.
- 5% If you washed your penis off with a beer.
- 80% If you used a rubber.

That would only leave you with a 5 percent chance of catching something, they said.

My mom sent me a can of baby blue spray paint I had asked for, and I sprayed my helmet. I figured that would give the VC a little color to shoot at.

SEAL Team One had rotated back and we'd been covering a lot of night time insertions and extractions. The weather had been terrible just like the SEALs liked it.

On one particular night we had been back about an hour after we had covered a routine insertion and our scramble bell went off. SEALs in deep shit. They had run into a large group of VC and were pinned down and running low on ammo. We were in the air and on theater in less than fifteen minutes. We could see the green and red tracer rounds and explosions in the distance. As we got close, the VC stopped firing. They did this quite often, hoping to avoid the wrath of a gunship on top of them. We made contact with the SEAL team leader, and he was whispering, so we knew right away that the VC were close. He told us the VC were as close as fifty yards and that he was going to give us a strobe. We were to lay down fire 50 to 150 yards west of the strobe. I heard the SEAL team leader, still whispering, implore, "No rockets! No rockets!" My pilot, who was the FTL, answered, "Roger. No rockets. Going hot on your mark." The SEAL team leader came back with, "On two." (Slight delay.) I held my breath, then one, two, I saw the flash. I tried to get some sort of reference point. The last thing I wanted to do was shoot up a SEAL team. It was pitch black with a light rain. We were rolling in with six machine guns blazing from our chopper and right behind us came the trail chopper with its six guns blazing. About this time, the ground lit up with green tracers coming at us. The SEAL team leader came on the radio, "You're on target, you're on target, and we are backing out of here." Why didn't we get shot down? I don't know. We covered the SEALs back to the extraction point and the waiting PBR. There would be a lot of missions like this one and every one of them was just as hairy as the first. During post-flight, we found bullet holes in both aircraft.

The next day, Moon River, our command headquarters, called in an airstrike in that area. The following day, we flew over the area to check it out. We found structures and bunkers exposed, so we shot up the area to see if we could stir anything up, but we didn't. The RVN later checked the area out. We never did hear anything about a body count.

The military has a savings program called the 10 percent interest program. I decided to put most of my paycheck in it every month. I didn't need much money here.

I was studying for my Third Class Petty Officer test in August every chance I got.

The USO put on a show at our club every once in a while. They just had a German rock band play and my fire team went. It was pretty good. A nice change from the norm.

A Man Returns

We were all getting lots of care packages from home. They came from family, friends, and even people and organizations we didn't know. Everyone shared and mail call was often full of surprises.

We got a new chopper. Well, it wasn't technically new, but it was in a lot better shape than the one it was replacing. It had the Seawolf logo on the front and NAVY in big white letters on each side. It took us all day to switch everything over. We also had to sight in the rocket pods and the flex guns on the pylons.

There was a road running directly from Nhà Bè to Saigon that we took when we wanted to go there. We usually took a jeep and most of the time, four of us went armed with handguns and M-16s. The VC knew a lot of Americans used it, so it was dangerous, with reports of several attacks along it. We would check out some of the bars along the route, but we were always on high alert.

Saigon—what a buzzing city. Bunkers, barbed wire, and military everywhere. Things were cheap and there were numerous people

Our haul from Saigon

trying to sell you something. I bought a handmade guitar for nine dollars and it was pretty nice. I had my mom send me a couple of guitar books and I learned to play the cowboy chords while I was there.

There were bars and girls everywhere. The girls stood outside the bars dressed in see-through negligees, inviting you in to buy them a Saigon tea. Saigon tea was nothing more than a shot glass filled with Kool-Aid. It cost fifty cents to one dollar and didn't last long. For a Saigon tea, a girl would sit on your lap. Not all the girls were prostitutes (those that offered you a little more than a lap sit). Some of the girls were working their way through college and some could speak a little English.

On occasion, we flew to Saigon and landed at Tan Son Nhut Air Base to buy cold drinks, beer, and booze. On my first such trip, we visited the PX and I bought a Sharp stereo for $140. In the States, it would have sold for $300. I couldn't afford a nice system yet. It was a combination AM/FM tuner with a record player on top and detached speakers. I also bought a seventeen-jewel Seiko watch and it was self-winding. We found out that you cannot wear a self-winding watch when you're firing a machine gun because it wound too tight.

We had an outbreak of hepatitis on base, and I had to get a shot. Mondays were known as "Malaria Monday" and most of us took a huge malaria horse pill. Some of the guys couldn't take it because it gave them the runs.

In July, the Viet Cong started a new offensive. We were flying a lot of operations and scrambles. SEAL Team Two had rotated in and we were doing a lot of night operations. They had one of their killer dogs with them. A huge German Shepherd; his name was Prince. His handler put on a little show for us to show what he could do. He had me get on top of a locker and then gave Prince the command to kill me. Holy shit! Just a minute ago, I had been petting him and suddenly, this crazed animal was trying to kill me. He kept lunging up at me, snarling and barking. His handler gave him the command to stop, so I could come down off the lockers. The dog settled right down, but I was a little apprehensive about coming down. Afterward, Prince let me pet him again with no problem.

August arrived and I finally took my Third Class Petty Officer test. I wasn't sure if I had passed it. My rate was ATN Avionics Navigation technician, so the test was mostly on electronics.

My mom sent another package with more records, including her new favorite Sky Pilot. She also told me she saw a documentary on TV about the Seawolves. I later found out they had filmed it just before I got there.

We finally received long overdue M60 and barrels. They had really taken a beating the past month. A few days ago on a mission, my gun had jammed and when I opened the cover, I had a cook-off. My hand took the brunt of it. The shrapnel cut through my gloves and into my hand in several places. None of the cuts were big enough for stitches though, and they healed on their own.

We had Mama Sans that cleaned, made our racks, and did our laundry for a very small fee. You couldn't beat that. They brought the weirdest foods for lunch besides their fish and rice and Nuoc Cham. I saw turtles, chickens, ducks, but no dogs. Rumor had it that they ate dogs, but I never saw that.

One morning a Mama San was trying to make an upper rack, and a gunner in the lower rack was messing with her and giving her a hard time. She finally had enough, and pulled out one of her breasts and sprayed him down. You would have thought it was battery acid. He jumped up, yelling and cursing and spitting and headed to the shower. We all clapped and cheered. The Mama San went on with making up the rack as if nothing happened.

That same gunner a few days later came back from the club smashed and passed out in his rack. We decided to play a practical joke on him. We had a case of scotch tape. (I have no idea what a box of scotch tape was doing in our barracks.) We decided to put it to good use. We ran the tape around and around him lying in his rack until he couldn't move. We left him like that until morning. It was a good thing we didn't have a mortar attack that night.

Several hundred Montagnard (sounds like "mountain yards") with several Green Beret divisions showed up at our base. They were going to do a sweep in the T-10 area of the Rung Sat Zone. Intelligence reports indicated that there was a large Viet Cong presence in that particular area. The advisors wanted to know if we would be available if they needed some support. We assured them that we would.

Montagnard were tribal people that still used bows and arrows and lived in the mountains. The U.S. government recruited thousands of these tribal people, and trained and outfitted them. They were trained and led by Army special forces advisors. They were fierce fighters and didn't back down from anything, unlike the South Vietnamese soldiers. It was said that they would kill a South Vietnamese just about as fast as they would kill a North Vietnamese. Racism and being cheated by the government had left a really bad taste in their mouths. There was a rumor that they got paid by the body count. I don't know if they did, but the ones we met sure showed off a lot of ears. (They cut them off their kills.)

The next night I had the duty. We had flown several missions that day and I was beat. Just about the time I was sound asleep, the scramble bell went off. Scramble one, Americans in trouble. We were in the air in minutes and found out it was the Green Beret advisors with the Montagnard. They had finished their sweep and had been headed to extraction when they were cut off by a large NVA force. As we got close to the area, you could really see the gunfire. It was the most I'd seen since I arrived. Pitch black with no rain, it was obvious where we needed to put our strikes in. My pilot contacted the Green Beret advisors and told them we were rolling in. You could hear the gunfire over his radio. We opened up as we made our descent and my pilot punched off four rockets. I thought for sure we were going to encounter a hail of gunfire but I think our gunfire was so on target and the barrage from the Montagnard so intense that they were keeping their heads down. All the guns were firing great and we broke around for our next run. This time we weren't so lucky. As we made our turn, we came under heavy fire. I don't know how no one got hurt. We circled back around and came in from a different direction. Again, we came under heavy fire. We unloaded the rest of our rockets and most of our ammo. We contacted the Green Beret advisor and told them we were headed back to Nhà Bè to rearm and refuel. They told us we had really damaged the Viet Cong and they were still taking heavy fire.

While we were doing our hot turn around in Nhà Bè, the Green Beret advisors called Moon River and asked if they could get the area lit up. They called in the Air Force. They sent a plane out to light the area with huge parachute flares. When we got back, the battle was still intense. We made three more rocket runs and managed to stay in the air. Just as we were leaving for another hot turn around, the Air Force showed up and started dropping flares. We did our hot turn around and checked the chopper for damage. A few bullet holes but nothing serious. When we got back, the place was really lit up and the battle had quieted down. We did three more rocket runs, covering a larger area. We took very little fire on those runs. The flares really mess with your night vision. We contacted the Green Berets, and they told us the VC were on the run and they were headed to extraction. They thanked us and told us the encounter could have turned out differently if it hadn't been for us.

We headed for Nhà Bè and refueled, rearmed, and checked the chopper real good. We had taken a few more hits on both aircraft, but nothing serious. All of us were wiped out and ready to crash.

The next day, we met with the advisors and the Montagnard. There was a lot of handshaking and gratitude. What a crazy tribe. This would not be the last time I met with the Montagnard. The next time would be bone-chilling.

One night, I was lying in my rack sound asleep. I didn't have duty, and it was just before midnight. We were abruptly brought out of a sound sleep by a huge explosion. We knew it was too big an explosion to be a mortar attack. We all headed out the end of our barracks and into our bunker as the base siren went off. We could hear the duty crew firing up the choppers and getting the helos off the ground. We stay in our bunker until the all-clear sounded. (If it had been a ground attack we would have grabbed our weapons and gone to our designated places at the helo pad to set up our defense positions.) It wasn't long before the all-clear sounded. Nobody knew anything and we could hear our helos returning. We got back to the barracks, dressed hurriedly, and ran to the ready room to see if the duty crew knew anything.

When we got there, it was chaos. People running everywhere and debris everywhere. The ready room was trashed. The ceiling was down and the windows blown out. About that time our choppers were landing, so we headed to the helo pad to see if they knew anything. It turned out that the VC had floated a five-hundred-pound bomb up to our shore. Three Seabees had been rigging lights around it so a UDT (underwater demolition team) could disarm it. Something had happened and it went off. The Seabees were blown to pieces, and several vehicles were destroyed along with several buildings.

We were busy cleaning up the mess in and around our ready room when a couple of MPs pulled up in a jeep. They were looking for volunteers to search for and collect the pieces of the Seabees. I and two of the other gunners volunteered. They told us where to report. As we got close to the area, you could smell the burnt flesh and my stomach did a flip-flop. I didn't want to vomit, but I came close. We picked up plastic bags and joined the other guys doing a walk down. I thought about the guys who were fighting on the ground, and how they have to deal with this regularly. I thought about my best friend, Lance, in the Marine Corp and wondered how he was doing. He carried a radio on his back.

In the dark, it was slow going, but we finally ran out of pieces and turned around and started back, searching as we went. I ended up along the shoreline, shining my flashlight back and forth when I thought I saw what looked like a head. I was almost afraid to shine my light back on it. I shined my light back again. It lay amongst some debris, and I about lost it. I didn't know if I could pick it up or not. When I got closer and put the flashlight on it again, I was relieved to find out that it wasn't a head after all. It was a large, hairy coconut. What a fucking rush. I made my way back to where we had picked up the bags and turned mine in. My buddies were turning their bags in, and the three of us headed back to the barracks. It was a quiet walk, all of us in our own thoughts. I wondered who those guys had been and about their families. I hit the shower and then the rack, but didn't sleep well.

The next day I had duty, but we all jumped in to get our ready room cleaned up and repaired. We didn't fly any missions, but stayed "on the ready" in case we got scrambled. As a result of the bombing, our ready room got a real makeover including new tile for the floor and cabinets.

We found out later that all the pieces of the Seabees were divided into three boxes with each of their names on them and sent home.

The Seabees built us a new revetment, including storage for rockets, ammo, smoke, and tear gas.

Speaking of tear gas, we were once on a regular search-and-destroy mission when we flew over a recently exposed bunker and tunnel complex in the T-10 Rung Sat area. It had been defoliated and blown apart by air strikes. We flew over low and slow, looking for signs of any activity when we spotted a couple bunkers still intact. Our FTL decided to drop tear gas into the openings and drop back to see what happened instead of wasting rockets on it. The FTL was going to drop the tear gas, so they headed down. I was in the trail bird, and we stayed aloft a couple hundred feet to cover them.

Normally the crew chief dropped the gas, grenades, or smokes. But this time, he decided to let the gunner get the experience. He got out on the skid with the CS gas and the pilot got into position. He pulled the pin and tossed it away, but he was concentrating too hard on the opening and the gas hit the step on the skid that the copilot uses to get in and out of the aircraft. From there, it bounced into the aircraft and down into the copilots chin bubble. There was no way to get it out of the chin bubble unless you were on the ground. I could see the gas billowing out of the aircraft. The FTL came on the radio and said he was having a hard time seeing, but was trying to find a clear spot to land. We stayed aloft to provide cover until he found a clear spot. He landed pretty hard and everyone bailed out. We got lucky. No Charlie. The canister burned out and they got it out of the chin bubble and got back in the air.

The incident was written up and headquarters got a hold of it. They sent an urgent memo ordering us to no longer throw hand grenades out of the aircraft. They figured if we could do it with a gas canister, we might be able to do it with a hand grenade. From now on we would use the M79 grenade launcher.

A Man Returns

September

Nhà Bè got a new base commander and he made a lot of changes for whatever reason. He didn't like where we were, so we had to pack up and move. Such was the military.

Charlie had been on the move lately, so we were really busy with regular scrambles and in-between special operations. They'd also stepped up their mortar attacks, destroying buildings and killing a few more civilians. We'd been very lucky at this detachment. Only a few birds had been shot up. Some of the other Dets had not been not so lucky. We'd lost a few brothers and a few aircraft. Every time we took off on a mission, we never knew if we were coming back, if this was going to be our last one. Each of us had volunteered for this job and could quit at any time, but we kept going. We believed in what we were doing. That's what kept us going, and we knew we were saving lives. We were a band of brothers—doing the job we volunteered to do.

I got a chance to go into Saigon again to the PX at Tan Son Nhut Air Base. I got a ride in with the other off-duty gunners. I had saved a little money besides what I put in the 10 percent interest program. I upgraded my stereo gear with two Pioneer speakers and a turntable, a Kenwood tuner, amplifier, and reverberator, and an Akai reel-to-reel tape player. I'd be sending all this stuff home when I left.

Most everyone here could put in for R & R (rest and recuperation). There was a list of destinations you could choose from. I had chosen Australia. But I decided to cancel my R & R and take the money and buy a new car instead.

I'd been looking at the Triumph TR-250. Over there, it was $2,300. In the States, it was $3,200. If you put 10 percent down, the Navy exchange would finance it for one percent interest.

In September, I found out I had flown over one hundred combat missions already.

We had a crew chief that would be leaving soon and I'd heard through the grapevine that they might try me out for his position. I had taken a crew chief course when I first got to Vũng Tau so that might help. Problem is, I was only an E3 airman, and you had to be at least an E4 Petty Officer to be a chief.

The crew chief was responsible for the aircraft and making sure that the gunner had his shit together. He decided whether the aircraft was flyable or not. He also kept up with all the maintenance. He kept tabs on the pilot, especially if the pilot was new, so he knew what was going on all the time. If I made crew chief, I was ready. It would look good on my record.

I received another letter from my mom. She sent some pictures of the family including pictures of our dog Shep, a German Shepherd. I carried Mom's picture and a family photo in my flight suit. She sent me a cross and I had it hanging in the helo, even though I wasn't very religious. She wrote that both my sisters, Lynn and Patsy, had new babies, so it looked like I'd have a new nephew and niece to visit when I got back. I also received a letter from my aunt Joyce, letting me know how the family was and that my cousin Harry had joined the Navy. She said she saw a nice write-up about me in the local paper.

At the duty briefing in the morning, the FTL surprised me by requesting that I try out for crew chief. And not just crew chief, but crew chief on *his* bird—*the lead bird*. The crew chief would take my spot as gunner. I accepted of course, but I couldn't believe he wanted me to man the .50 caliber. That was the prime seat to have. I was so excited. I thought for sure I would be on the trail bird, manning the twin .30 calibers. The crew chief whose position I was taking was a great guy, an excellent crew chief, and skilled with the .50 cal. I was glad he was on the aircraft, just in case I needed something.

Author behind the .50 caliber

As crew chief the first thing you did when you got to the aircraft when you were getting ready to take off was to untie the rotor blade from the tail rotor stinger. You pulled the rotor blade around to the front of the aircraft, so the pilot could see you. That way he knew he could fire up the aircraft. He first hit the battery switch, then the fuel switch, followed by the igniter switch. The jet engine then came alive.

I could feel the pull on the rotor blade. I hung on until I knew the rpms were up to the point where the blade would not flop around. It was a fuel thing. I tossed the tie down into the aircraft and armed the rockets, connected the barrels to the flex guns, and made sure the ammo was in the receivers. Next, I put on all my gear and climbed aboard. I checked the gunner and got a thumbs up from him. Then I turned my attention to all the instrument gauges to make sure they were all registering the right numbers. When the rpms reached about 6,600, the pilot pulled the stick and we were off the ground. Oh, did I love that feeling. The pilot would normally do a hover check at four to five feet, and then, we both checked the gauges again. Then the pilot keyed his ICS button and asked the crew chief (me) if it was clear to move out of the revetment and into the helo pad. During this time, the copilot was turning on all the radios: VHF, UHF, FM, and the nav aids. The VHF hooked us up to other tactical support groups. FM allowed us to talk to troops on the ground and the VHF let us talk to other aircraft and our command center.

Normally we would have to back down the runway and kind of get a running start. We were so heavy and underpowered we couldn't lift straight up like you would think a helicopter would be able to do. During the day, it was very hot and the air was thin. At night, it was cooler and the air was not as thin, especially when raining. We had the river at the end of the runway and we didn't want to end up in it, like we'd seen other choppers do. Since I'd been there, two Army choppers had ended up in the soup. One of the crashes killed the pilot.

The FTL informed us that we were going to fly a couple of H & I missions, which stood for Harassment and Interdiction. They said the new guy on the .50 caliber (that was me) should get some experience. I was all for that. I performed my crew chief duties flawlessly, and we were now airborne, and headed for the Rung Sat Special Zone.

From takeoff until the time you touched back down, you had to be ever so vigilant. Looking for anything out of place: a muzzle flash or a B40 rocket coming at you. We were ready to throw a smoke at any time. The quicker you spotted something could be the difference in whether you lived to fly another day.

Trail bird

The wing bird pilot radioed us to let us know that his gunner had spotted a hooch and dropped a purple smoke near it. We did a 180 and flew back over the area. We knew the smoke would be forward of the target but we did not see anything. The trail bird flew back over the area again. This time the gunner got a yellow smoke almost on the target. The FTL decided to put a strike in on the area. Our run would be east to west, firing four rockets with a break to the right. About that time, your adrenaline started pumping. You never knew if you were going to take a hit or not.

We rolled in, machine guns blazing, while the pilot punched off rockets. We blew the holy hell out of the area with no return fire and no secondary explosions. When we flew back around to take a look, we found the large hooch on fire along with two smaller ones also on fire. As we looked more closely, we saw two more very small structures about three hundred yards to the east of the others. My pilot keyed his ICS button, saying, "Smith, I'm going to circle back around. Let's see what you can do with that .50 caliber." I told him I was going to load a box of incendiary rounds and set them ablaze. He thought that was a good idea. He radioed the wing bird to let them know what we were going to do. He told the pilot to have his crew chief pump some .30 cal into the area.

I emptied a hundred-round box into the structures and the surrounding area, setting everything ablaze. I was setting in another hundred-round box when the radio went off. It was tactical command Moon River. They said that a couple PBRs were in serious trouble not far from us. They had gone up a small canal looking for VC and had found nothing, but when they turned around to come back out, they had been heavily ambushed. They were cut off and the tide was going out. We made contact with them and advised them that we were six minutes out. You could hear the gunfire on their radio. Needless to say, he told us to hurry. We still had plenty of rockets and ammo, but we weren't so good on fuel. The PBR captain told us the VC were all on the south bank. You could hear the stress in his voice.

We soon spotted the PBR, and there was a lot of gunfire going on. We knew we were going to take some heavy fire. We contacted the PBRs and told them we were rolling in and that they should keep their heads down because we were going to use rockets. My pilot keyed his ICS: "Going hot, six rockets, break left, here we go." Looking forward, I could see the rockets hitting their mark. As we broke left and gained altitude, the wing bird came in right on target. My gunner was firing away, putting cover fire down under the wing bird. As we came around, we spotted two sampans loaded with VC headed for the mouth of the canal. My pilot told me, "Smith, they're all yours." He knew we didn't have enough to do a strike on them.

They would have been beached and lost in the cover and the jungle by the time we came back around.

As my pilot rolled the Huey over on its side, the only thing keeping me in the helo was inertia. I was looking straight down the barrel of my .50 cal at the two sampans, and they were headed straight toward the shore. I squeezed down on my butterfly trigger, and at the same time all hell broke loose. A shower of incoming rounds severed the mount on the .50 caliber, almost taking me out the door with it. The .50 cal, plus the one hundred rounds of ammo, and part of the mount weigh over a hundred pounds, so it was an armload. I had not stopped firing, so I let the barrel rest on the deck while I held the other end in my lap. As I looked down the barrel, still firing, I couldn't believe it. I had shot both sampans and they were on fire. I had still had the incendiary bullets in the gun, and they had done their job. The crew chief on the wing bird was tearing the area up with the twin .30s.

In the meantime, the gunner/crew chief informed the pilot about the .50 cal situation and was bringing the helo around so the gunner could put the M60 on the VC that remained. I was getting the .50 situated on the deck when the gunner/crew chief's M60 jammed. He laid the gun on his lap and opened the cover. At the same time, he had a cook-off right in his face. He had raised his dark visor, so he could see the problem. He yelled that he couldn't see. I moved over to help him and keyed the ICS to let the pilot know what was happening. He had several cuts on his face, and he couldn't see. There was not much I could do for him except talk to him and keep him calm.

Our pilot contacted the PBRs to see how they were doing and to let them know about our situation. They were okay and had slipped by the VC as we were rolling in. We informed them that we were low on fuel and had an injured gunner. We were headed back to Nhà Bè for a hot turn around, but could be back in about forty-five minutes. They told us they were leaving the area soon as they were low on ammo. We radioed Nhà Bè, saying we were coming in for a hot turn around and had an injured gunner on board. We also told them that the .50 cal was down and that we would need another M60 with a box of ammo along with a replacement gunner. It took about fifteen minutes to get back.

The fuel truck was waiting along with two corpsmen to take the injured gunner to sick bay. One of the off-duty gunners took his place, and a couple of other gunners helped us rearm. I pulled the .50 cal out, stowed it, and started checking the aircraft for damage. Our bird and the wing bird both had quite a few bullet holes, but nothing serious—just sheet metal repairs. One of our flex chutes had taken a round and I was repairing it when I sliced my hand on a jagged edge. It was a bad cut, blood everywhere. I notified my pilot right away and one of the off-duty gunners stepped up right away. He headed to the barracks to get his stuff. By the time he got back, the chopper was ready. I headed to sick bay for stitches. After I got my five stitches, I checked on my gunner/crew chief. He was still there. They had medicated his eyes and said he should be better in the morning. We walked together back to the barracks. We both had the next three days off and he fully recovered.

On the way back to the PBR ambush, my helo lost oil pressure and had to make a landing in the jungle. Right after they landed, the engine froze up. No one was injured and the wing bird was able to cover them until an Army slick came in and picked them up. An Army Chinook was called in to pick up the helo and carry it to Vũng Tau. I found out later that it was caused by a bullet.

Wow! My first day as crew chief and my first day on the .50 caliber. I wondered how this chain of events would affect my future as a crew chief. The maintenance department in Vũng Tau had another aircraft for us and were able to rebuild the .50 cal mount. Those guys

Celebrating 21st birthday with my buddies

had a hell of a job keeping the Hueys flying with all of the problems they had getting parts.

On my twenty-first birthday, I and a couple buddies went into Nhà Bè, had a few drinks, and got laid. In fact, I got laid twice; after all, it was my birthday. When we got back to the barracks, the rest of the crew joined us for a proper birthday party.

October

My turn with mail call was up and I handed the responsibility to one of the new gunners.

At the morning briefing they told me I made crew chief. Hot damn, I made crew chief and as an airman. That was pretty good. Apparently my first day trying out for crew chief had not deterred their decision. They did decide to put me on the wing bird on the twin .30s. The crew chief on the wing bird was a short-timer and headed to Vũng Tau in about a week—about the same time as the crew chief on the lead bird. One of the other gunners had a little more seniority than I did. He was a Third Class Petty Officer. I did not have a problem with that. He was a great guy and an excellent door gunner. I couldn't wait to get on the twin .30s.

The crew chief checked me out on the twin .30s. Now all I needed was some firing time on them. Like everything else, they had their little idiosyncrasies. We also went over the entire aircraft. I already knew it pretty well from my time as a door gunner. It had a few minor problems and he went over a few things I needed to pay special attention to. One of the things that the aircraft had was an above-average vibration in the rotor blades. The balance needed to be checked to see if the trim tabs needed adjusting. This procedure was called "flagging the rotor blades." I had never done or seen it done before. Well, he had and he was happy to show me. It was quite an operation and a little bit dangerous. Imagine sticking something into a turning rotor blade. You first brought the blade around and mounted the top of it with a pole using a bow. The bow was strung with special string (I don't remember what it was). You brought the blade around and picked a spot to stand the pole up. There were tie-down clips at the end of the rotor blades. You touched the bowstring to the end of the clips, positioned the pole straight up and down from there, and marked the ground. Using different color grease pencils, you rubbed the end of the clips: one color on one clip and a different color on the other clip. You then fired up the chopper. You set the base of the pole on the previously marked spot and slowly tilted the bow into the rotor blades ever so slowly until you heard a *tic tic*. The bowstring was now marked and you could check how close together the marks were. If there was a separation in the marks, you had to shut the chopper down, adjust the trim tabs a bit, and start all over again. It wasn't right until you got the marks on top of one another. It turned out that our rotor tracking was spot-on so maintenance in Vũng Tàu would tend to it.

A Man Returns

Charlie had been really keeping us busy. Besides flying H & I (Harassment & Interdiction) flights, we'd been flying a lot of cover missions for different operations. We had also been dropping a lot of propaganda pamphlets—thousands of them.

I'd flown so many combat missions that I'd already been put in for six air medals!

A couple of the new gunners and I went into Saigon. I told them they were in for a treat. We took the local bus, and what a trip. Being so close with the locals was strange: they were so little, so different, and so poor. We did a little souvenir shopping to send home to friends and family. Then, a little barhopping. I introduced them to the Saigon tea girls. We checked them out up front and close.

On the way from one bar to the next, we came upon this very old man dressed in white robes. He had very long white hair and a beard. He stopped us and asked us in English if he could read our palms for a dollar. He took my hand, turned it over, and gasped, telling me he had never seen a palm like mine, and he needed to read it. I was immediately interested. I gave him a buck just to satisfy my curiosity. On both my palms, there is a line that runs straight across. The man said there should be two lines—a heart line and a head line. The fact that they were running together as one line was very good, he said. Then he started reading my palm; it was so interesting. He surprised us all by writing it down as he went in English on rice paper. Funny thing is that, as my life went on, his predictions were pretty much on the money. My day of celebrating making crew chief turned out to be an interesting day.

My mom sent me another package. Besides the regular goodies, she sent me a bag of maple leaves, all dressed in their fall colors. Everyone had to breathe in the fall aroma. I gave everyone a couple leaves, and we taped them to our lamps to bring out the colors. After the leaves all turned brown, I gathered them up and we burned them in a hub cap in the barracks over a few beers—well, maybe more than a few. That way we could get the final fall effect of back home.

It had been a little quiet around here lately, so our commander decided to spice things up a bit and fly Operation Firefly. This was an insane, suicidal way to piss Charlie off and get him to show himself. We had a bracket on the port side doorway on the lead bird that a specially made light ring fit into, along with a cannon plug that plugged into the aircraft. A light ring was about four feet in diameter and the whole circle was covered with lights. It was mounted on a swivel so the gunner could direct the light anywhere he wanted. We got it all hooked up, and just after dark, took off. We headed out to the T-10 area of the Rung Sat Zone to see if we could find any Charlie to piss off. You could pretty much count on getting shot at when you flew the Firefly. The head bird with the light flew at about 500 feet, while the wing bird flew at 200 feet with lights out and about a quarter mile back. This particular night must have really pissed Charlie off. I was in the wing bird, manning the twin .30s, when out of the pitch black night came a B40 rocket straight at the lead bird followed by a hail of green tracers. The rocket barely missed, but I couldn't tell about the tracers. We went into rocket run mode immediately. The lead bird told us he didn't take any hits; he was lights out and climbing. We unloaded in the area with no return fire which was common. By this time, the lead bird had come around and was putting fire down in the same area. We circled, and put some .50 and .30 caliber into the area with no return fire. Like so many times, we didn't know if we did any good or not.

October 16

Hot damn! I got the message today that I made Third Class Petty Officer. Time to party. That's what I did. I headed to the club along with most of the fire team and several SEALs. We proceeded to drink buku amounts of beer and tell lots of lies. The only problem with making rate in the Navy was the taking on the crow tradition. That entailed everyone taking their turn punching you in the left shoulder in the area the crow would be worn. The good thing was that this was usually done after you were so drunk that you could hardly feel it anyway. Everyone took their turn and soon my shoulder was hamburger meat. Hey, what were good friends for if not to help you celebrate? Needless to say, my shoulder was very sore for the next few days and I had to fly with it.

I had bad news from home. My cousin, Johnny Calton, only son of my Aunt Maddie and Uncle Bill, was killed in a car accident while home on leave from the Marines. His next duty station was Vietnam. Johnny had given them a very hard time as a teenager, but then out of the blue he up and joined the Marine Corp and became a changed man. They were so proud.

All the gunners and pilots coming and going had finally stopped. So it was looking like all the guys here now would be the ones I'd fly with until I left the country. I was glad. They looked like a great group of guys.

Coming back from a routine patrol, we came under heavy fire from the river bank just across from Nhà Bè. The lead gunship had dropped smoke on it and was circling back. We immediately rolled in on it. As we came in, we took heavy fire from the tree line. The lead bird came around and put down fire right under us, covering our break. There was still fire coming from the tree line, and as the lead bird broke, we covered them. We did this routine two more times until everything quieted down. We headed for Nhà Bè. When we landed I jumped out. Usually, the first thing you did was pull the barrels on both flex guns. I flipped both levers and grabbed both barrels. Since I was just coming in from three rocket runs which had happened just minutes ago, the barrels were still red hot and I wasn't wearing my gloves. The hot metal fried both hands and I dropped the barrels on the ground. It was very painful, but I was more pissed at myself for making such a rookie mistake. I didn't go to sick bay. I figured I would just deal with it.

The next day my bird had to make a maintenance run to Vũng Tau. Periodically, we had to make maintenance or admin runs to Vũng Tau. The crew chiefs liked to make these runs because sometimes the pilot gave them a little stick time. Because my hands were in bad shape, another crew chief volunteered to take my place. I told him I appreciated it.

Later that day, we got very bad news. My bird, the one that had gone to Vũng Tau, had lost power and crashed into the river. The pilot and the crew chief made it, but were banged up pretty good. The copilot died. The crew chief was knocked out on impact, but the pilot was able to pull him out of the aircraft before it went under. The copilot had survived the impact, but the pilot thought that he had got his flight suit hung up on the pylons and went down with the bird. My recollection may not be totally accurate, but that's the way I remember it. Two PBRs were in the area and saw the chopper go down and were on them in minutes. By the time they arrived on scene, the crew chief had regained consciousness. The PBRs brought them into Nhà Bè, and they were checked out and released. They found the copilot's body about a week later, washed up on shore and completely covered in leeches. My motto has always been that's it's better to be lucky than good. This was just one more time I cheated death.

November

Aw! Another trip into Saigon, the land of the Lambretta, the three-wheeled workhorse scooter. I'd seen them loaded with a family and their entire house stacked on in sections. While we're talking houses, the Vietnamese, besides making all kinds of toys, hanging things, and decorations, flatten cans out for roofing shingles and siding. Nothing like seeing a Pabst Blue Ribbon or Budweiser house!

On the way into Saigon, we liked to stop at some of the local bars. It was a little dangerous. You just had to be on guard all the time, and we were used to danger. Everywhere you went, you attracted the children. They were very curious. Sometimes we bought them candy.

When we got to Saigon, we checked out the USO and there was not much happening there, so we ended up doing the usual thing— barhopping and checking out the Saigon tea gals.

In Saigon, the National Police were everywhere. We called them "white mice" because of their white uniforms. You didn't want to mess with those guys. Most of them were corrupt, and most of them didn't like Americans. If you got drunk or caused a disturbance, they could be really bad to deal with. The good thing was that they would take a bribe.

Just before we got ready to head back, a Vietnamese boy approached us with a beautiful Amazon parrot in a handmade bamboo cage. He wanted five dollars for the parrot including the cage. I don't know what I was thinking, but I bought it. I sure didn't know what I was getting into. I wasn't used to having to be responsible for anything. All the feeding and cleaning was a pain in the ass, and all it wanted to do was bite me.

About two months into the ownership, we were sitting around one evening drinking, telling lies, and smoking cigarettes, when I decided to let the parrot out. I can't remember what I named the parrot. It was such a short relationship. Well, the first thing it did was take out a big chunk out of my thumb. Well, that was it. Mixed with the right amount of alcohol and the number of times it had bitten me, this was the last straw. Our tiny fridge had a small freezer compartment hanging down from the top. I wrapped the parrot in my T-shirt and stuck it tail first into the box with its head hanging out. During the course of the evening, every time someone got a beer out of the fridge, it squawked. The next morning, it was frozen solid and I tossed it in the river.

I look back on that day, and think about how life didn't mean much to me then. We didn't know if we were going to live or die one day to the next. It took me many years to finally put a value on life, and realize how valuable life is.

Just after that, I and six other guys got colds. It was hard to believe we got colds when it was so freaking hot.

I had to catch up on my shots, and got a cholera and plague shot. My arm was sore.

I had turned in my second class course and I just needed my practical factors signed and I'd be ready for a second class field promotion.

I was socking some money away now that I was getting third class pay plus hazardous duty pay which amounted to just over $300 a month. I took only $40 a month out of that, hoping to have a nice chunk of change in the bank if I make it home.

With three squares a day plus mid-rats pretty often, not to mention all the beer we consumed, I'd put on weight. I was up to one hundred eighty pounds to be exact. We didn't get much exercise, so that didn't help either. I could hardly get into my dress blues. I got a new set of dress blues tailor-made in Saigon for thirty dollars. They were not Navy regulation, but they were gabardine and would have cost sixty to seventy dollars at home. I had gold eagle liberty cuffs sewn in.

In the middle of November, I received a Christmas package from the Gouldsboro Ladies Auxiliary, ladies from my hometown. How nice was that! It was packed full of candy, peanuts, soap, a flashlight and pocketknife, nail clippers, and assorted odds and ends.

A Man Returns

My new ID showing my new rank came, and I was glad to get rid of the old card with the buzz haircut. My hair was a lot longer than Navy regulations, thank goodness. Out here on detachment we didn't have watches; we didn't have a muster, and no one said anything about your uniform or haircut.

I took my yearly flight physical and passed. I had been worried about my hearing, as my right ear was not doing so well.

I sent my mom fifty dollars for curtains and a bedspread she'd been wanting along with some other odds and ends.

I also got to vote for the first time, absentee of course, and I voted for Nixon.

They'd had a bombing halt in effect for a while, and the action here sure picked up. We'd had twice the number of scrambles. At this morning's briefing, I found out we had to go into Vũng Tau. Just a quick administrative trip. My pilot told the gunner and copilot to take it easy as I was going to fly with him as copilot. Hot damn, how exciting! I didn't get to take off or land, but I got to fly all the way to Vũng Tau and back. He let me do all kinds of maneuvers. Climbing was fun, but the descents were a little scary, as you had to try to level off without putting too many Gs on the rotor blades. Breaking left and breaking right, and trying to keep the rudders in the right position was also a little hairy. Needless to say, it was a memorable trip.

They opened up a Special Services here and we checked out a couple fishing poles. We stopped by the galley and picked up some hot dogs and bacon and headed to the PBR docks. We fished for a couple hours, but the only thing we caught were leeches.

We checked out a ping-pong set and that became one of our favorite pastimes. They also got an electric guitar, and I checked it out. They didn't have an amp for it, but I was able to back feed it through my stereo amp and out my speakers. It worked pretty good. One of

PBR docks

the new gunners played the guitar and he took time to teach me more. He was a great help in learning to play.

I was smoking over two packs a day. They were only ten cents a pack and I figured I'd quit whenever I got home. Well, I didn't. I didn't quit until I was twenty-five years old, and the main reason for quitting then wasn't my health. It was the fact they went to fifty cents a pack and I couldn't afford them.

My mom was always sending me poems she had written. I decided to try my luck at writing one and surprise her. I named it "My Secret."

> *Each time I climb*
> > *Into my faithful little bird,*
> *I say a little prayer,*
> > *And I know I am heard.*
> *We fly through the Rung Sat*
> > *And kill one or two,*
> *And I hope that He realizes*
> > *That this we must do.*

A Man Returns

We face many dangers

In our one-hour flight,

But I know He was there

Through all of the flight.

It seemed like we were always changing pilots. Most pilots didn't spend a year flying, so they were always coming and going. They were always in training for the next seat. Copilots wanting to certify as pilots and pilots wanting to be the FTL (flight team leader). Today was just such a day. We had just got a new CO (commanding officer). He was taking my pilot's position as FTL and my pilot was going to fly the nugget seat, which is what we called the copilot on the wing bird.

We took off mid-morning on a routine search-and-destroy mission. We were in the air about ten minutes when we got a call from our command center, Moon River. PBRs near our location were under heavy fire. The boat commander had been killed and there were four wounded sailors, two of them in serious condition. We told Moon River we were on our way. My copilot dialed up the PBRs on the radio and made contact. The radio on the PBR was loud with gunfire; we could barely hear the sailor on the other end, and he was very stressed. Their boat was dead in the water. One of the seriously wounded sailors had a bad head injury and had lost a lot of blood. The other PBR was running low on ammo and trying to keep the heat off the other PBR. About that time, we had them in sight and could see they were taking heavy fire from both sides of the canal. We rolled in with rockets and machine guns blazing, tearing up the river bank lined with VC. We were taking heavy fire. At the end of the run, we rolled up and over and came down on the other side of the river, doing the same damage to slow down the attack on the PBRs. We could hear the sailor on the PBR trying to get a medivac. The closest chopper was thirty minutes out, and they needed a landing zone (LZ) and there was none.

We circled above the PBRs and all the door gunners poured fire into the VC positions. The new FTL was deciding what to do next when we noticed the wing bird had broken formation and was headed down. The FTL radioed the wing bird to find out what he was doing. My pilot, who was flying copilot, had taken command of the wing bird and was going to try to somehow pick up the two seriously wounded sailors off the PBR. The FTL ordered him to abort and fall back into formation. The wing bird responded: "Negative, I'm going to unload the rest of my ordinance into the river bank where the VC are still firing from. I would appreciate some overhead cover." The FTL said, "No. Abort right now. It's too risky! That's a direct order." I could see the wing bird dumping his rockets into the river edge and the door gunners unloading into both sides of the river. The PBRs were still firing at the VC. The FTL took our chopper to a couple hundred feet above the wing bird. I opened up again with the .50 cal. I could see the VC hiding behind the trees along the riverbank. My gunner was firing on the other riverbank with his M60. PBRs are only thirty-one feet long and the wing bird copilot was trying to land on skid on the stern. The PBR was moving with the current, plus the rotor wasn't helping, not to mention we were all still taking fire. He finally got it to stick and I saw the gunner jump out into the PBR. It was a good thing the gunner was a stocky fellow. He handed the first sailor up to the crew chief and then the second sailor up to the crew chief and jumped back in the chopper. He grabbed his M60 and the crew chief got back on his twin .30s and they both started firing again. The VC were persistent, following the PBR, and popping up off and on to fire on it. The chopper slid off the stern and my heart skipped a beat as the skids went into the water with the two sailors on board. Even with getting rid of most of his ordinance, he was almost too heavy in the heat of the day. Then the chin bubble went into the water causing more drag. It was going with the current trying to get lift. I thought for a moment that they were going in, but somehow he managed ever so slowly to break free of the water and start climbing. We headed to the nearest Army field hospital near Saigon. They sure didn't look good. We called ahead and the ambulance was waiting when we landed. We found out later from the PBR officer-in-charge (OIC) that they both made it and were going home. One of the Army fuel trucks filled us up and we headed back to Nhà Bè. Unbelievably, we only had a few bullet holes and nothing serious.

The other PBR was able to tow the disabled one back to Nhà Bè. Both PBRs suffered quite a bit of damage.

At debriefing, shit hit the fan. The new OIC got into it with my pilot. He told him he was going to see to it that he lost his wings. Nothing ever came of it and later he was awarded the Silver Star for his actions. My pilot was well-liked, and the new OIC started off on a bad foot.

We were used to having newspaper journalists and magazine people coming in and out, but whenever you had a special incident happen (and news travels fast), they came out of the woodwork. Quite a few reporters came by over the next couple weeks. We even had official Navy writers and photographers drop in. I remember a woman journalist coming by. She was pretty cool. Her name was Helen Musgrove. She was from Jacksonville, Florida, my next duty station. She was very interested in the Seawolves and interviewed each of us.

A lot of these individuals wanted to fly on a mission with us. From time to time, we took somebody, and depending on the character, we might have some fun with them. This mainly consisted of us just pulling an autorotation on them, making them think we were going in. For some reason, they didn't think that was very funny.

The crew chief on the wing bird manning the twin .30s was currently on the way to Vũng Tau to finish out his tour, and not by choice. He had a bad temper and was known to start fights. He had even tried me and trained me. He was an excellent crew chief—the best I'd seen on the twin .30s. Well, this incident was his last. He came in the barracks late one night drunk. He was looking to start something with someone, and that someone happened to be the biggest guy in the room. He and I had gone through all of our Seawolf training together, so I knew him as an easygoing guy. We tried to settle him down but that wasn't working. He had grown up on the streets of New York and was known to be a dirty fighter. He took a swing at the gunner and hit him in the gut. The gunner grabbed him, and they ended up on the floor. The gunner got his legs wrapped around the guy's neck. The gunner only had on his boxer shorts, and the crew chief chomped down on the inside of the gunner's leg, tearing a piece out of his leg! The gunner turned him loose. It looked really bad. One of the guys called for shore patrol. The crew chief jumped the gunner again and this time they went out the door and onto the ground. The gunner was bleeding pretty bad, and they were punching each other on the ground. The SPs showed up and the gunner had the crew chief in a choke hold. The crew chief had one of the gunner's fingers in his mouth and clamped down to the bone, blood everywhere. The SPs were yelling for them to break it up. The gunner released the crew chief, but the crew chief would not let go of the finger. The SP hit him in the head with his nightstick and he still would not let go. Finally, after several more blows to his head, the crew chief turned the gunner loose. Wow! They were both covered in blood. They put the crew chief in the jeep and sped away. We wrapped the gunner's leg wound with a T-shirt and took him to sick bay. He had a nasty hole in his leg and his finger was nearly bitten off!

A Man Returns

It took a long time for both wounds to heal and that's why the crew chief was on his way to Vũng Tau.

In my free time, I threw darts, played ping-pong, strummed my guitar, and recorded music on my reel-to-reel. Special services had records you could check out, and I'd been taking advantage of it. I'll tell you, 1968 and 1969 was a great time for rock and roll music. I also recorded off the radio American Forces Vietnam Network (AFVN). They played a lot of rock and roll too. Hanoi Hannah also played rock and roll—along with her propaganda. I think the most-played song in Vietnam was "We Got to Get Out of This Place" recorded by the Animals. Nothing like listening to rock and roll while on a mission. By the time I got home, I'd have plenty of music on my reel-to-reel.

Again, we had to move, and what a pain in the ass that was with all the stereo gear I now had.

I'd been trying to grow a mustache but it was so blond, you couldn't see it. The only time you could see it is was when I came back from a mission because it was black from gunpowder. I took some real ribbing about it, so I finally shaved it off.

One of the crew chiefs was one of my best friends, and like me, an avionic tech. He decided to get into the Thanksgiving spirit by putting on a little holiday production—pilgrims, Indians, the whole works. With a little help, he managed to pull it off. It was a nice change from the norm. This same crew chief later extended his tour in Vietnam and was transferred to another detachment. I got word shortly after I got back to the States that he had been killed. The thing I remember most about him was his infectious smile. He seemed to wear it all the time.

December

A Sikorsky CH54 Tarhe, also known as the Flying Crane, had to make an emergency fuel stop at Nhà Bè. He landed okay but when he tried to take off, he lifted the PSP runway planking and caused big ripples in it. They had to use a caterpillar to smooth it out flat again.

We used Chinooks to pick up our Huey and the Flying Crane to pick up the Chinooks. They could pick up as much as ten tons, so they were a powerful helicopter.

We had another good reason to party (as if we needed a reason) when my pilot made lieutenant. When it came to partying, there was no officer/enlisted separation. Nothing like flying with a hangover.

One of the gunners got a new puppy and named it Ralph. One day he decided to take Ralph into Saigon to get its shots. Upon arriving,

Damaged UH-1B headed to maintenance

they stopped at the USO club first to get something to eat. Well, they wouldn't let him in with the puppy. He found a Vietnamese boy whom he paid to watch Ralph while they ate lunch. When he came back out to get Ralph, the kid and Ralph were both gone. They checked the surrounding area with no luck.

On his next day off the whole crew started "mission impossible" and went back into Saigon to track down Ralph. They started at the USO, and lo and behold! There was the boy! He didn't see them coming and they were able to grab him. Without any problem, he led them down a couple alleys to a cage full of puppies. My friend didn't see Ralph at first and was calling his name when from the back of the cage came Ralph, ears flopping and a big smile on his face. So our mission impossible ended up possible. He got real lucky.

Our gun cleaning station (yeah, the one where I lost my graduation ring) was behind the ready room and had no roof. During the rainy season, it was a real pain in the ass to clean your weapons. One of the gunners decided we needed a roof and took it upon himself to get one built. He spent about two weeks scavenging here and yonder for materials, and actually managed to build a roof over the station. Now we were not only out of the rain, but also in the shade.

In early December, everyone got lots of packages and goodies. Today at mail call, there was more of the same, except today I received a large package from my mom. I was pretty excited. Upon opening it, I found some more guitar books which I really needed, but the real kicker was astounding and I knew she put a lot of effort into doing it: it was a real live Christmas tree! The tree still had its roots and she had wrapped them wet and bagged them. The tree looked very fresh. She had also bagged the tree. When I opened it, the pine fragrance filled the whole barracks. Along with the tree, she had sent lights, decorations, and even a nativity for underneath the tree. The tree became real popular, real fast. Guys heard about the tree and came by just to get a whiff of a real Christmas tree. What a special Christmas gift.

As mentioned before, my motto has always been: "Better to be lucky than good." Well, luck came through for me again. The Bob Hope Christmas was coming up on December 23 at Xã Long Bình. I didn't have duty that day and it looked like I was going to get to go. What a special treat. I was ready for a break. I'd flown over two hundred combat missions so far and this would be a nice distraction. I was not taking R & R, so this would be my one day of it.

Security must have been something. With over 30,000 guys, the place was packed. Bob Hope really put on a show. He had Ann-Margret shaking her booty all over the place. Then there was Penelope Plummer, Miss Australia, who was crowned Miss World 1968, and the show was mighty fine. And of course, the Golddiggers with Les Brown and his Band of Renown. They put on quite a show and it was over way too soon. Back to the jungle.

From a dead sleep to wide awake in seconds. The scramble bell was going off. It was a scramble two: RVN in trouble. We were airborne in about two minutes, adrenaline flowing. After we got airborne, we found that it was one of the outposts that we'd been scrambled to more than once. There were several outposts in our area of operation, and they were constantly getting hit. This time they said they were in serious trouble. The VC had used the cease fire to move troops into the area and the outpost was being overrun by hundreds of NVA troops. We could see the outpost in the distance and it was not good. The firefight was very heavy. I knew this was going to be a bad one. We made contact with the outpost and they had taken heavy casualties. Two walls had already been breached. The FTL decided to surprise Charlie, by coming in on the deck below the treetop level. The perimeter around the outpost had been cleared of all trees for obvious reasons.

A Man Returns

We flew along the south wall just above the ground, NVA everywhere. The copilot had the four M60s blazing, and the pilot was punching off rockets. We were so low, we were flying through our own rocket debris. The door gunner was tearing up the clearing and the tree line. I was taking them down along the wall. As we came to the end of the clearing, we pulled up, rolled around, and did the same thing down the other wall. Instead of coming back around to the first wall we hit before, we flew down the tree line. This allowed the pilot to rocket the tree line and the copilot to strafe it. My gunner and I stayed busy with targets everywhere. We were just finishing dropping the last of our ordinances on the second tree line when a team of Army gunships arrived.

It was the Gunslingers. We had worked with these guys on several occasions. We told them to have at it. We were out of ammo and low on fuel. We headed back to Nhà Bè to do a hot turn around. Upon landing, the first thing I did was check the aircraft for damage. Again, we were lucky. Both aircraft took several hits, but nothing serious. We fueled up and reloaded, heading back to the outpost. When we got there, the Gunslingers were gone and the outpost was recovering. NVA troops had retreated into the jungle. We stayed for a while, covering the Army medivacs removing the dead and the wounded. We found out later they counted over sixty North Vietnamese killed.

January 1969

Wow! New Year's Eve and I didn't have duty. The EM club (enlisted man's club) was putting on a party and a show. I thought I would have a good time. By the time midnight came around, I was pretty smashed. I was so smashed that a couple of the guys had to help me back to the barracks. I had something else going on too though, because I stayed sick for a week and a half. I never missed any missions, but it was a very rough week and a half. Of course, I swore I'd never do it again.

I got a big kick out of the Vietnamese rock bands. They didn't speak a lick of English, but they could sing all our songs in English with a funny accent.

Our detachment was selected to try out a new experimental starlight video camera system. In Vũng Tàu, they mounted this system on the front of a Huey gunship. It consisted of a metal frame with a starlight mounted in the middle connected to servo motors. It stuck out from the front of the nose about three feet. It was operated by the copilot who used a joystick to move the camera around. He also had a CRT (cathode-ray tube) screen between his legs. I think it was about a ten-inch screen. It made things just a little tighter in the cockpit. They wanted us to try it out for a couple of weeks. Lucky us. We

Starlight camera mounted on UH-1B

A Man Returns

flew into Vũng Tau early because we knew it was going to be a long day. We parked our chopper near the starlight bird. We had to move everything from our bird to the starlight bird. Goodbye, .50 cal (the starlight bird does not have a .50 cal mount). That's alright. I really liked the M60. It would be nice to be on the "60" again for a while. I hated changing choppers. Just as you got used to all the little things that made your chopper tick, something happened and you had to learn a new one.

As the crew chief I had to check the operational status of the chopper. I got with maintenance and checked the chopper service record and any gripes it might have had. Thank goodness, the bird was pretty clean. Our maintenance guys again were doing a great job. We spent the afternoon getting checked out on the operation of the starlight system. Since I was the detachment electronic technician, it was necessary that I checked out the troubleshooting end of it. It was a pretty simple set up. My pilot and I were pretty concerned about the extra weight. Not only did we have all that weight hanging out the front, but they also added a weight to the stinger to balance everything out.

For the next two weeks, we were very busy. Besides our scrambles and regular operations, we were flying two missions a night, checking out the starlight camera. I knew Charlie had to be wondering how in the hell we could see them at night. We spent most of the time flying the canals in the Rung Sat and T-10 areas. The camera worked pretty well. The copilot would spot a sampan (or sampans), and if we couldn't get visual on them, we would open up with our M60s and he would talk us in by watching the tracers on the screen. I don't remember how many sampans we got in the two weeks we had the starlight camera, but I know we got several of them and it freaked Charlie out.

The weight was the biggest problem. Our UH-1B was way underpowered to carry it. Everyone was kidding my pilot about stubbing his nose on takeoff. Overall, the system was pretty good, but it needed a more powerful bird. The two weeks went by pretty quick—we were so busy flying. Now it was time to head back to Vũng Tau to swap aircraft again and get my .50 cal back. Lookout sampans.

Boy, was I pissed! I couldn't believe it! During the night someone walked through the barracks and walked off with my .38! When Iwasn't not wearing it, it was holstered and hanging at the head of my rack. Well, that little incident cost me a Captain's Mast, which didn't look good on my record. I had to go to Vũng Tau for the Captain's Mast. It wasn't bad. They knew shit happened, but I had fifty dollars deducted from my pay.

I'd been thinking about extending six months, but I finally got a letter from my best friend, Lance, that changed my mind. He was up north and he'd been having it pretty rough. He was a radioman in the Marine Corp infantry. He was due to go home June 1 so I decided to just extend two months and go home on June 3. When he found out what I was doing, he was pretty happy because we'd both have thirty days off to raise hell. But on the other hand, he said, he would feel really bad if something happened to me in those two months. I told him I had planned to extend six months anyway, so this would cut out four months of exposure.

February

I definitely decided to not take any in-country or out-of-country R & R. Instead I saved that money for a new car. I was thinking about a TR250 Triumph, but hadn't made up my mind yet.

We'd been really busy. Charlie was on the move with Tet just a few days away. I had been really racking up the combat missions, especially with guys taking R & R.

A Man Returns

SEAL Team One was back. I was always glad when they showed up because it meant we were going to get a lot of night action and they had quite a few operations scheduled. Some of them were body snatching. They grabbed someone and brought them back to Nhà Bè where they had an interrogation room with a team of interrogators. Operations wanted to see if they could find out what was going on in the delta with Tet coming on.

The SEAL teams used our gun cleaning station and our test firing area. This was very cool because we got a chance to fire some of the weapons they carried. My SEAL weapon of choice was the stoner. What a fine machine gun. The CAR-15 was pretty nice too, and it probably didn't weigh over six pounds. It was amazing how much fire power a team could carry. I liked watching these guys get ready for an operation and noting the amount of equipment they carried. It was pretty awesome. Most of them wore the tiger stripe cams and they all had different headgear. The camo face paint was the final touch—the touch that scared the hell out of any VC unlucky enough to come in contact with one of them.

Besides our regular daytime operations, we spent the next week carrying out body-snatching operations almost every night at different locations. Some of them went pretty smoothly, but others were pretty hairy. They got some pretty good intel and we were able to head off some of the VC Tet operations as a result.

I was sending voice recordings back and forth to my mom since they were able to use my dad's tape recorder. I was surprised he let them use it. It was pretty cool because not only did I get to hear everyone's voices, but I could also hear our parakeet and our dog, Shep, in the background at times.

I didn't have my orders yet but I could still start my short-timer's calendar on February 20. On that day I'd have ninety-nine days and a wake-up. The calendar was called a FIGMO calendar and it stood for

My FIGMO calendar

Fuck It, Got My Orders. There were all different kinds of calendars. Mine had a female genie coming out of an oil lamp. She had large breasts and her hand was reaching out, touching the wake-up spot (the penis of a sleeping sailor). Her body was made up of ninety-nine spaces that you colored in as you counted down the days. My mom was very cool. I sent her one so she could count the days down too. She saved this calendar along with all the letters I had sent her.

We had just returned from a mission and refueled and rearmed. We were headed to the chow hall when the Seawolf scramble bell went off—scramble one: Americans in trouble. Upon getting airborne, we found out that a company of Montagnard along with their Army Ranger advisors had come in contact with a large NVA force. They were currently pinned down and running low on ammo. Upon getting there, we made contact with the advisors to find out where we would do the most good. The area was a little different in that there was elephant grass everywhere. We decided on the best plan of attack and rolled in, rockets blasting and all the machine guns chattering away. We came under heavy fire right away. We cut a swath down though the elephant grass and could see the NVA troops scrambling everywhere. The smoke was already heavy and getting worse. We rolled in several times from different directions and the return fire slowed down. This allowed the Montagnard and Rangers to advance. The Montagnard were fierce fighters.

The Rangers radioed us that the NVA had suffered heavy casualties while they had captured a high-ranking NVA officer, but he was badly wounded. They didn't expect him to live much longer and they wanted us to evacuate him back to Nhà Bè for interrogation. We radioed Moon River and they asked us to pick him up and bring him in. We were low on fuel and ammo, so we were a lot lighter.

My pilot keyed his ICS button and wanted to know if we were all in to fly with a hot LZ and pick up a prisoner, and of course we were. It was all part of the job. The Rangers popped a smoke and we headed down. I strapped on a fresh hundred-round box of ammo on my .50 cal and got ready for anything. I was sweating like crazy, and smoke was swirling everywhere. We came in fast and hit pretty hard.

My eyes were straining to see through the smoke, gunfire everywhere. I had both thumbs on the butterfly trigger, adrenaline flowing and sweating profusely. Then out of the smoke came a couple of Montagnard; I was wound so tight, I almost opened fire on them. As they came out of the smoke, I could see they were dragging bodies by the hair of their heads. Then several more appeared, also dragging bodies, and came toward the chopper. My door gunner keyed his mic and told us that the Rangers were loading the NVA officer on his side. He was hooked up to a couple of bags and the gunner handed them to me. I hung them from the ceiling. I turned around and saw that the Montagnard were trying to load the bodies into the chopper. I yelled, "*Di di mau!*" That meant "get the hell out of here" and the next thing I knew, the guy in front of me pulled out his machete and chopped the guy's head off! I keyed my mic and told the pilot, "We're clear! Let's get the hell out of here!" The NVA officer was thrashing around and my gunner was holding his .45 on him and yelling, "*Di di Mau! Di di Mau!*" at the Montagnard. Meanwhile, they were chopping off heads and trying to throw them in the chopper. On my side, one of the heads made it into the doorway. I picked it up by the hair and I sat it on the injured officer's stomach. His eyes got big and he stopped thrashing around. I left the head there, surprised at how heavy it was. At the same time, the pilot radioed our wing bird, who had been keeping us covered, to let them know we were lifting off so they could cover our ass. As we slowly lifted above the elephant grass, we started taking fire. We both opened on them and so did the wing bird. I don't know how we made it out of there. We had used the last of our ammo and it was going to be close on fuel getting back to Nhà Bè. We took a lot of hits but we were still in the air. We radioed Nhà Bè to have an ambulance standing by as well as an interrogator, if possible.

We made it back to Nhà Bè alright and the ambulance was waiting. When the medic got to our chopper, they were surprised by the head still sitting on the officer. I remember my pilot shouting, "No pictures! No pictures!" There was so much blood in our chopper we had to have the fire department hose it out. We found out later that the officer died, but not before they got some good information from him.

After refueling and rearming, we all headed to the chow hall. We were starving. After we ate, I did a thorough post-flight on the aircraft. We had taken quite a few hits but all and all, we came out pretty good. We just needed some minor rewiring and repairs and some hole patching. We were mighty lucky again. At this time, I had almost three hundred combat missions. Even so, every time we took off, my adrenaline started pumping and I wondered if this was going to be the one that got me.

A few days later, the Rangers, along with their company of Montagnard, arrived at Nhà Bè. The Rangers came by to thank us for saving their asses again. I was off duty so I asked them about meeting some of the Montagnard and they said not a problem. I followed them back to the edge of our base where they had set up camp. The Montagnard were a pretty rowdy bunch, but seemed excited about talking with me when they found out I was one of the gunners with the Seawolves. I talked with them through one of the Rangers' interpreters. They showed me what they were cooking for dinner too. It was quite an array of stuff they had gathered as they walked through the jungle. It was so interesting talking to them. I got a rise from the whole company when I told them about the Apollo moon mission. It was daytime, but the moon was nearly full and bright in the sky. I pointed up at it and told them about sending a manned mission around the moon and back. Then, I told them the next mission would actually *land* on the moon and a man would walk on the moon. They all laughed, calling me "*dinky đầu,*" which meant crazy. I was a crazy American.

There was a rumor going around that the Montagnard were getting paid by the body count. I asked the Rangers about it, and they had no comment. It was said that they kept track of the dead VC by cutting off their ears. I personally saw several guys with ears that they claimed they got from Montagnard. I asked the Rangers about the head-chopping incident we ran into while evacuating the NVA officer. Did that have anything to do with a body count? He said it did.

The Rangers had my respect—trusting their lives to a bunch of natives who just the other day were using spears, bows, and arrows, and now were suddenly firing machine guns and rifles. The Rangers said they were fierce fighters and did what they were told.

March

My gunner and I were ready for a one-day R & R. We decided to go into Saigon to have a few beers and find a massage parlor and check out the women. We had heard they really treated you right in the massage parlors, and we wanted to find out for ourselves. I had three girlfriends that I usually went to for a good time: Kim and Kai were in Saigon and Sally was in Nhà Bè. They spoke English and were working their way through college. Kim was half-French and drop-dead gorgeous. Sally and I wrote back and forth for several months after I got back to the States. They would tell me, "You no butterfly me." That meant you don't go to other women. But today I was looking for some strange girl and a good massage.

We took the local transportation into Saigon which was an adventure in itself. We no more than got off the Lambretta when a taxi cab driver hailed us. He spoke very good English and wanted to know if we were looking for a good time. We told him that that was exactly why we were there. What did he have in mind? Of course, in the back of our minds we were wondering if he was a VC.

A Man Returns

Author on his way to Saigon

He told us his brother owned a massage parlor, and of course, had the prettiest girls in Saigon. He said we could have our pick of the girls and everything would be free. Well, we knew that was too good to be true. What was the catch? Oh, that. Well, he also had a little business venture he thought we might be interested in. Besides the massage parlor and the girls, we could make some easy money. He proceeded to explain in detail what we would be doing. He wanted us to do a little black marketing. If we were to get caught in this little business venture, we would have had to do some brig time followed by a dishonorable discharge. That didn't sound like anything I wanted to get involved in. Well, he went on to explain how it worked. First they took your ration card and painted a clear chemical on it. It didn't change the color of the card and was completely invisible. When the cashier at the BX inked out the little square for the item you were purchasing, they would just paint another chemical on it and the ink disappeared. He said he would take us to his brothers, pick up a van, and then take us around to the different BXs and PXs to get a list of the different items he wanted us to pick up. We talked it over and decided we had enough adventure in our lives already. Neither of us wanted to take a chance on a dishonorable.

We told him we had decided not to do it, but would still like to check out his brother's massage parlor. He said fine. We got into his taxi which was a tight fit and headed to his brother's. It didn't take long to get there and the place was pretty nice. He had about ten cycles parked at his place. He told us he was in that business too. The cycles are like a carnival ride. You sit right up front and become a human bumper. I never rode in one. He introduced us to his brother who invited us in. He didn't speak much English, but he spoke enough to get by.

There were seven girls, and if I remember correctly, all but one was French/Vietnamese. True to his word, we both got to pick a girl. They were all very nice looking and dressed in nothing but a see-through nightie. We made our choice and then there was a quick introduction. She did not speak any English, but it wasn't necessary; we didn't need to talk. She took me by the hand and led me down a hallway to a small cubicle. Then she started undressing me. When I tried to help her, she stopped me. She hung all my clothes on a hanger and gave me a pair of flip flops to wear. After getting me completely undressed, she picked up the hangers with my clothes on them and my boots, and nodded for me to follow her. I wasn't sure where we were going, but I knew it couldn't be far. After all, I was naked as a jaybird. She led me to another small room with a shower in it. The whole place smelled of incense, but this room had an entirely different scent. It smelled strong of herbs and spices. She hung my

A Man Returns

clothes up and turned on the shower. It was not much more than a drizzle, but apparently, they had hot water because she kept testing the temperature. Then she motioned for me to step in. The water was warm and felt good. A wooden shelf next to the shower was loaded with different kinds of soaps and oils and whatnot. She took off her nightgown, selected a bar of soap, and proceeded to wash me down. The soap was very strong smelling and made my skin tingly, especially in the more sensitive areas.

After getting me thoroughly washed, she toweled both of us off and slipped back into her nightgown, motioning me to follow her again. I followed her through a beaded doorway into another room. This room was dark except for a single candle burning and more incense. There was a table with a mattress on it covered in brightly colored sheets. It had a small transistor radio which she turned on. She motioned for me to get on the table which I did. I stretched out and waited for the magic to begin. She massaged me with different oils, humming along with whatever was playing on the radio as she did. Before long, I was on cloud nine and I stayed there a while until the happy ending. It was all over way too soon, and I just laid there enjoying the moment. For a short while, the war was a long way away. She helped me get dressed and I followed her back out to the lobby. My gunner was sitting there with a big smile on his face; next to him was the taxi cab driver. He wanted to know if we wanted a ride back to the base. He said he would do it for two dollars each. I countered with three dollars for the both of us and he agreed. His brother came out from the back and asked if we had enjoyed ourselves. I told him I'd had other massages, and this, by far, was the best. He told us to be sure and tell our friends and to come back. We said we might just do that. We each gave him four dollars and I gave my girl an additional dollar. The taxi cab driver gave us a ride back to the base as well as his number, in case we wanted another massage or wanted to do a little black marketing. All we had to do was just give him a call.

We hadn't eaten all day yet, so we headed to the chow hall to see if we could get something. We told the other gunners about the massage place and about the offer to do a little black marketing.

I was still getting lots of mail from everyone, including people I didn't even know. Good news came from my mom: her new eye doctor had found out what was wrong with her eyes. The other doctor had told her she was going blind and scared the hell out of her.

Mid-March

Besides putting money in the 10 percent interest program, I'd started buying government bonds. I was saving about $300 a month. I was still looking at buying a Triumph, but instead of the 250, I was looking at the TR-GI GT. I really liked the look of them. The IT was $3,100 to $3,200 in the States, but here I could get one for around $2,600, depending on the options I chose. I sent my mom a picture of it, and she really liked it. The only problem I had was finding one that fit my time frame in going home. You had to have a certain amount of time left in country for them to be able to ship it, so that it got there when you were home on leave.

I finally bought a nice camera—a Petri MR IV 35 mm SLR. Along with it, I bought a slide projector with a remote control. I was having all my pictures put into slides, which meant I needed a projector. Our helo pad had been very busy with lots of Army gunship traffic. The VC were on the move again and we'd been busy doing a lot of operations with the Army. I called many of them door-to-door operations because that's kind of what we did. The Army would land two or three slicks full of troops at a rice paddy hooch and check the place out for VC. We covered from the air. Every once in a while, all hell broke loose and it got pretty hairy. We'd do several hooches like this in one operation.

My gunner and I were walking towards the helo pad to check our revetments' ammo and rocket supply. When we were just about there, an Army gunship, the Mad Dog, landed in the middle of the pad directly in front of us. Just to our left was a fuel truck parked next to a helo, and the fuel guy was filling it up. Suddenly, I heard the most horrible sound right in front of us. An Army slick, the Greyhound, had forgotten to tie down his rotor blade to the stinger. The Army gunship's rotor blades connected with the rotor blades of the other chopper in the revetment, and pieces started flying everywhere. We dropped for cover behind the revetment and the fuel guy took off running towards us. He had only gone a few feet when one of the big weights from the end of the rotor blade caught him on his backside, nearly cutting him half. He went down on the pad, guts hanging out and blood everywhere. One chopper caught fire and there was debris everywhere.

Guys ran for cover. My gunner and I got to our helo, grabbed a battle dressing, and ran over to the fuel guy. We lifted his head off the hot PSP, wrapping the dressing around him the best we could, but he was already gone. A couple of gunners were coming out of our ready room. Someone yelled at them to call an ambulance and fire truck. A couple of the Army guys had minor injuries and the helo pad was a mess. Some of the other Army helos had minor damage too. We checked both our birds and they were fine.

The fuel guy used to tell us how crazy we were to be flying around out there, hanging our asses out, and getting shot at. He said it was less dangerous for him. He was happy with the job. The only thing he had to worry about was dodging a few mortars once and a while. He was also a short-timer. I think he had only a couple weeks left in

Receiving first air medal

country. A couple months after I returned to the States, I heard they had dedicated the helo field in his name with a formal ceremony.

I received a message from personnel that Vũng Tau had called. My orders were in and I needed to pick them up. My leave date was still the same: June 3. I'd have a thirty-one day leave, and then was supposed to report in at NAS Jacksonville, Florida, on July 5. I'd be going to VW-4 Hurricane Hunters and then would attend radio school. I'd be flying as a radio operator. To do that, I'd have to learn aircraft radio procedures, the Morse code, and teletype. It also meant I would serve my entire four years in the Navy and never have gone to sea! In the event that I got crazy, and shipped over, I stood a very good chance of being stationed on a bird farm, also known as an aircraft carrier. I'd be flying in all kinds of weather. In the summer, I'd be flying into hurricanes, tropical storms, and tropical depressions; and in the winter I'd be flying out of Bangor, Maine, and into the northeastern snowstorms. I'd also be flying weather for all the space launches. At least nobody would be shooting at me.

It sounded exciting and my cup of tea, but not what I put in for. Coming from a combat zone, you were almost guaranteed your choice of orders. And that's the key word here—almost. In this case, my luck didn't hold out. I had put in for Quonset Point, Rhode Island; Lakehurst, New Jersey; or Philadelphia, Pennsylvania. My overseas choice was Japan. *I had put in for a change of orders*, I thought. *Surely they've made a mistake.* Nope! They said my qualifications were perfect for VW-4 and that's where they were sending me. Look out, Florida, here I come! Land of sunshine beaches and best of all, beach babes. When I was in Memphis, I kind of liked the way the southern girls talked. Of course, this would only happen if I finished my tour without getting killed.

I was twenty-one years old and they were calling me "the old man." For good reason. I'd been here at Nhà Bè Det 2 longer than anyone else, including the pilots, and I still had two and a half months to go. We were starting to change out pilots and door gunners again. By the end of the month, we'd likely have mostly new gunners and pilots again.

I received a letter from my buddy, Lance, and now he was thinking about extending six months. In his last letter, he said that he hated it there and couldn't wait to leave. I considered extending six months for the extra money and extra leave, but started thinking about a possible new car and that I might be pushing my luck. We'd already lost quite a few pilots and door gunners. I didn't want to be on that list.

I also knew my family would flip out. If Lance extended six months, I knew another family that was going to flip out. I did extend two months to be home at the same time as Lance so I hoped he was taking that into consideration.

I now had $1,670 saved and I'd have another $600 before I left. That did not count my stocks and bonds.

Pennsylvania was offering an incentive for guys that were getting out of the military. If you took up residency there, they would give you $300; and if you served in Vietnam, you'd get an additional $25 for each month you were in Vietnam.

I ordered the RCA home study course. I planned to check out the RCA plant in Scranton when I got out to see what they were offering. My background in electronics (along with the home study in my back pocket) might just give me enough edge to get hired. I also might try the Army signal depot in Tobyhanna. I had friends working there, and they told me that if you were ex-military, it helped in getting a job.

Mine Division 112 was stationed in Nhà Bè. They had the boring job of running up and down the Mekong River, sweeping it for anything Charlie put out there to blow up ships. Slow moving, they made easy targets for Charlie whose favorite weapon of choice was the B40 rocket. Needless to say, the sweepers called on us quite often. The VC usually fired several rockets at the minesweeper. Whether they hit or missed, they immediately went into hiding, knowing the minesweepers would call us. By the time we got there, the VC were nowhere to be found. The minesweeper would give us a general idea of where the attack came from, and if there were no friendlies in the area, we would call Moon River for clearance to put in a strike in that area with the hope of drawing them out or maybe getting a secondary explosion.

A Man Returns

"Scramble the Seawolves, scramble one!" A minesweeper about ten minutes south of us was under attack. The VC had opened up on them from the shore with AK-47s and B40 rockets. A B40 rocket had hit them and they had a couple of guys with minor injuries. They were still underway, putting some distance between them and the VC. As we headed down the river just above the water, I couldn't help but think that maybe this time we'd get them. By the time we got there, the minesweeper was well out of range and around a bend in the river. My pilot contacted them. They were headed straight to Nhà Bè to tend to the injured and start on repairs. They gave us the position the attack came from and we headed that way. It only took us a couple minutes to get there. It was all jungle, but when we looked closer, we saw a very small canal almost out of sight. My gunner spotted it and pointed it out to our pilot. We didn't need clearance, but let Moon River know what we were doing anyway.

My pilot decided to fly straight down the canal. Maybe we'd get lucky and catch them on it. Sure enough, a minute later there they were—unloading at the end of the canal. They bailed into the jungle on both sides of the canal. My pilot keyed the ICS, "Going hot!" That's all we needed to hear. He radioed the wing bird and told them, "Four rockets!" We were going down the middle, straight at the sampans. Guns blazing and down low. I just knew we were going to take some hits. The pilot punched off rockets—two followed by three more. My pilot told me to concentrate the .50 on the sampans. As we made a fast turnaround, I had a clear shot of both of them. I opened up on them. Suddenly, *kaboom!* Holy shit! I hit something good. As we closed in, more explosions. My pilot waved off the strike and told the gunner to keep putting down fire. I was still concentrating on the sampans. Keeping our distance from the sampans, we put all of our fire into the jungle. I could see the sampans off and on. They were both ablaze, and still things were exploding. My pilot came on the

mic, saying, "I think we've done all we can. Let's head to Nhà Bè."
On the way back, we could see the minesweeper up ahead. My pilot
told us we were going to do a close flyover. And we did, very close; the
captain blasted his horn, and everyone was waving. We got lucky that
time and found them. There was no telling how many KIAs we got,
but we definitely knew we had destroyed some supplies. We landed
back at Nhà Bè and checked the aircraft. No bullet holes, yes! Then
we did the usual: refuel, rearm, clean out the aircraft, brass and clips
and post flight. At debriefing, my pilot had found out (through our
intel guys) that they believed something was going on in that area.
They ordered air strikes there. They would send in fighter bombers
off a carrier sitting offshore in the South China Sea. After the air
strikes, they'd send in defoliant planes and spray Agent Orange over
that whole area. I couldn't wait to see what they uncovered. Finding
those two supply sampans helped them make their decision to check
the area out. It turned out later that they found a whole tunnel and
bunker system loaded with supplies. I loved to watch the fighters
come in and drop their load. First you saw them as a pinpoint in the
sky; the next moment they were dropping load. They were so loud!

At that point, I was wearing the gold aircrew wings and I was just
awarded the combat aircrew wings. These wings were gold and silver.
Very nice looking. The Navy hadn't given us their approval yet, but
it was just a matter of time. There were only a few sailors who could
wear the combat wings so I was really proud to wear them.

Late March

Things were really heating up near the Cambodian border near the
Ho Chi Minh Trail. The amount of supplies and troops coming
down the trail stepped up. The detachment I was assigned to before
I got to Nhà Bè Det 6 Đồng Tâm took a terrible mortar pounding.

The duty crew had scrambled to get their helos off the pad when a mortar round hit the ammo dump. The explosion took out both helos, killing the copilot and injuring several men. Another brother paid the ultimate price. The mortar attacks here picked up too. It put everyone on edge.

Three of our best pilots were leaving soon; one of them was my pilot. I was not happy about it, but all I could do was hope my luck carried me through. That left us with only two experienced pilots. I knew these new guys were the best of the best, but once you got used to someone, it was hard to change. You could usually tell right off if someone was going to make it or not. Most of them did, thank goodness, but there was always one or two that "just ain't got it."

I received a St. Patrick's Day card from my mom. It really surprised me because I had no idea it was St. Patrick's Day. I think it was just an excuse for her to send me a card. My dog, Key, had her pups. She dropped the first one in the middle of the room and the next six under the desk. Our other dog, Ralph, didn't know what to make of it and I didn't think he liked it.

March 27

I'd been to Saigon a couple times in the past month. I was trying to find and buy a Triumph, but it looked like a no-go. We couldn't get the time frame right. I'd been eyeballing a Dodge Charger. I know, but what the hell. I guess you can go from a Triumph to a muscle car! Big deal. I really liked the look. I liked it so much that I bought it at the PX through Military Car Sales Corp. It was a 1969 Dodge Charger for a total (with extras) of $3,415.50. I put $1,415 down and financed $2,000 at 1 percent interest through the Navy Credit Union. My payments would be $69.93 a month for thirty-six months. Wow! I couldn't believe I had bought a car. The wait was going to be unbearable. All I had was a bunch of pictures and a piece of paper saying I owned a 1969 Dodge Charger.

It had a bright blue, metallic paint job. It had a two-door hard-top 383 with the Hurst offset shifter four-speed. White interior, three-quarter cam red line, tires, x-racing suspension, and the speedometer went up to 150 mph. *Hell! That was faster than our Huey!* The price included all the paperwork, including shipping. The only thing it didn't include was fifty cents for the temporary tag in Trenton, New Jersey. I was lucky again in that Trenton being a shipping terminal was not very far from the Pocono Mountains.

I had to have car insurance before I could pick up the car. I sent all the info to my mom to see if she might be able to get my insurance there in Gouldsboro at Matthews Insurance Agency. This was the kind of stuff my mom didn't do. She was uncomfortable doing stuff like this. She'd never driven a car herself, but I tell you what, my mother got me car insurance. When I got home, I hoped Lance would be there, and we could catch a Greyhound bus in Tobyhanna to Trenton. I couldn't wait.

No letup in the mortar attacks. We just got two new gunners, and just like it had on my first night in Đồng Tâm, they had a mortar attack their first night. It didn't hit anything or anybody. Thank goodness.

Our flight surgeon, a hell of a nice guy, extended another year! Wow! He was working on a training program for the Vietnamese medics. We got to know him from his visits at Nhà Bè. From time to time, he would fly center seat, also known as "dead man's seat." They said that if it crashed, the rotor post would come right through the middle. The flight surgeon flew with us to get his flight hours in. He stayed in Vũng Tau most of the time. He visited other detachments too off and on.

They told us the '69 Tet Offensive was over, and as expected, it was nothing like the Tet of '68. There were still a lot of lives lost. Our job was to save lives. I only hoped that we did our best to keep the numbers down. All the detachments were a lot busier than usual.

April 1969

"Scramble the Seawolves. Scramble two, RVNs in trouble." I was on duty, and sound asleep. The next thing I knew I was airborne. I'd done this so many times that I could do it in my sleep. Ha! Ha! I was still in the lead bird, manning the .50 cal, but I had a new pilot and he was flight team leader. The copilot contacted Moon River. One of the outposts was under attack again. We've been to this one many times. It only took a few minutes. It was black as hell and pouring down rain. Charlie decided to take advantage of the weather, which they very often did. My pilot made contact with the Green Beret advisor. They were being overrun. They had breached two walls and were in the compound. Hundreds of them. I could see the assault ahead, and it looked bad.

We were there in a matter of minutes and made contact with the outpost again. By that time, he told us, "What walls? They are coming over them. They're in sight!" We wasted no time. Rolling in, the pilot came on the IC: "Going hot!" *Holy shit, there were VC everywhere— hundreds of them!* I'd never seen so many. Firing away on the .50 cal, I looked straight at the wall and concentrated on it. There were too many friendlies in the compound to fire in there. This was a time when you really had to concentrate on not burning your barrel out. You wanted to put enough fire out to get the job done, but you had to pause just enough to keep the barrel from getting too hot. Unlike the M60s, we didn't carry spare barrels. They were hard to come by. We broke out of our run, climbed, then rolled over, and came down the other side. By this time, they knew we were there, and tracers started coming our way. You couldn't worry about incoming; you had to concentrate on what you were doing. We did several more runs until we ran out of ammo and were low on fuel. We'd killed and wounded a bunch, and yet they still kept coming. We contacted the advisors to let them know we were hauling ass, and would be back as quickly as we could. They had regained some ground, but were still in trouble.

We headed for Nhà Bè. On the way, we radioed Moon River to let them know how bad the situation at the outpost was. My pilot told them that they might be overrun by the time we got back. They said they would see what they could do. We also radioed Nhà Bè to let them know that we were coming in on a hot turn around. When we landed, some of the guys were there to help reload. The fuel guy was waiting with the fuel truck and pulled right up with the blades just a-roaring. I checked the aircraft for damage and found a few holes, but nothing serious, so we got lucky again. By the time we were fueled up, we had finished rearming.

We were back in the air and contacted the advisors on our way. They were in bad shape—barely holding their ground. They had a lot of dead and wounded, and the VC were breathing down their necks. We radioed Moon River to see if they had gotten anybody and they said they were working on it. They were trying to get Spooky out of Tan Son Nhut Air Base and waiting on a call back. "Spooky" was their call sign, but they were known as Puff the Magic Dragon, a real fire-breather. The VC called them Dragon Ships. When they fired at night, the rounds came out so fast that they looked like streams of liquid fire. They were old Douglas DC-3s converted to a new number—AC-47 (Attack Cargo 47). They carried three mini-guns: two mounted in windows and a third mounted in the cargo door. They usually carried around 60,000 rounds of 7.62, the same bullet that the M60 and the M-14 used. They fired anywhere from fifty to a hundred rounds per second. This had to be done in about six-second bursts to keep it from overheating. The Air Force converted fifty-three DC-3s into Dragon Ships. They proved to be bad to the bone and often had Charlie on the run in a hurry. The only problem was that they were very slow which made them vulnerable to rocket fire. (Fifteen had been destroyed by enemy fire.) They also carried a load: mainly MK-24 parachute flares. In fact, the Air Force once used these planes as flare ships. They converted them to a new number then too: the FC-47, a Flare Cargo ship. As I mentioned before, one of these MK-24 parachute flares could light up a huge area. On our chopper, we carried the small pop flare. It was pretty good, but nothing like the MK-24. I used them on our choppers, and we usually only carried them for special night operations. Their light capacity was two million candle power and they burned for about three minutes.

A few years back the Oriskany CVA-34 had a major accident on board: one of the sailors dropped a MK-24 flare and its salty lanyard was inadvertently pulled. Then another sailor picked it up and tossed it into the munitions locker. Things got really bad after that. Many men were killed and wounded with lots of damage. The chutes were fifteen feet in diameter and made a great cloth shade. I brought one home, and used it on the beach in Florida.

April

We'd worked with Puff on a number of occasions. A couple of them were with outposts being overrun. Puff was exactly what we needed to turn the tide.

We were coming in right on the deck. My pilot radioed the outpost to see how they were holding up and to let them know we were minutes away. I don't remember exactly what the advisor said, but I know he was very happy to hear we were back. He said they couldn't hold them much longer. At about that time, we broke into the clearing. We were right on the deck and the outpost was directly in front of us. We knew we were going to catch hell and adrenaline was running high. We came in from the opposite side this time—along the wall. This put the wall on the gunner's side and he was hosing it down, targets everywhere. I had the .50 cal pouring out lead all over the clearing and the tree line. We were taking hits and I figured if there was a time that I wasn't going to make it, this was probably it. Especially being short. (I only had sixty days left in country.)

My pilot was punching off flechette rockets. I had had the guys load half-flechette and half-explosive heads. I knew he had to be taking people down with those flechettes. When you loaded different rockets, you had to let the pilot know what rockets were in which tubes so he could choose which ones he wanted to fire.

We stayed at treetop level and broke around to the right. I let the .50 cal sing while covering our wing bird as it made his break. The VC started retreating back into the jungle, so we made a close turn and came back down on top of the tree line and let them have it again. The pilots punched off the last of their rockets. There were still a lot of VC everywhere.

About that time we got a call from Moon River. Puff was airborne and on its way: ETA fifteen minutes. We climbed to about 500 feet and the door gunner worked the area over until we ran out of ammo. My pilot got Spooky on the radio and gave them the rundown on what was going on. We told them we were headed back to Nhà Bè for another hot turn around and would be back shortly. Again, we didn't shut down. I checked the aircraft the best I could with it running. More bullet holes with a couple of very close calls. Again, we had help rearming and were back in the air in minutes. As we got closer, we could see Spooky hosing the area down. I couldn't help but wonder what it was like on the ground when those mini guns rained down. Spooky had the area lit up with flares. We contacted the out-post. They still had VC in the compound that they were dealing with, but they hadn't taken the compound back. We radioed Spooky. When we were ready to roll in, he was going to back off and let the guns cool down. I had loaded all flechette warheads on our rockets: 2,400 darts in each head. We were going to tear up some jungle along with some VC. We contacted Spooky and told him we were rolling in.

He told us that when we finished our runs, he was going to roll back in and finish off his ammo. About two hundred yards in from the tree line, we started taking fire. We must have really pissed them off. As we broke around to come down the other side, two B40 rock-ets came flying by us, just missing us. They had led us too far, maybe because we slowed to make our turn. My pilot radioed our wing bird to see if they knew where it came from. They did and were getting ready to roll on it. We came around to cover their gunner, spraying the jungle down just beneath them. As they broke out, we rolled in on the same spot. All of a sudden, the area started exploding. Appar-ently either our helo or the wing bird had hit something good. We came back around again and rolled in on the other tree line adjacent to the other wall they had breached. My pilot let go with the rest of our rockets and we hosed the area down. We came out of the run and climbed to a safe altitude. We were almost out of ammo and low on fuel. Things were pretty quiet and Spooky fired off two more MK24 flares to light up the compound. We radioed Spooky as we flew back over the area to let him know we were headed back to Nhà Bè. As we flew over the area, we saw bodies everywhere. Spooky was already hosing down the area again. What a sight it was to see them in action. I could hear Army medivac choppers talking on the radio. They were on their way to the outpost and the outpost was secure. We had done our job well tonight and saved a lot of lives. It was too bad we had to take a lot of lives to do that. Just before we landed, my pilot got a hold of the Army medivac choppers to see if they were going to need any cover, but they said they had Army gunships covering them. I think we were all happy that we didn't have to go again.

Of course it had often happened that we thought we were done for the evening and the scramble bell rang. We were all pretty tired and hoped the bell didn't go off. As we touched down in our revetment, it was just beginning to get light. By the time we were refueled, rearmed, and had pulled a post flight, it was daylight. More holes in both aircraft but nothing serious. I'd be getting off soon and I'd have plenty of time to catch up on sleep right after breakfast.

I was still eating and drinking the same, but we'd been busting our asses so much lately that I'd gone from 186 pounds to 174. I felt much better. I had felt a little sluggish. I didn't want to go home fat.

I sent a letter to my mom asking her if the phone was turned back on at the house. I wanted to be able to let them know when I landed at the airport in Scranton. If not, I needed the phone number of a couple friends, so I could call to let them know I was home. My mom couldn't get insurance for my car. I was going to talk to the legal officer and see what he suggested. My car was ready in Detroit, waiting on the insurance before they could ship it.

I got a letter from my sister, Patsy, letting me know that my old girlfriend was getting married this month. Now I didn't have to worry about any of that drama when I got back. We had given away four of Key's pups and had three left. They were so cute and fluffy. At feeding time, I gave a whistle and they all came running.

We were so busy that the time was just flying by. I was getting shorter and shorter. It was April 24 and I only had thirty-eight days and a wake-up. All the original guys I came with were already gone. You would think it would feel strange, but it didn't because you became like a machine.

A Man Returns

I was supposed to report to Vũng Tau and spend my last thirty days out of combat, but it looked like I was staying right here. I'd much rather do that and leave straight from here.

We'd been very busy and lost both men and choppers to the point that we were shorthanded. I was not only flying on my regular duty days, but also flying on my off days, training new gunners and crew chiefs.

May

May was a blur. We were so busy. I was getting a lot of flight time. I only sent one letter home to my mom and they didn't publish a Wolf-gram that month.

It looked like my gunner was going to stay on Det and we'd be leaving at the same time. I was excited and on edge. I kept thinking about going home and climbing into my new car. That wasn't good. I needed to stay focused.

Operations wanted us to fly a few propaganda missions—this time using a tape recording and speakers instead of the usual pamphlets. I'd flown these before. Operations had an area in the T-10 zone where there had been a lot of reported activity. We usually did this over the small villages where VC (and VC sympathizers) were believed to be hiding out.

We flew with the lead bird flying in the dead man's zone, blasting the speaker. (The dead man's zone was the altitude at which they could reach you with small arms.) You wanted to be on the deck or above small arms fire. This way we doubly pissed them off and might draw some fire. You stayed on your toes. The wing bird stayed a ways back and on the deck, watching to see if the lead bird drew any fire. This way they were in good position to drop down on them.

We had flown two missions out to the T-10 area and hadn't seen anything. All was quiet. It was late afternoon and we were on our third mission with the speaker. We had just got over the area we were supposed to fly. My gunner had just turned on the tape recorder when all hell broke loose and we were taking fire. I tossed smoke right away and keyed my mike, "Taking fire three o'clock, going hot!" My gunner and I opened up. My pilot headed for the treetops. The wing bird had already picked up on the tracers coming up at us and they were rolling in. I could see the wing bird light and punching off rockets. What a beautiful sight! While I was covering the wing bird's break, my pilot rolled in for a strike and we unloaded on them. When we made a break from a rocket run, the Gs were quite strong, and with all the weight we were carrying, it was quite a pull. The rotor blades sounded like they were going to break off, popping. This is the point when we were most vulnerable. Today was one of those days. Just as we made our break, we started taking serious fire. We let the wing bird know, but he had already seen it. We came around and rolled in again. This time all was quiet. We made one more pass, but I guess Charlie had had enough. As we headed back to Nhà Bè, we suddenly realized that our speaker had been on the whole time.

When we checked both birds during post-flight, we found bullet holes in both birds. Again, how lucky could we be? I was way too short for this shit! I had a new car waiting! So much for the gravy run.

May 13, 1969

I only had twenty days and a wake-up left to go. I was supposed to leave from Tan Son Nhut Air Base on June 3 at high noon on Braniff Airlines, Flight B2A4A. Home sweet home was getting close.

In the last letter I received from my mom she wanted to know what I wanted for my first supper home. I didn't have to think about it. I wanted red boiled potatoes, sliced up in the skillet with their skin on and lots of butter. Then you broke three eggs over that, and just before you took them off the fire, you sprinkled on a generous handful of scallions, finishing with lots of salt and pepper. I still enjoy that for breakfast now and again today. Only now I like it with cheese on top too.

I made a trip to Saigon to say goodbye to my two girlfriends. I was very sad, and of course, they both wanted to know if I could possibly come back. I was honest with them and told them that I doubted it very much.

I also finished the rest of my souvenir shopping for friends and family. I'll admit it sounds funny, but it also felt funny. Here there was a war going on all around you and you were souvenir shopping.

My mom finally got me my car insurance with a little help from some friends. All the paperwork had been turned in and the car was on its way to Trenton, New Jersey! I don't remember what it cost, but I do remember that when I found out, it was like taking a bullet.

We finally found homes for the rest of Key's puppies. I was glad as I had been really worried about not finding homes for them before I left. Also, one of the new crew chiefs I had trained stepped up and was going to take over Key after I left. That made me so happy, as we had become really close. After I got back to the States, I often thought of her and the pups, wondering how they were.

Most of our fire team went into Nhà Bè to celebrate my gunner and I leaving. I also had to visit Sally one last time and say my goodbyes. We exchanged addresses and vowed we would write each other. And write we did—for several months and then the letters got fewer and fewer. It was really weird writing her and hearing about everything going on there.

Before we headed back to the base, we had to visit Fat Cat one last time. Fat Cat was the self-proclaimed blow job queen of Nhà Bè, and I think we all pretty much agreed with her.

You didn't want to contract any kind of venereal disease when it was time to go home. Most guys stopped screwing the whores when they got down to thirty days left in country. After that they went to see Fat Cat.

There was stuff out there that they didn't have a cure for. One of your checkouts before you left the country was the medical department. If they found something, you got to leave the country but did not go home. Instead, you had to go to the hospital in the Philippines and you didn't go home until you were cured.

I was so short that it was time to ship my stuff home. I shipped all my stereo gear, slide projector, guitar, souvenirs, ten rounds of linked 7.62 ammo, and a few other things to my mom's address. They would arrive at the rail station in Tobyhanna about ten miles from my hometown. They were supposed to get there about the same day I got home.

May was kind of a blur, as we stayed so busy. I was living in a day-dream about home, seeing everyone again, and picking up my new car. I was flying a lot of missions. At this point, I was way over three hundred missions and still flying training missions. Home was so close that I couldn't help thinking about getting killed. The occasional mortar attack took on a whole new feel. I did not want to get taken out by a mortar. If I was going to go, I wanted to go out with my machine gun in my hand, and taking a few with me.

When we did get time off, my gunner and I stayed drunk a lot of the time. We talked about our families and what we were going to do on our thirty-day leave. We could start talking about things like that now. Before this, we didn't know if we were going to make it, so we just didn't talk about it.

A Man Returns

On one of those particular occasions while we were sitting around, talking and telling lies about each other and getting drunk, we decided to make tapes—one for each of us.

Forty-five years later, I still had my tape and wondered if he had his. So I got a wild hair and decided to see if I could find him and send him a copy of my tape. I got his address through another gunner, made a copy of my tape, and sent it off. Then I waited to hear his reaction. And I waited—nothing, not a word. To this day I have not heard from him. Then I thought that maybe he didn't want to remember those days. We all handled our Vietnam experiences differently.

It was hard to believe my tour was up, and I'd flown my last mission. My fourteen months were up and I was going home. It was scary and exciting at the same time. I had gotten used to being out of the regular Navy, and hoped I could adjust to all the rules and regulations.

On the other hand, the realization that I was still alive, had beaten the odds, and was going home was pretty exciting. Not only that, but I was getting ready to start a whole new adventure and fly into hurricanes.

The guys had a short ceremony at the club for my gunner and me. I was used to going to these, but this one was for me. It was primarily another reason to get wasted. After it all was said and done, they presented each of us with a nice plaque. It was decorated with metal helos, Vietnamese flags, and had the Seawolf logo in the center. At the bottom, there was an engraved brass plate which had the number of combat missions you had flown. Mine read 385 missions.

I didn't sleep much that night. My mind would not shut down and I kept thinking about getting mortared. The next morning, my pilot flew my gunner and me to Vũng Tàu. We had to do our check and get a medical release. We also had to pick up our orders. We walked around to see if there was anybody left that we knew, but we didn't find anybody. I crossed off the "100" on my FIGMO calendar, so the only thing left now was the wake-up.

We were headed home in the morning, and I thought I would be flying my last flight with the Seawolves, but found out they had an operation in the morning, so that was out.

I took a look at my orders and yep, it was official. I was going to be a Hurricane Hunter! NAS JAX VW-4 Hurricane Hunters was my position. I was going to be a radio operator. I would first have to pass radio school and learn Morse code. Then, I would be assigned to a flight crew—aboard a WC-121 Super Connie. I would be flying into hurricanes during the summer, and snowstorms in the winter. They also flew a lot of special operations—like flying weather for all the space shots from the Cape. Not only did these guys fly into hurricanes, but they did it at very low altitudes (between five hundred feet and one thousand feet). How crazy is that! Like I said, I thought it was going to be exciting. I hoped I could sit in a classroom all day and pass the course.

Freedom bird and headed home

A Man Returns

I finished packing my seabag and spent the rest of the day walking around and saying goodbye to everyone and hanging out at the ready room. It was so different when you were the one saying goodbye, and you were the one getting on the Freedom Bird.

My gunner and I spent the evening and half the night at the club, telling lies and getting drunk. After the club closed, we somehow made it back to the barracks, got a second wind, and stayed up the rest of the night drinking and smoking.

The next morning as we watched the long awaited sunrise, I colored in the wake-up on my FIGMO calendar. Whew! I was headed home today.

During breakfast, which included lots of black coffee, the guys commandeered a jeep from somewhere. We said our final goodbyes and good lucks, grabbed our seabags, and headed to Tan Son Nhut Air Base. We made the trip without incident, and they dropped us off in the middle of chaos. After some time carrying our heavy seabags around, we found out where we were supposed to be. We were just finishing checkout, when I saw it—our Freedom Bird. It was a great big green jet airliner with the word "Braniff" in large black letters over the passenger windows. A plane never looked so good.

A crowd of us were standing around too nervous to sit down in the boarding area when a woman came up and told us to follow her. We headed out the door onto the hot tarmac and onto the Freedom Bird. Now if we could just make it down the runway without getting blown up, we'd be on our way. I stepped aside at the top of the gangway and took one last look and smell of Vietnam. You could hear the war going on in the distance. I flashed back to my first night there on top of the hotel, manning a machine gun and seeing, hearing, and smelling the war going on in the distance. What a difference between then and now. Before I had wondered if I was going to leave my life here, and now I was going home. After sitting there for what seemed like an eternity, we finally took off, and were in the air. I looked out the window at Vietnam for the last time. I could see smoke here and there in the distance, reminding me of what I was leaving.

The stewardesses were unbelievable. It was amazing how well they were able to handle a plane full of drunken men all pumped up about going home that hadn't seen a white woman in a long time. There were no incidents that I can remember. We'd been two days with no sleep, so I thought I'd get some sleep on the plane. Not a chance! We were all too excited in the air.

We flew the same route we took when I came to Vietnam: Vietnam to Japan to Alaska and finally Travis Air Force Base in California. Good old USA! It looked a lot like Tan Son Nhut with thousands of men coming and going. I was surprised at how fast we were able to check in. It felt good having good old American greenbacks in my wallet again. My gunner and I and another sailor shared a cab to San Francisco airport. We headed out into traffic and across the Golden Gate Bridge. We thought the taxi driver was going to kill us. We hadn't been in traffic in a long time. He was hauling ass and cutting in and out of the traffic. I was so glad when he dropped us at the airport. I felt like I had cheated death again.

My gunner was headed to Kansas and I was headed to Pennsylvania, so we gave each other a big hug and vowed we'd keep in touch. He went down one corridor and I another. I found my departure gate and decided to call Mom. The phone was working! My mom answered. I remember a lot of crying and gasping, and after a short time, I could finally talk to her. We said our hellos and it was so nice to hear her voice; she sounded very happy. I know I was. I was ready to get this flying over with. I gave her my flight number and arrival time at the airport in Scranton/Wilkes-Barre, Pennsylvania.

We finally took off. It was a long flight, but again I didn't sleep. I was too wired. The flight seemed to take forever. We finally landed in

A Man Returns

Pittsburgh, Pennsylvania. Now it was only a hop, skip, and a jump to Avoca Airport. I didn't have much layover time, so I was on my way pretty quickly. It was early morning. I'd been flying all night. As we were coming in, I could see the mountains on each side of us. Scranton and Wilkes-Barre are located in Wyoming Valley. We touched down, and as we taxied toward the terminal, I could pick out my family and friends already jumping up and down and waving. There were other people doing the same thing, as we had other military guys on board.

My father wasn't there, but I didn't expect him to be. Mom got one of her work friends to take her to the airport to pick me up.

As the plane finally arrived at the terminal, I got such a wonderful feeling, knowing the rich earth of Pennsylvania was under my feet, and straight ahead family and friends were waiting on me. I was home.

We all kissed and hugged and cried. Everyone was talking a hundred miles an hour. We finally got the cars loaded up and headed to Gouldsboro.

After I got caught up with the rest of the family, Mom made a large iron skillet of potatoes, eggs, and onions. She said that after we ate, I was sitting on the couch talking, and just fell over mid-sentence sound asleep. I slept for almost twenty hours. I was pissed that I'd missed part of my leave.

Lance stopped in, and we said our big hellos. Then we went to say hello to his folks. Like I mentioned before, they were like my second parents. That was a nice reunion.

I called the dealer in Trenton to let them know I was coming to pick up the car, and they said no problem. I needed a driver's license and the bill of sale. Lance's brother, Jay, gave us a lift to the Tobyhanna bus station. I was so excited with anticipation. In just a few hours, I would be driving the car in the picture. It seemed forever before we got to Trenton. The car dealership wasn't far from the bus station so we decided to walk. As we walked through the gates of the dealership, I saw a blue Charger in a row of cars up against the fence. We both took off running. "It's my car! I know it's my car!" I was so excited. A man came out of the building. He asked if I was Mr. Smith. When I said yes, he said, "That's your Charger." Holy cow! I could actually touch it. Then he said they did have a problem. The girl that did the paperwork had to leave early and we'd have to come back tomorrow. We both froze. We couldn't believe what we just heard. I answered, "No way! We are leaving here with the car one way or another." He started to apologize for the inconvenience, but I cut him off. I said, "You see all those shiny new cars out there in the lot? If I have to come back tomorrow, you had better keep an eye on them." He asked, "What do you mean?" I told him he knew exactly what we meant. Man, all of a sudden, he was so pissed and was yelling at us, "Are you guys threatening me?" I told him, "Yes. We aren't coming back tomorrow." I told him that all I had was a picture of this car for months and it was time I drove it. Of course, he already knew that. I'm sure there were a lot of guys from Nam picking up cars.

The next thing I knew he told me to follow him and we headed to his office. He didn't say a word; he just started doing the paperwork. It took a while, but he finally took care of us and handed me the keys. Yes! The keys to a brand new 1969 Dodge Charger, four-speed Hurst shifter on the floor. We eased out of the dealership and headed to Gouldsboro. I did thank the guy for going above and beyond the call of duty. Look out, world, here we come!

There was a fifty-mile break-in period. It was so hard not to open her up. (I think it was a fifty-mile break-in period. I'm not sure.)

My thirty-day leave was mostly a blur. We drove fast, drank a lot, and looked for girls. It was different now. Everyone was gone. You know the old saying: "You can never go back." It was true. My old girlfriend, Sue, stopped in to see me. She's the one whose mother sent me the "dear John" instead of her. She was married to a jerk. In fact, when he found out she had come to see me, he beat her up. We just made small talk and said we'd keep in touch, but that didn't happen. We drove around a lot visiting. We did do some fishing and swam a few times in the reservoir. The reservoir was where most everyone in town swam.

One day the town constable stopped, telling us we'd been driving through town a little too fast and doing a lot of drinking. He said he would not arrest us this time, but if he caught us, we would have to listen to his sermon.

There were three beer gardens and three churches. We never went into any of the three churches but we did visit those three beer gardens a lot.

Unlike many others, we were treated like heroes in our small town. We very rarely bought our drinks. My buddy, Lance, who was underage in Pennsylvania, where the drinking age was still fixed at twenty-one, had no trouble buying or drinking beer in the three bars. Lance was a Vietnam vet and a Bronze Star recipient, but couldn't buy booze? What a joke! Thanks again to our government.

All my stuff from Vietnam made it home except my guitar. Wow, was I pissed! The rest of my stuff was in good shape though. I'd have to leave all my stereo gear with my mom until I got a place off-base in Jacksonville.

Before we knew it, it was time to say goodbye. What a difference this time was compared to when we were headed to Nam.

AIRBORNE EARLY LEARNING SQUADRON:

HURRICANE HUNTERS

pointed the Charger south and let it eat up some asphalt as we headed to I-95. Lance had to be at Camp Lejeune in North Carolina on July 3 and I had to be in Jacksonville on or by July 5. We decided I would drop him at Camp Lejeune on my way to NAS Jax, the naval base in Jacksonville. It was a hectic ride because of the Fourth of July traffic but we made it. I dropped him at Camp Lejeune and headed for Florida.

It was getting late and I was yelling at myself, blasting the radio, and hanging my head out the window—anything to stay awake. I-95 hadn't been finished yet, so I had to keep taking detours which really hurt my time. The worst were in Georgia. On some of those detours, I felt like I was back in Louisiana because of all the swamps and Spanish moss hanging from the trees. It was like a scene from a scary movie.

I was getting near the Florida-Georgia line and my gas gauge was getting close to empty. I finally came upon a small station in the middle of nowhere. Thank goodness! I pulled in and the first thing I saw were two big signs, saying NO CHECKS! *Shit, that's all I had!* I went in the tiny building and explained that I was on empty and I had no cash. He said, "Sorry, station policy." I told him I was in the Navy, just back from Vietnam, and headed to NAS Jax and the Hurricane Hunters. He smiled and basically said, "Why didn't you say so?" I got filled up plus ten dollars cash! *Man, what a nice guy.* He took down all my info plus my squadron's name, just in case the check was no good. What a lucky break for me. I thanked him and continued south.

A Man Returns

I finally crossed into Florida and there was still just swamp and Spanish moss. It was two o'clock in the morning and I still had a way to go. I pulled over for coffee and a couple sugar donuts and checked with the cashier that I was on the right road. "Yep, US-17 takes you straight to the base." Thirty minutes later, I found NAS Jax, but I decided I was too tired to check in, so I drove on by. I found a wide grassy area, parked, jumped in the back seat and was sound asleep in minutes. I was so exhausted. I was sawing some Zs when suddenly, I heard a train whistle. It was so loud I thought it was in the car. I sat up. The car was totally lit up. It took another blast on the whistle, when I understood the danger. *Holy shit. A train and it's coming straight at me!* I must have parked on the railroad tracks and didn't know it. I had been so tired. Well, I was wide awake now and trying to get the key in the ignition to get this baby off the tracks. Too late! The train was on us! It blasted past with only a couple of feet to spare. Wow! I had an adrenaline rush like in Nam. I had parked on a curve, so it looked like the train was coming right at me. It turned out that there was a railroad crossing just up the road. He had been blasting for the crossing. Yikes! I made it through Nam and then was almost taken out by a train. So much for anymore sleep. I found an all-night diner and had breakfast. I knew it was going to be a long day.

I got to the main gate at sun up, and the Marine guard told me how to get to VW-4. I found it without a problem and parked by the hangar. There they were: three WC-121 Super Connies with the Hurricane Hunter logo on their sides along with the aircraft number. I was already excited. I walked across the taxi area to the water's edge. The St. Johns River flows right by the base. I sat down and watched it flow by, waiting until the base woke up.

Time to check in and back to regular military life. Check-in went smoothly. Everyone wanted to know about my tour in Vietnam; apparently they had very few Vietnam vets in the squadron. The barracks was new with only four men to a room and a gang shower and head. Last stop was my work center: Work Center 210 Avionics. I met the chief and a bunch of the guys; everyone seemed nice. Our job in avionics was to keep the radios and navigation equipment operating on the WC-121. We primarily just changed out black boxes. I couldn't wait to get aboard the aircraft and see what it was all about.

They had a total of six aircraft, and as I would find out later, just kept one aircraft up and ready to fly if there was a problem. The aircraft were x-rayed on a regular basis to make sure their structure was sound. They took such a beating in the storms. The WC-121 was a very distinctive aircraft with three vertical tails and two huge ray domes, top and bottom. The bottom ray dome was the long range horizontal radar and it covered 200,000 square miles. The top ray dome was the short range vertical radar. The four huge engines were

WC-121 Hurricane Hunter

A Man Returns

Wright Turbo-Compound engines which would develop 13,000 horses. The 8,500 gallons of fuel would allow it to stay in the air for almost twnety-two hours. That was pretty good considering the plane weighed 145,000 pounds. It had been in use as a Hurricane Hunter since 1958 and had always brought her crews home. The only Hurricane Hunter to go down was in 1955. It was on a P2V Neptune. They entered the eye of Hurricane Janet and never came out. The plane and the entire crew were lost.

The interior consisted of the pilot and copilot seats with the flight engineer sitting behind them. There were several racks on boards for those long flights and a galley. They didn't do much cooking; it was mostly box lunches. On the wing port side sat the radio operator with a multitude of different radios. On the wing starboard side sat the navigator. Besides all the nav gear, he also had a radar scope. Further back towards the tail were several large radar scopes and electronics. In the back of the plane was all the meteorological equipment. Below deck was all the equipment that helped keep the aircraft flying.

I started radio school in a couple of weeks and was not looking forward to sitting in any classroom all day. At this poitn, I was helping whoever needed me do whatever.

The country was excited as Apollo II had put men on the moon. Our squadron got to cover the launch. We wouldn't cover the splashdown because they were coming down in the Pacific. The squadron was busy. They'd already had a couple storms: tropical depressions and Tropical Storm Anna.

I'd been going to the beach a lot and dating. My first date was the dental hygienist who cleaned my teeth. She was a Navy WAVE. I met the other girls I dated at the EM Club; it was called the Crow's Nest. I was really starting to like Florida, especially the accent of the southern girls!

A lot of the guys didn't have cars. I found out that if you owned a car, you'd have lots of friends in a hurry. I spent a lot of my days off going to the beach. Jax Beach was okay, but when I had the time, I preferred Daytona.

We had just returned from one of our trips to the beach and I was taking a shower when I heard over the intercom, "If you have your windows down, it's getting ready to cut loose." I had left my windows down so I grabbed my towel, wrapped it around me, and hauled ass to the parking lot and rolled my windows up. As I was, it cut loose with a heavy deluge. As I was running back to the barracks, my towel came off. I was almost there, so I just threw it over my shoulder and headed for my room. A short time later, the intercom blasted, "Would Ben Smith please report to the office." As I approached, I could see two MPs standing in front of it. I walked in and told them I was Ben Smith. What did they want? He said the officers wanted to talk to me. They asked me if I owned the blue Charger in the parking lot, and I said, "Yes, is there a problem?" He said they had a report that someone rolled up the windows on that Charger and then streaked naked across the parking lot. (Streaking was very popular at that time.) I told them I didn't know anything about that. He asked, "So you didn't roll up the windows on that Charger?" I said, "No. It was probably some good Samaritan that did it." They asked again if it was me and I denied it. Then they turned around and walked out of the barracks.

I found out later that a woman had dropped someone off at the barracks. As she was leaving, she happened to see the dropped-towel incident and reported it to security on her way out the gate. I never heard any more about it.

One day I was at the beach with a couple of buddies. We were pounding down the beers as usual and tossing a football around when I cut my foot pretty good. I wrapped it up with my T-shirt and kept playing. One of the guys playing football had a Chevy SS396 and he'd been bugging me race him. When my buddies and I got ready to leave, we saw him coming. "Let's do it!" he said. I answered, "Fine. Follow me out." We got out on the hard road and we both took off. The race was on. Suddenly there was traffic, so we had to let up some. Then, he got caught by a red light, while I kept hauling ass. Next thing I knew I had blue lights in the rearview mirror and I backed off. He hit his speaker and told me to pull over. I did and I just knew I was in a world of shit.

He came to the window, asking for the regular stuff, and wanted to know where the fire was. I told him I was in the Navy and had cut my foot pretty badly. I was headed to the base to get it taken care of. He told me to get out of the car. He wanted to see my foot. I still had it wrapped with the T-shirt, and it was soaked with blood. He took one look at it, handed my cards back, gave me a short lecture on speeding, and sent me on my way. Wow! What a close call! My buddies couldn't believe he let me go. I think the main reason he let me go was because I was in the Navy.

I started radio school and it was going to be rough. I just couldn't concentrate. I had to learn radio procedure, Morse code, and teletype. Teletype was not a problem. I never thought the two years of typing in high school would come in handy, but it did. Listening to dots and dashes all day though was going to be rough. The only thing that kept me going was that I wanted to fly, and this was the only way I was going to be able to do that. I did have one thing going for me—the instructor had also been in Vietnam so we hit it off real well. We became good friends and he told me that if I just applied myself a little, I did not have to worry about graduating from radio school. I finally got into the groove of things and back into Navy life.

Another storm was taking shape near the Cayman Islands and one of our crews was going to take a look at it. I talked to my instructor to see if it might be possible for me to fly along with the crew and get some on-the-job training. He talked to the pilot and he agreed. I spoke to the radio operators and found out the departure time and what I could expect. The storm was Camille. It had reached 60 mph and was headed north towards Cuba. The morning we took off I was so excited. The radio operators took the time to show me all the things that were going to be expected of me once I became an operator. My head was spinning, trying to take in all the information. The flight to the storm was pretty routine, but once we got within a hundred miles of the storm, things started changing. Watching it on the radar screen as we got close was pretty cool. Everyone was busy doing their job. The navigator used his radarscope, and talked the pilot into the storm by giving him the headings to take to avoid the roughest parts of it. We were flying below 1,000 feet. The civilian and Air Force usually flew into the storm between 10,000 and 12,000 feet. As we got close, the rain was more intense, the ride got rougher, and visibility was almost zero. As we neared the eye wall, the navigator had the pilot zigzag through the softer spots and the meteorologist was starting the dropsondes. This device sent back data like pressure, temperature, and humidity. The radio operator stayed in contact with the Miami Hurricane Center and transmitted our position every fifteen minutes while we were in a storm. We broke through the eye wall and it was just like everyone said it would be: blue sky and sunshine. You were completely surrounded by a dense wall of clouds! The pilot flew back and forth within the eye until the meteorologist found the center of the storm. Once they did that the navigator looked for a soft spot to exit the storm, which he did. It could be a rough ride out if the wall closed up and you couldn't find a soft spot to exit.

Camille was now 75 mph so I was in my first hurricane. It was pretty darn exciting, but not as intense as I expected.

A Man Returns

I'd been in a couple of hurricanes before, but never in an airplane. The first time for me was in 1955. I was nine years old when Hurricane Diane slammed into northeastern Pennsylvania. Our house sat on a hill in the fork of the road at the end of town. I remember looking out my bedroom window on the second floor. The entire town of Newfoundland was completely under water. The second was Hurricane Wilma in 2005. My wife and I were living on our sailboat in the Florida Keys at the time. We got off the sailboat and hunkered down in a hotel not that far from where our boat lay at anchor. Wilma took a hard right turn, came straight into the Keys, taking our sailboat thirteen miles up the coast and leaving it on the rocks..

Our squadron penetrated Camille several times as it headed for the coast of Mississippi. It ended up being the worst hurricane to hit the U.S. at that time, packing winds of 175 mph.

Several more storms were brewing, and I couldn't wait to finish radio school and be assigned to a crew. I was ready to do some more flying and check out some more storms. I didn't know it at the time, but there would be plenty to check out.

One evening my buddies and I were hanging out at the Crow's Nest when I happened to look over at the entrance. Two girls had just walked in. Guys were already hitting on them with no luck. I told my buddies I was going to give it a try. The one girl was very cute, so I introduced myself. She told me right away that they weren't staying. They were waiting on a friend and then heading over to the Officer's Club. I kidded her about enlisted men not being good enough, and asked her name. She told me her first name was Kitty, but wouldn't give me her last name. I tried to get a telephone number, but all she would say was that she worked at the Jacksonville airport for National Car Rental. About that time her girlfriend showed up and the three of them left for the Officer's Club.

When I got back to my buddies, they all kidded me about striking out. I told them I had struck out tonight, but I wasn't done. I would be making a trip out to the airport. I knew there was something special about her, so I was going to give it another shot. Even though I wasn't an officer, I was going to get a date with her. They all laughed at me and thought I was crazy.

A few days later I drove to the airport. I didn't bother calling. I figured this was something I needed to do in person, and that I might stand a better chance getting a date in person. On the way there, I stopped and bought a long-stemmed rose. I thought that that might help break the ice and open the door to at least get a telephone number. After arriving at the airport, I found the National Car Rental desk but she wasn't there. My first thought was that she had told me a line of bull. I walked up to the desk and I asked the girl there if she knew a girl named Kitty that was supposed to work here. I was so relieved and excited when she said yes. Kitty was on break and would be back in a few minutes. About that time I saw her coming down the hall. When she saw me, she broke into a great big smile. I hoped that was a good sign. She thought it was sweet that I had brought her a rose, but I still couldn't get a date. However, I did get her phone number.

I don't know how I did it, but I finished radio school. Our instructor told us that if we thought that we might ever be interested in becoming a ham radio operator, now would be the time to do it with the code fresh in our minds. I didn't think I would ever be interested in something like that so I passed on it. Years and years later while living on my sailboat, I kicked myself in the butt as I found myself studying Morse code again to get that very license.

The squadron had five crews with approximately twenty men to a crew, and I was assigned to crew two. I would stay in crew two during the entire time I was with the squadron. They issued me two flight suits, the same as I wore in Vietnam, a crew name patch, and a pair of brown aviation boots. Now all I needed was a storm to fly in, and that came right away.

September had eight storms, so I got plenty of experience quickly. I was very lucky. I liked all the guys on the crew and they accepted me right away, especially when they found out about my previous duty station.

They had five more storms before I graduated. Hurricane Debbie, a Category 3, then Tropical Storm Eve, followed by Hurricanes Francelia and Gerda, both Cat 3s followed by Holly, a Cat 1. My first chance to fly into a storm as a second radio operator was with Tropical Depression 29.

The first thing the radio operator did before a flight was to check all the radios to make sure they were operating. We also made sure the intercom was working at all stations. Then I believe it was radio station WWV in Colorado that we dialed up to set all the clocks on the planes at the exact same time. We also checked the radio book from the squadron duty officer, which contained all the radio frequencies that we would need. One of the nice things about being a radio operator on a plane was that you heard everything coming in or going out.

Tropical Depression 29, formed in the Gulf of Mexico, made landfall at the Florida panhandle. It was a good storm for me to get my feet wet because things weren't too hectic. A piece of cake.

With the next storm, Hurricane Inga, I got to fly to Bermuda and spend a few days exploring the island. Inga turned out to be one of the longest lasting hurricanes on record, lasting twenty-five days. It became a Cat 3 with winds of 115 mph. It stayed in the Atlantic, brushing Bermuda with 80 mph. We flew into Inga twice.

September proved to be a very busy month with eight storms. The last three storms were Hurricane Ten, Tropical Depression 11 and Subtropical Storm 1, and I was able to fly in all three.

After several weeks and several phone calls, I was finally able to get a date with Kitty, the girl at National Car Rental. As it turned out, she was going to college and working there part time. I set up a date and got her address. She lived on the north side of Jacksonville. It was a little bit of a run from NAS Jax. On our first date, I took her to dinner at Jax Beach followed by a movie: *True Grit*. Just as we were leaving Jax Beach, I was sitting at a light and thought it turned green. I took off, but it turned out the green I saw was the green arrow to turn left. The next thing I knew, there were blue lights behind me. A Jax Beach cop pulled me over. I was not having very good luck with the Jax Beach cops. First thing he said was, "Had your mind on something else, didn't you?" I said, "I guess you could say that." I told him it was my first date with this girl. I showed him my license, military ID, and I think that he decided to let me go because of my military ID and the fact it was my first date with this girl. I couldn't believe it! Twice now the Jax Beach cops had given me a break.

When I dropped her off, I asked if she would consider going out with me again, even though I wasn't an officer. She was impressed with my car and the fact that I took her out to dinner and a movie, so she said she might consider it.

Again after several calls, she finally said yes. After that, we started dating regularly. My buddies did not like it one bit. I was no longer their beach or drinking buddy.

October proved to be a busy month with five storms. I got to penetrate three of them. Most of my flights were fairly routine with the usual rough rides. I did get to experience some unusual events while flying though. The first incident I remember was losing an engine cowling. Another time while we were making a routine landing at

A Man Returns

NAS Jax, we lost our brakes and ran off the runway and almost into rush hour traffic on US-17. The only thing that stopped us was the soft ground at the end of the runway. It took two D-8 caterpillars to pull us out.

The worst one was the fire below deck. Heavy smoke was coming up through the floor. Our pilot took us down to a low altitude so we could depressurize. The smoke got so bad that we had to pop the windows. NAS Jax was the closest airport and we made it back without it getting worse. It turned out to be a motor that caught fire. Other crews had their scary encounters too, but the old WC-121 always brought us home.

You hear about weird things happening in the Bermuda Triangle. I had an incident there while flying in it. I lost all communications! I couldn't get out with any of my radio equipment. I had to resort to my telegraph key. We had one at the radio station and I had used it before, but only in practice. I had to send out our position every so often, or they'd send out search planes to look for us. Well, my Morse code training came in handy, and I was able to get through with the telegraph key.

One of the things the crews liked to do every so often was to stop at one of the islands and load up on booze. You could buy a gallon of Ron Rico rum wrapped in wicker for five dollars. We'd stash all the booze below deck. When we landed at NAS Jax, customs would come aboard and walk front to back of the aircraft but never look below deck. The wicker jug made a real nice candle holder, with the wicker catching all the melted candle.

One of the things we did in between flying weather was something we called touch-and-gos. A lot of the radio operators didn't like to do these; they considered it boring, so I volunteered to do as many as I could. After all, it was flying. And I loved to fly. In training new pilots, they did touch-and-gos at different airports. You approached the runway, touched down for a short distance, then you taxied around, and took off again. We did this at NAS Jax, NAS Cecil Field, NAS Mayport, and the Jacksonville airport. When flying the WC-121 you had to have a pilot, copilot, flight engineer, and radio operator, so I got to fly these quite often.

Kitty and I were dating pretty regularly and I thought things were starting to get serious. My buddies were all giving me a hard time, telling me I needed to break it off before things got too serious.

One night after a movie, I was taking her home, and just before her house, I pulled down a dirt road to do a little necking. We weren't there but a few minutes when a police car pulled in behind us. An officer came to my window, asking, "Whatcha doing there, young man?" I don't know why, but I came out with, "Looking for gators, sir." He started laughing and said, "I don't think you're going to find any gators where you're looking." Then he told us how dangerous it was being parked here at night. He could have been somebody else looking for trouble. He told me to get off my hip and take the young lady to a motel where it's safer. I just said, "Yes, sir," and he got back in his car and left, and so did we. We joked about looking for gators for years.

My pilot reminded me of the pilot in Vietnam that I flew most of my missions with. He was young, very personable, and didn't sweat the small stuff. He was a radio ham and made the long flights to a storm less boring. He knew ham operators all over the world, and on these long flights, he would have me dial up different frequencies and talk to all his ham buddies all over the place and I got to listen. It was pretty interesting.

The navigator on board was also a great guy, and also young with a great attitude. He sat across from me on the starboard wing, so we talked a lot and became friends. My rate was Avionics technician navigator, so we had a lot in common. He was really into navigation.

A Man Returns

He liked to practice with the sextant. On long flights he would take nav readings and I would help him by doing the minutes for him. We had a small port in the overhead and he would screw his sextant into it to take all of his readings, pending clear skies. That was a lot of fun and I got to learn something new.

We were also involved in the space race in a kind of roundabout way. We flew over the cape and monitored the weather for all the space launches. I got to fly weather reconnaissance for the Apollo 12 launch and got some nice pictures of the launch out of the window of our aircraft. We were also involved in all the booster recoveries.

Another operation we did (which I considered a lot of fun) was Operation Fountain of Youth. We would fly up and down the Florida coast at low levels, searching for fresh water springs boiling up in the ocean. They were concerned about Florida losing its fresh water to the ocean. There was talk about blowing these holes up to try and stop the run off. No one could come up with enough facts to support the idea that blowing these holes up would work. They were also worried that if it did work, it would affect the water table in Florida. We mapped a lot of springs, but as far as I know, they never did anything. Flying the coast was a lot of fun, seeing all the sharks and big fish in the water. What amazed me most was how many sharks there were in the surf where all the swimmers and surfers were.

I also got to fly in Operation Storm Fury. This involved several other government agencies. It involved seeding clouds with silver or potassium iodides. They normally did this to try and make clouds rain, but we were trying to see what effect this would have on hurricanes. We tried it on two hurricanes—one off the coast of Barbados and the other off the coast of Florida. There was never any conclusive evidence that it affected the hurricanes at all.

Thanksgiving rolled around and the hurricane season was coming to an end. The 1969 hurricane season proved to be the busiest storm season on record, having eighteen storms. I knew I was ready for a break. I took advantage of the Thanksgiving holiday. I took the plunge and asked Kitty to marry me. I took her to the beach. While sitting in the Charger taking in the beautiful view, I popped the question. She said yes! A whole new adventure opened up. Later that evening, we drove back to her house and told her mom. She was overjoyed. I was already tight with her mom, so I knew that wouldn't be a problem. Her dad was a different story. I didn't know him very well. Later when he came home, I caught him in the garage. I was nervous as hell, but I came right out with it, and asked for his daughter's hand in marriage. He stared at me for a bit, but before he would give me an answer, we had to have a little talk. The talk was mostly questions, but after it was finally over, he said yes. The biggest problem was that I was not religious at all and they were strict Catholics. I didn't consider this as a problem, but they did. I had to start taking lessons to become a Catholic. That didn't bother me. I figured one religion was as good as another. I wasn't a very religious person. Let the lessons begin.

After the holiday I went back to work. I told my buddies what I had done and most of them were happy for me, but a couple of them couldn't believe I did it, and would barely talk to me.

The Hurricane Hunters used to be stationed at Roosevelt Roads, Puerto Rico, and moved to NAS Jax, I think, in 1966.

Crews took turns deploying to Roosevelt Roads for usually a one-month stay. When my crews turn came around, I had to leave my new fiancée for a month. She was not happy about that and neither was I. However, I liked new adventures, and Puerto Rico turned out to be alright. It was a pretty relaxed atmosphere with enough time off to check the place out. We were told that Puerto Rico could be dangerous because Americans were not welcomed everywhere. There were a lot of places off limits for us. Old San Juan was one of them, so of course, that's the first place we went. We mainly hit the bars there and we always traveled with several buddies. I really enjoyed the forts—La Fortaleza and Castillo San Felipe del Morro. They were the first forts built by the Spanish. Later, in 1783, they finished their third fort, Castillo de San Cristobal which was huge. I visited the forts several times. I also enjoyed hiking in the jungle where I ran into my first land crabs.

I remember spending New Year's Eve in San Juan and getting so drunk that I threw up in the bus on the way back to the base. It smelled so bad that we had to get off the bus. We couldn't get another and we had to walk several miles back to the base. I had never seen land crabs before, and that night they were everywhere—many squished on the road. The next day all of us were still pretty screwed up.

Our lunch room had a microwave, and it was the first one I'd ever seen. I had heard about them and what they could do. We had to try this one out, so we put all kinds of different stuff in the machine just to see what would happen.

We spent most of our time there doing maintenance on the aircraft and flying training missions.

Kitty and I wrote a lot of letters back and forth while I was there. We talked about a wedding date. I was thinking spring and she was thinking Valentine's Day. After I got back to Jacksonville, we talked more and we settled on Valentine's Day. Her folks were not happy about it as they wanted a big Catholic wedding, and Valentine's Day did not leave them much time to prepare.

In the winter, we flew snowstorms, the big nor'easters. I did not care for that at all. At least in a hurricane, if you went down and survived the crash, you still had a chance of being rescued. It might be a very slim chance, but it was a chance. If you went down in a snowstorm, you could kiss your ass goodbye. I only had to fly in two snowstorms, thank God. We flew out of Maine and came up from Florida to Maine. It was damn cold. On these flights, one of the added things the navigator and I had to do was check the deicers on the leading edge of the wings periodically. At night the pilot turned on the wing lights so we could check them. If the deicers ever quit and the leading edge of the wing iced up, there went your lift and there went your ass.

Valentine's Day was coming up fast and there were lots of preparations to be done. I asked several of my buddies in the squadron to be ushers. All accepted except one. He just refused to be a part of me getting married. I asked my best friend, Lance, to be my best man, but he was still training troops for Vietnam at Camp Lejeune, and they wouldn't let him take leave. I asked Russel, my other best friend back home, and he said yes, he could make it.

It took five priests for us to be able to get married. We had to get permission from the priest of the Immaculate Conception Church in downtown Jacksonville to use the church to get married in. He said yes. Then the priest that my fiancée wanted to marry us was not her parish priest so we had to get permission from her parish priest for the other priest to marry us. He said no! He said she was too young to get married! (She was nineteen at the time.) It boiled down to this: he was just pissed because she was getting married out of his parish. The priest that she wanted to marry us said he could get around this, but he didn't want to make waves. I went to my squadron priest. He said making waves was not a problem for him. He would contact the priest and get it taken care of, which he did. The fifth priest to be enlisted was the priest in my hometown. Even though I was not Catholic, I had to send a form to my mom that this priest had to fill out. Basically, it stated that I had never been married before. What a whole bunch of bullshit! But there you go: five priests! I couldn't believe it. The only other problem we had was getting all the flowers

A Man Returns

we needed because of the wedding being on Valentine's Day. I don't know what all that entailed, but they were able to get the flowers.

My mom really wanted to come and we really wanted her there, but she couldn't afford to miss several days of work and she didn't drive.

I had no problem getting leave for the wedding or honeymoon; I had leave saved up and storm season was over. My commander signed my leave papers without a problem.

Valentine's Day was on a Saturday and the big day was coming up. I got a call from my friend, Russel, on Wednesday with a big surprise. He was leaving early Thursday morning, picking up my mother and my baby sister, and bringing them down with him. Oh, my God! Was I ever surprised and happy! This was going to be a big trip for my mom and sister. They'd never been out of our hometown. They were going to leave right after the wedding so they could be back at work on Monday.

Friday was busy and spent getting the last of the details worked out, like picking up the tux. Russel, with my mom and sister, got to my fiancée's house late morning, and my mom and future mother-in-law hit it right off. They both had two boys and three girls, so I guess they had something in common right off. It was so good to see my mom and sister. I was thrilled that they would be attending the wedding. In the middle of the goings on, my mom had a special request: would it be possible to see a Hurricane Hunter plane? What could I say? I told her sure, but we would have to make it fast.

There were two of our planes sitting on the tarmac. We walked around checking them and my mom took a few pictures. Next thing I knew, this security vehicle came speeding up. A security guard jumped out and started yelling at us that this was a security area. No pictures were allowed. He asked my mom for her camera. I told him to wait a minute. We took pictures of these aircraft all the time. What did he think people were doing when we took these planes to an air show? He got real nasty and wanted to know if I wanted to go for a ride to the security office. We were pressed for time, and I didn't want to get hung up in all that bullshit. So he took my mom's camera, took out the film, and handed it back to her. He said we needed to leave. I was so pissed and embarrassed that I couldn't stand it. I started to have words with him, but my mom stopped me. She said, "You're getting married tomorrow. You don't want to end up in the brig." We left, but I was fuming; my mom had other pictures on that camera. I later took the issue up with my chief and he couldn't believe it. I didn't get the guard's name, so not much could be done.

We got back just in time for the rehearsal and rehearsal dinner. After dinner, the guys wanted to take me out for a few drinks like a bachelor's night out. My future in-laws, my mom, and my fiancée weren't too happy about that. My fiancée asked me to please get back early and not drink too much. We did just that, but when we got back Lance was there! He had gone AWOL and hitchhiked down from North Carolina! He said he wasn't going to miss my wedding. What's the worst they could do? Well, that meant that we had to go back out again (which we did), and we closed the bars down and all of us were feeling pretty good. My future mother-in-law was pretty pissed. The next day, we all felt pretty bad. But long story short: I did get married and it all went well.

We had a small wedding luncheon afterward. Right after the luncheon, Russel, my mom, and my sister said their goodbyes and headed back to Pennsylvania. My new bride and I headed out soon afterward. My Charger was all decked out with toothpaste and shave cream. They also filled the engine compartment with balloons which all started popping as we headed down the road. They also tied a bunch of cans to the back bumper. We headed to Pennsylvania and the Pocono Mountains which everyone knows is the honeymoon capital of

America. But that's not the reason why we were headed to the Poconos. We were headed there because that's where my hometown was, and I wanted my new bride to meet all my family and my relatives.

We headed north until almost dark and pulled off the interstate and got a motel. When we pulled off, my car acted like it didn't want to stay running. The next morning, it wouldn't start. The Charger was a stick shift so there we were in the parking lot trying to push it to get it started with the car all painted up saying: Just Married! Finally, a couple of guys helped push the car and I got it started. It was still acting funny, so before we got on the interstate, we drove into the little town to a mechanic's shop. He found the problem right away: apparently the balloons had knocked a wire loose that was plugged into the alternator. Thank goodness, it wasn't a major problem. The guy did not charge us and we were back on the road.

I was in a hurry to get home, and I was letting the Charger eat up the highway. Not paying attention and just cruising along, I looked over and there was a state trooper cruising right alongside me. I glanced at my speedometer. I was doing just over 80 mph. I about shit. He looked at me and I looked at him. He smiled, motioned for me to slow down (which I did) and sped on up the road. We figured the "Just Married" all over the car saved us.

I only had a few days leave so we were quite busy seeing everybody and having some fun ourselves. My new bride had never experienced snow before and we were in the mountains, so it was very cold. She was sick on the second day, but it kind of came and went. We thought it was maybe all the excitement or the thinner mountain air.

Before we knew it, it was time to head back to Jax, back to work, and the fun part, setting up our own household.

After we got back, Kitty was still getting sick and finally went to the doctor. What a surprise we got! She was three months pregnant and her due date was in September. Wow! Did that change things! I was going to be a dad.

We rented a duplex located halfway between her work and the Navy base. She already had a new MGB so transportation was not a problem. I got a housing allotment and a small jump in pay which really helped. Plus we could shop on the base.

We settled into married life. She was working every day, and when I wasn't flying, I was doing maintenance on the aircraft.

We had a change of command ceremony and the squadron turned out on the tarmac in full dress blues. During the ceremony the new commander presented me with several awards that I had earned in Vietnam.

In April, we got to fly weather again at the cape for the Apollo 13 launch. It was an exciting time in the space race, and Apollo 13 got a lot of attention with the aborted moon landing because of an oxygen tank failure. It was touch and go for a while for their safe return.

Spring arrived and my crew got to do an airshow in Houston, Texas. That was a lot of fun: you sat at your station and as people filed through the aircraft, you told them what you did, and answered a lot of questions. The kids were the really funny; they could come up with some crazy questions.

Hurricane season arrived early with Alma on May 17 forming in the southwestern Caribbean. It made landfall on May 25 near Cedar Key as a tropical depression and petered out in North Carolina. Several crews (including mine) got to check this one out.

June was quiet, and we didn't have any storms that month.

The squadron had another ceremony, and again I received several awards for my service in Vietnam.

In July, things started picking up with Becky, a tropical storm, then a tropical depression, followed closely with Celia, a Cat 3 hurricane. Taking off to check out Celia, we lost an engine and had to fly out over the ocean and dump fuel until we were light enough to land. Usually if an engine was going to go, it would go on takeoff because of the strain put on the engines to get all that weight off the ground.

On the first of August, the squadron offered a deep water survival school put on by the Air Force at Homestead Air Force Base. Only a few guys signed up for it. Everyone heard that they tried to drown you and that it wasn't much fun. I talked one of my buddies into signing up with me. It was a two-week course. You spent the first week in school and the second week in the field, mostly in the water.

Kitty was getting really big and doing fine. She was getting regular checkups at the base, and she was still working. She wasn't due until September, and since she was doing fine, I didn't see any reason not to take the course.

A few days later, we were on the road and headed to Homestead Air Force Base. I drove, and my buddy rode with me. We got there midafternoon and got checked in, and they showed us to our rooms. Guys from all over were taking the course. There were about thirty of us—officers and enlisted men. The first week was alright, just a little boring, but we offset this by checking out the Miami nightlife. I'd never been to Miami, so it was very interesting. Besides the survival bookwork, they also prepared us for what was coming in the second week.

The first day of the second week, you learned about not cutting your parachute loose until you hit the water. Over the ocean, there were no reference points, so you had nothing to let you know how high above the water you were. Guys would release their chutes too high and be killed on impact. The reason they wanted to get rid of their chutes right away was because they were afraid of being pulled under the water by their chute dragging them. This trained you to wait until your feet hit the water before releasing your chute.

You wore sneakers for all your water activities. If your sneakers were white, you had to pull your navy blue socks over them. They didn't want any white feet dangling in the water to attract sharks. They also issued all of us Air Force flight suits with no rank on them. Everyone was treated the same. We had to climb a ninety-foot tower next to the water. It had a cable connected to it, and the other was connected to a post in the water. The cable was on an angle of about thirty degrees. You put on a parachute harness and connected it to the cable, then you jumped off the platform, and slid partway down the cable until you came to an abrupt stop. This simulated your chute opening.

You would then go through the routine of checking to see if your chute was open, take off your oxygen mask (if you had one), and pull the cord to deploy your life raft. When the instructor saw that you'd completed all of that, he released you, and you zipped toward the water, releasing your parachute harness when your feet hit it. You would then swim over to a life raft, like the ones that would be attached to you, and climb in. We all went through this several times.

Next we had the parachute drop. They had a fully opened parachute raised above the water. In this exercise, you learned how to get out from under a parachute if it came down on top of you. Men had been known to drown trying to get out from under their chute. When it was your turn, you swam out so the center of the chute was directly over you, then they released the chute and it dropped on top of you. This was where your classroom training kicked in. You simply flipped over on your back, taking hold of a seam, and followed that seam until you came out from under the chute. Pretty simple, if you knew the trick and didn't panic.

We learned how to properly get into many different life rafts and what you could expect to find in different-sized rafts. You also learned how to use all the different survival gear—from the simple signal mirror to a watermaker.

Learning how to get picked up out of the water by a helicopter was a little more difficult than I thought it would be. They took us by boat to the middle of Biscayne Bay where it was a little choppy. Then you jumped out of the boat and the boat moved away. A chopper came in with a cable and lift collar. You had to make sure that the chopper discharged the cable in the water before you grabbed it to avoid getting shocked. With the chopper overhead, the water became very turbulent. With the water stinging your face, it was very hard to see. You slipped the collar under your arms and away you went. Once you reached the doorway, you let the crew bring you in, and you didn't try to help them.

The next adventure with the chopper was being hoisted through dense mangrove swamp. They gave us a radio and a smoke. When the chopper got close, we popped the smoke and talked to the chopper until it was right above us. Then the chopper would lower the jungle penetrator down through the mangroves. The penetrator was like a steel capsule. The sides were folded down to sit on, and the top section folded up to protect you as you came up out of the trees. It was very important to lock the top part in, so it didn't collapse on you when they were hoisting you through the trees.

So far I was really enjoying the training and it was going to get even better. The next phase of our training took place in the middle of Biscayne Bay. They had a barge anchored there with a wire mesh screen standing vertical on the one end. On the middle of the barge was a red line that you stood on. Here you put on a parachute behind you. They would then raise the parachute up on the wire screen, and the wind would hold it in place. You were then hooked up to a boat out in front of the barge. When you were ready, the instructor would wave a red flag at the boat, and boat would take off, pulling you off the barge. As you were being pulled forward, the chute would inflate with air and you were airborne. They towed us up to 300 feet, and after you went through the same routine you did at the ninety-foot tower, they waved a red flag on the boat, and you cut yourself loose by releasing two gooseneck connectors. After hitting the water, you released the chute and they picked you up with the tow boat. That one was a lot of fun. I could have done that all day long.

Our next exercise was not as much fun. This exercise would simulate the wind blowing you and your parachute across the water. We all boarded a boat and headed out on Biscayne Bay. On the back of the boat, they had an I-beam that stuck out over the water. They put you in a parachute harness, and then hooked you up to a cable connected to the I-beam. Then you stepped off the back of the boat and hung suspended over the water. The boat was moving though the water at five to ten knots. The instructor pushed a button, which released you from the I-beam and you dropped into the water. The slack was quickly taken up, and now you were being dragged through the water. In class, they taught you how to bend your knees, arch your back, and bend your arms in, and hold them straight out to your side. If done correctly, instead of being pulled underwater, you planed across the top. Once you achieved this position, a chase boat picked you up. You did this a couple times and then you did it blindfolded to simulate a night situation. I have to say that it was a weird feeling, dangling off the back of the boat blindfolded, spinning, and waiting for the drop.

On our last day of training, we left the dock very early and headed out on the ocean until we were out of sight of land. They dropped us off in the water in six-man groups with a life raft capsule. It was a six-man life raft, and after we inflated it, we all climbed aboard. We couldn't see the other groups, so we felt quite alone not being able to see land. We spent the entire day there. We checked out the survival gear on board and set up the watermaker. There was fishing line and hooks in the survival pack.

About midafternoon, a storm blew in and the sea got pretty choppy; we got tossed around a bit, but it didn't last long. We got a little chilly from being soaked, but the sun popped back out and we dried off pretty quickly. Two guys in our raft got seasick, and the fish guts didn't help matters. Late afternoon, the boat picked us up and we hauled ass in. Everybody was hungry and thirsty.

It was our last night there, and even though we had had a long day, a few of us decided to go out and celebrate finishing the survival school without drowning. The next morning we headed back to Jax and stopped to pick up beer on the way.

We were cruising up the Sunshine State Parkway. Depending on traffic, I ran the Charger up to 100 to 110 mph off and on. The speedometer ran up to 150 mph. The Charger cruised so nicely at that speed, and it felt good.

It felt good until I spotted a faint blue light in the heat mirage way back in my rearview mirror. I told my buddy to hide the beer. We had company. I took my foot off the accelerator and checked the mirror. He was coming on fast. By the time I had slowed down to about 75 mph, he was on my ass and I pulled off the road. He pulled up behind me and I got out of the car. He walked up to us with a little smile on his face and said, "Let the old fuzz sneak right up on you?" I couldn't believe he was joking with me. I said, "Yes, sir, I guess I did." I handed him my driver's license and registration. He asked why I had a Pennsylvania license and New Jersey tags. I explained that I bought the car in Vietnam and it was delivered to New Jersey, but I was a resident of Pennsylvania. Then I showed him my military ID and that answered his questions. He took a look at my car and asked me what I had in it and I told him. He said it was a nice car, but it was a good thing I didn't try to run. It turned out that he was driving a Plymouth with the 426 Hemi in it. He'd have caught me and then I would have been in big trouble. He asked me about Vietnam and where was I headed so fast. I told him about the Seawolves and the Hurricane Hunters, and that we had just finished a deep water survival school. It turned out he was an Army vet with two tours in Vietnam. Like I always say, better to be lucky than good. We talked a little about Vietnam and then came the lecture, which ended with, "I'm going to let you slide." Hot damn, I couldn't believe it. He told me to slow down and not get myself killed after making it through Nam. I thanked him and he got in his car and smoked the tires on down the road. I couldn't believe my luck. That could have turned out real bad, and I'm sure my new bride would not have been happy. We held to the speed limit back to Jax.

My bride was happy to see me and me, her. We'd settled into our little duplex and liked our neighbors. Most everyone was military. It was sure nice living off base.

August was pretty quiet with only two tropical depressions and two tropical storms and they were all close to the U.S., so I got to spend a lot more time home.

Towards the third week in August, Kitty started having pains off and on and didn't feel well. She had to quit work, and her mother started coming by and spending the day with her. She had finally gotten over the fact that Kitty had gotten pregnant out of wedlock and was getting excited about the grandbaby coming.

On August 28, her mom was due to come, but hadn't made it yet, and I needed to get to work. Kitty was fine, so I went ahead and went to work.

A couple hours later, I was out on the flight line working on an aircraft when one of the guys told me the chief wanted to see me. I went into the shop and the chief said someone called and said your wife was about to have a baby and left a telephone number. I called the number and it was a restaurant. I looked at the chief. I told him that that wasn't very funny and that I didn't appreciate that at all. I started to walk out of the shop, but he yelled for me to come back. This was no joke, he said. Someone, a woman, said your wife was about to have a baby. I called home and there no answer. I called the base hospital to see if my wife had been admitted and they said no. My chief told me to drive over there and check it out. I hauled ass over there straight to admitting, and asked the girl if my wife had been admitted. She checked and said no. I asked if she was sure. Another lady sitting there said there was chance that she came in through the emergency entrance and they hadn't told us yet. I had them call emergency and sure enough, she had come in that way, and was on the maternity floor. I asked what floor and where the elevators were. I would never forget, getting off the elevator and almost running into my mother-in-law and the look of panic on her face. She was pissed. She was on her way to a phone to call my shop again to let me know that Kitty had a baby girl, and both were doing fine. I followed her back to Kitty's room, where she was holding our new baby girl, Kathleen. Wow, what a feeling! I was so excited I was shaking. Kitty held her out for me to hold, and what a beautiful feeling.

My mother-in-law was still fuming, and wanted to know why I left before she got there. First of all, I had to make muster; second, Kitty was doing fine when I left; and third, she wasn't due for another month. It turned out that they had messed up on the due date. Kathleen came out full term.

My mother-in-law had arrived at the house shortly after I left, and Kitty started contractions shortly after that. She got Kitty in the car and headed to NAS Jax. She made it almost to the base when traffic came to a standstill. At that time, there was major construction going on. They were widening US-17. My mother-in-law went into a panic, and just by chance, one of the workers saw how upset she was, and walked to the car. He assisted her in getting off the main road and onto a construction road, and told her it would take her all the way to the gate. At the gate, they told her they would call the hospital, so they would be waiting for her at the emergency entrance. Kitty almost had our baby in the elevator. So Mom had good reason to be a little stressed, but she soon settled down, and we both got to indulge in the new baby.

Kitty only spent two days in the hospital and we got to take our little one home. The hospital charge was five dollars and twenty-five cents, and that was for meals.

Friends and family had given us just about everything for a new-born baby. We also found out that the Navy Relief had large starter kits for new babies, so I went by and picked one up. It was loaded with just about everything you would need for a newborn. It was times like these when I was thankful that I made it back from Nam. I had a new appreciation for life. I thought about Nam a lot and won-dered how I ever made it through all that I did. I thought about my brothers in Nam and wondered how they were doing. Things here had changed so much for me in such a short period of time that I could hardly believe it at times.

September proved to be a very busy month, and thank goodness my wife and baby were both doing great. I was gone a lot: we had one Cat 3 hurricane, five tropical depressions, and two tropical storms. September was a blur.

October was not so busy. We only had one Cat 1 and one Cat 2 hurricane so I was home a lot more.

One day my division officer called me into his office to discuss my career in the Navy. I had less than four months left, and he wanted to talk to me about some options. I came to find out that the Navy was offering an early-out program. It seemed that they had too many people and needed to let some people go. He wanted to know if I was going to ship over. The Navy was decommissioning the WC-121s and changing over to the P-3 Orion in 1971. The Hurricane Hunters were getting four aircraft and already sending guys to transition school. That was one of the reasons he wanted to know what I was going to do. They didn't want to send me to school if I planned on getting out.

He told me the Navy had a lot to offer because I was in a critical rate—both an air crewman and a radio operator. If I were to sign up for another six years, they would give me several thousand dollars and another stripe. I told him that I had thought a lot about it, and that if it weren't for the chicken shit and ass-kissing, I would stay. He said he was sorry I felt that way. If I wanted I could get a 120-day early out. That would mean I would get out November 2, which was right around the corner.

When I joined the Navy, they had so many guys signing up to avoid the draft that I had signed on and been delayed, first for 120 days and then another 30 days, so it was kind of crazy that I was getting a 120-day cut now. I told him that was what I wanted and he said he would run the paperwork. When my wife found out, she was excited because I wouldn't be taking off somewhere all the time.

I had one last flight to take, and it was to Barbados. We would then fly out of there to the African coast. The whole trip went well until we took off to fly back to NAS Jax. We had just leveled off when the starboard engine quit. We turned back to Barbados, dumping fuel on the way, and landed without a problem.

It turned out to be like a vacation. They put us up at the Royal Caribbean Hotel for five days while they worked on the engine. The only thing we had to do was take turns standing guard on the aircraft, and the rest of the time was ours. I climbed my first coconut trees. We'd pick the coconuts and take them to the hotel bar. The barkeep would drill a hole in it and pour rum in there.

We mostly hung at the pool and took it easy. I did do a lot of hiking around the island. We didn't pack to stay anywhere, so clothes were a big thing. There was a show bar called Harry's which claimed to be the best show bar in the Caribbean. One night, a bunch of us had to go and check it out. I have to say I have been to a lot of bars and Harry's ranked right up there.

They repaired the engine and our vacation was over. I have to say that I enjoyed my last flight with the Hurricane Hunters. It was a nice vacation after the hectic month of September.

When I got back, my wife was not too happy; the Navy would not tell her anything. She wanted to know why I didn't at least write her. I told her I did, but she didn't really believe me. About a week later, my letter arrived, thank goodness.

We had a big problem. I didn't have a job to go to, and was getting real close to the end of my Navy career. My chief was letting me off a lot if I didn't have duty, so I was out looking for work. I was still doing my Bell and Howell TV repair home study, so I concentrated on TV repair. The biggest problem I had was that the job market was saturated with guys getting out of the military. The Vietnam War was winding down and Jacksonville was a big military town, so a lot of guys were getting out here and staying.

I put in applications everywhere, not just TV repair places. A lot of places wouldn't even take applications. I finally got a job at a small two-man TV repair place. They liked my electronic background and said that I would catch on pretty quickly. The starting pay was terrible, but it was a start. We both had a little money saved up, so we would be okay for a bit.

November 2 was check-out day, a day of mixed emotions. When I went by my division officer's office, he tried to talk me out of it, but I told him I was done. I went by my work center, Work Center 210, checked out, and said my final goodbyes. Checking out at administration, I found out that I had flown nearly six hundred hours in the Super Connie. I can't say the Hurricane Hunters were as exciting as the Seawolves, but it did have its moments.

A few years later in April 1975, after going through the experience of changing the squadron over to the P-3s, the Navy decommissioned the Hurricane Hunters. The Navy Seawolves were also decommissioned in March of 1972. In fact, I think they were the only squadron that was commissioned and decommissioned outside the United States.

Wow! Civilian life and a new job. The new job wasn't working out. After a couple months, all they had me doing every day was putting up antennas, with a raise nowhere in sight.

I started looking for another job and found one with an electrical contractor. I could start as an apprentice. The starting pay was a little better than the TV repair place: I would be making one dollar and seventy-five cents an hour and taking home sixty-four dollars a week.

Things were pretty tight. Kitty was not working and I didn't want her to work. I wanted her to stay home with the baby, so to save some money, we sold her MGB to her dad. About a month later, I bit the bullet and traded in my Dodge Charger for a four-cylinder Dodge Colt. It was really hard to do, but between the gas and the insurance, I had to do it.

We also started saving a little money by moving from our nice duplex, which cost $130 a month, to an unfurnished garage apartment at $60 a month. Again, friends and family helped us out with necessary items, like a table and chairs, bed, dresser, and a crib. We bought the rest of our furnishings from used furniture places and thrift stores.

The people from whom we rented the apartment owned a roofing business, and I was able to work some weekends doing roofing.

Our new baby was doing great, and my wife stayed busy painting and making the apartment our own. It hadn't been in the best of shape when we moved in.

The work I was doing was fine, even though a lot of it was grunt work. I was learning a lot about construction.

P2V Neptune Sub chaser

VP-62: AIRBORNE EARLY WARNING SQUADRON:

FLYING THE P2V NEPTUNE SUBMARINE CHASERS

I really missed flying. My Hurricane Hunter buddies still came around, but they were all single, and it wasn't the same anymore. I told one of them about how much I missed flying and he told me about VP-62 at NAS. It was a reserve unit and they hunted Russian subs. I checked into it, and Kitty and I talked about it. We decided it would be another nice little income.

I went into NAS Jax one Saturday morning and talked with the commander of VP-62. What a nice guy! He was so impressed with my service record that he welcomed me aboard right then. He told me that if I signed on now, he would pay me for the weekend, and guaranteed that I would fly every weekend. He told me that if my name wasn't on the flight schedule, I should call him and he would take care of it. He also told me that because I had already fulfilled my military obligation, I didn't have to sign up for any particular length of time.

Not only would I get paid for the weekend, but I would also get flight pay. One of the cool things about VP-62 was that they flew the P2V Neptune, a very cool-looking aircraft. I couldn't wait to get airborne in it. This aircraft was the original aircraft that the Hurricane Hunters used, and it was also the only aircraft they had ever lost in a hurricane.

My job on the plane was to be radio operator, for which I was already qualified and the main reason the commander hired me.

A Man Returns

My training period was pretty short; all I needed to learn was their procedures.

One day a friend called me up and said he'd won a radio contest. It was a certificate for a jump class for two, and I was the only guy he knew that might be interested in something like that. I didn't hesitate, and told him, "Hell, yeah." A couple of weeks later, he picked me up and we were on our way.

We spent several hours in the classroom and then several hours outside on their training course. After the training was all said and done, we were supposed to do a jump, but weather had moved in, so we couldn't. They told us we could come back tomorrow and do the jump. Wow, we were disappointed. The jump school was a long ride, so we weren't looking forward to having to come back the next day.

My buddy picked me up early, so we could be in the first groups to take off. Well, we got there plenty early, but what they didn't tell us was that we had to wait for one of the jump masters *and go through a refresher course* before we could jump. At the time I thought, *What a waste of time!* Little did I know that in a short while I would appreciate the review.

The weather was good and one group had already jumped. Our jump master finally arrived and ran us through the course.

Five of us boarded the small plane. I was the first to get in, which meant I would be the last to jump. We took off and climbed to 3,200 feet. The first two guys jumped and then my buddy. Everything was going like it was supposed to go. As I got to the door of the plane, I could see the three parasails below us. The jump master had me check my rip cord, so I could see that it was attached to the aircraft. He then asked me if I was ready. I said yes. I stepped out on the small platform and held on to the wing strut. He asked again, "Are you ready?" I said yes. The pilot cut the engine and I let go. As I fell away, I felt the ripcord pull my main chute away, but I didn't feel it opening. I just felt myself falling through the air. I looked up and my chute was all tangled up. In class, they had told us that it took approximately twenty seconds to hit the ground without a chute from 3,200 feet. The tangled chute was causing me to spin around and around very fast. I grabbed hold of the shroud lines on both sides and yanked as hard as I could several times, but nothing happened. I knew right away that I had to get rid of the main chute. You had to make sure the main chute was gone before you released the reserve chute, or the reserve chute would just tangle in the main one, and then you were screwed. My life didn't flash before me and I didn't say any "Hail Marys." I was just remembering what I was supposed to do in this situation. I never did look at my altimeter. It didn't matter. I only had a few seconds to do what I needed to do. I knew I needed to get my reserve chute deployed before I reached about 1,500 feet. I looked at my breakaway handle on my right side, and pulled hard. As it released, I felt my speed increase by quite a bit. I stuffed the handle in my flight suit. Then I looked down to my left and got a good hold on the reserve D-ring and pulled hard. At first, I didn't feel anything, and I had a sick feeling instantly that they didn't pack the reserve chute. No sooner did I have that feeling when the reserve chute popped open. And when I say popped, I mean you had better have your straps in the right place around your gonads, because it was quite the jolt. It felt like you came to an abrupt stop. When your main chute opens, it's a parasail chute. It has a slider bar on it that slides up when your chute opens, reducing the jolt. This was very different. I stuffed that handle into my flight suit. I did that because they told us that if this ever happened and we lived, we would be charged twenty-five dollars each for the handles. As I did this, I looked down for the first time, just as a paved road was coming up at me. I went into a parachute landing fall (PLF) and landed hard on my feet, rolling with it to my hip, and then to my shoulder with my helmet hitting hard on the road. *Son of a bitch, I was still alive!* At the time I didn't realize how hard I had landed. I was on the road that ran along the fence around the airport. I rolled up my reserve chute and I saw my main chute hanging from some trees a short distance away. About that time, a truck from the jump school showed up. The trouble was that he was on the other side of the fence and had to go all the way back around. They asked if I was alright, and I said I thought so. I was walking. I walked over to my main chute and rolled it up and headed for the airport. I found a small gate and it wasn't locked, so I opened it and cut across the field to the airport. I didn't see the truck and found out later that that part of the road had a locked gate and they didn't have a key. Lots of people were coming towards me, most of them cheering that I was still alive. My buddy came running up, and told me he had pictures of me coming down. My jump master came to see how I was doing. He almost fell over when he saw the two breakaway handles sticking out of my flight suit. He couldn't believe that with everything that was happening, I had the composure to save the handles. I told him I wanted to go back up right now and jump again. He told me I was crazy. I assured him that I was not joking. He said okay, and got us a chute. A plane was loading up. He walked over, told two of the guys they had to catch the next plane, and they motioned for me to board. We took off and he told the pilot to go to 4,000 feet. As we were climbing, he kept asking me if I was okay. When we got to 4,000 feet, I clipped my ripcord to the ripcord ring and I was first to go out the door. The pilot cut the engine, and I released my hold on the strut and fell away from the aircraft. I felt the ripcord release my main chute, and holy shit, the same thing. *(No, I'm kidding.)* I looked up to see a full parasail. I was flying. As I descended, I tried some of the things they taught us in school: pulling on the shroud lines, I steered myself to the left or right, and if I pulled down hard on both sides at the same time, it would give you a short stall. I practiced this several times because that's what you do upon landing to soften your contact with the ground. I could see a crowd of people watching. I guess they wanted to see if my chute opened this time. I turned and flew right down the runway and made a perfect stand-up landing in front of the hangar and the crowd of people. Again, everyone was clapping and cheering and congratulating me on a perfect jump and landing. My jump master told me that on average, you had a malfunction about every 175 jumps, so I figured I was good for a while.

When I got home, Kitty was not happy to hear about what had happened, and she really didn't want me to jump again. The results of my hard landing really started to show up that evening. I was unable to go to work the next day. Both my feet to above my ankles turned black and blue. My leg (from my knee to my butt) turned black and blue as well as my whole shoulder area. I also had whiplash from my head hitting the pavement. I was able to go to work on Tuesday, but I was a hurting puppy. I did go back to make several more jumps without incident. I also talked to a couple jump classes about my jump and the importance of all the training. I finally stopped jumping—not only because my wife wanted me to but because the cost was high, the distance was far, and sometimes the plane had problems or the weather would change by the time I got there.

My job was going okay as far as the work, but they were giving me the runaround about getting a raise. My foreman would say that I should be getting a raise next week and then it wouldn't happen. I asked him about it, and he'd tell me he'd check on it. Finally I went into the office and talked with the boss. He told me my foreman had to recommend me for a raise. Of course, when I talked to the foreman, he said he had. Well, I was getting really pissed. I was working my ass off, wanting to get ahead.

My VP-62 reserve meetings were going okay, and I was flying every month. We would fly up and down the Atlantic coast searching

A Man Returns

for Russian subs. We dropped sonobuoys in certain areas and listen for pings. The buoys were about three feet long by five inches in diameter. They were deployed through a tube in the rear of the plane and floated to the surface by parachute.

I really enjoyed the flying, even though it could be a little boring at times, but that was only until you found a sub. Then it got pretty interesting.

I told my father-in-law about my problems at work. He was a union pipefitter and worked for a very large union mechanical contractor. He told me they were hiring laborers. If I was interested, they were paying a lot more than I was making now.

I talked it over with my wife and decided to make an appointment and talk to them. They told me they were hiring and I could start anytime. The pay was two dollars and fifty cents an hour. I told them I wanted the job, but needed to give my employer two weeks' notice.

I went into my employer's office the next day and gave them notice. They said I could leave now, which I did, so I started with the mechanical contractor the next day.

After a couple months, they asked me to join the labor union, so I could work on the government jobs they were doing. My pay jumped to over three dollars an hour, which was very nice. I really enjoyed construction and liked working with the plumbers, pipefitters, and welders. After working for nearly a year as a laborer, I put in for the plumber's apprenticeship program with Local 234. I think the fact that my father-in-law was a union member helped me get in, but I also think my military background really gave me the edge. I was accepted. I can't begin to tell you how happy I was when I found out. That meant my future was secure and my family's future was secure.

Being a veteran came through for me again. My apprenticeship training was for five years and the VA gave me a check every month. As an apprentice, you could donate blood regularly to the local union, and then you didn't have to pay union dues, so I took advantage of that.

Shortly after I started apprenticeship training and my new job, we started looking for a house. We found a three-bedroom, two-bath in Cedar Hills, a suburb of Jacksonville. We had saved up a little money, and using the VA, we were able to buy it. We got it for $17,500 and our mortgage payments were $124. I remember thinking, *Wow, I hope we can afford all that comes with owning a home: like insurance, taxes, water, sewer, and electric.*

My job with VP-62 wasn't going so well. I really enjoyed the flying, but I wasn't getting along with the guys. I just didn't seem to fit in. One of the reasons I got out of the Navy was because of the ass-kissing, and some of the guys felt that was exactly what I was because the boss, our commander, made it known that I was to fly every weekend. The other guys didn't like it.

One weekend I came into the shop, and instead of the flying they had scheduled, I had, of all things, corrosion control school. This was a direct slap in the face. I thought about it for about two seconds, then told them to kiss my ass, and walked out. I never did look back, and so ended my Navy career.

When I had joined the Navy in 1966, I had no idea that the next six years would have so much adventure in them. I never felt much like a sailor because I had never been aboard a ship. I spent six years hunting—hunting VC, hunting hurricanes and storms, and then hunting Russian subs.

The Navy gave me a great start on life. My experiences in Vietnam still haunted me, but the bond I formed with the guys in the Seawolves still lives on today. I volunteered for Vietnam and the Seawolves because I believed in what we were doing over there and so did all the guys that I flew with. We had no idea at the time that it was all political, and that in the end, our government would let us down. I'm fortunate. I came back. But I am so bitter towards our government. To this day, I hold them responsible for all the men and women who paid the ultimate price.

While in Nam, I served my country proudly and did the best job I could do. While there, I'm proud to say, I earned fourteen air medals, the Air Medal Bronze Star, a Presidential Unit Citation, Good Conduct ribbon, National Defense ribbon, Vietnam Service Medal with four bronze stars, Republic of Vietnam Meritorious Unit Citation for Gallantry, Republic of Vietnam Meritorious Unit Citation for Civil Actions, the Republic of Vietnam Campaign Medal, and the Cold War Recognition Certificate. Along with these awards, I also earned the gold aircrew wings, the combat wings, and the aviation warfare specialist wings.

On November 4, 2005, in a ceremony aboard the aircraft carrier USS Yorktown, I was inducted into the Enlisted Combat Aircrew Roll of Honor. This was a very proud moment in my life—to have my name included alongside combat aviators from both WWII and the Korean War. Many of my Seawolf brothers were on this list, and I'm sure that there would be a lot more, once they were located.

Today, after all these years, the Seawolf brotherhood is still going strong. We have regular reunions and a Seawolf website, so everyone can stay in touch. Our Seawolf website is Seawolf.org.

On September 4, 2018, on the flight deck of the USS Midway, Arbollo Entertainment showed the world premiere documentary, *Scramble the Seawolves,* narrated by Mike Rowe. I know it took a lot of hard work and a lot of donations, but I have to say it turned out pretty darn good. Yours truly appeared in it. The documentary DVD is available on the internet.

FAMILY LIFE

In the next five years, Kitty and I had two more children, both boys, and I finished my apprenticeship training. I turned out as a journeyman plumber/welder, and later took a course on pipefitting. My wife still wasn't working. We decided to wait until the last child was in school. I was making good money and getting a lot of overtime, so we were doing pretty good.

Once my last child started school, my wife got a good job as a rural mail carrier. This was a really big help, so we were able to put a little money aside.

I raised my children going camping and fishing. We also kept them busy with all the sports activities that were offered. When they were old enough, I bought a boat and had them all scuba-certified. In the summertime, we fished and dove the ocean, and in the winter, we dove the springs all over Florida. We took many dive trips to the Florida Keys. I just loved the Keys. When I was with the Hurricane Hunters, I got to visit many islands, and really loved that. The Keys were like the islands without all the beggars.

I have lots of adventure stories with my kids, but I couldn't possibly write them all down. However, one particular trip off St. Augustine sticks in my mind. We were nine miles off the coast of St. Augustine. We were going to dive on a sunken tugboat. It was in sixty feet of water, so it was a nice easy dive. The current was running pretty good when we got there, so we decided to do some fishing and wait for the current to let up. While we were fishing, a large school of spadefish showed up, hanging around the boat checking us out; they were very curious. My youngest son, Chris, and I decided to get in the water with our spear guns and try our luck at a couple of the larger ones.

A Man Returns

When we first got in the water, they all took off, so we just floated on top of the water, hoping they would come back and they did. I picked out a large one and dove on it, releasing my spear when I got close enough. Perfect shot right through the middle of the fish. I was down about twenty-five feet, and I started back up with the fish in tow. Well, it had other ideas, and headed down for deeper water, taking me with it. I tried kicking for the surface, but I was in its element and running out of air. We had been free breathing! I finally had to let go of my spear gun and head for the surface. I couldn't believe it. I'd lost my spear gun to that fish! At the same time, my son had speared a large one too. In his fight for the surface, his cable broke on his spear gun and the fish took off with it too. We couldn't believe what had just happened.

The current finally let up and we all put on our scuba gear to make the dive. As the tug came into view, I couldn't believe it: there was the spadefish on the bow of the boat, still alive but just barely moving. I slowly dove on my spear gun and got it, and the fish still had enough life in it to try to make a break for it. However, this time, I was able to pull it in and stick it in my dive bag. With my gun back, I was able to shoot two more fish. The tug (like any structure offshore) was loaded with fish. My son saw the whole incident and decided to look for his fish with the spear sticking out of it. He started swimming around the tug, moving out a little farther each go-around and I'll be damned if he didn't find the fish lying on the bottom and still alive. He was able to get hold of the cable, pull it in, and stick the fish in his dive bag. It turned out to be a good dive trip after all. Everyone got fish.

We lived in our first house fifteen years. By building up some nice equity, we were able to get a loan to build a new home. We bought an acre in Fruit Cove, Florida, and started to build a 3,600-square-foot, four-bedroom, five-bath, two-story log home. I remember the day the logs arrived: all 850 of them came on five tractor trailers. We built the home ourselves. My children got to learn a lot about how a home was built and really appreciate what it took to build one. Our old house sold before we finished our new house, so we camped out in the new house for a couple months. It took me well over a year to finish, working evenings and weekends. It still took a couple more years to finish all the small stuff.

About a year earlier, I had taken the Florida state plumbing contractor's test and passed, and it was burning a hole in my pocket. I decided to start my own company and named it Sunshine State Plumbing. I gave my employer six months' notice; and during those six months, I got all my ducks in a row. I talked to my union business agent and was able to take leave. I had fifteen years in the union, so I didn't lose my pension.

I hired a helper right away, and for a little better than a year, we worked out of my house. My business was picking up, so I bought another truck and hired another plumber and helper. Soon after, I was able to purchase an old auto parts store in a great location. I opened a plumbing parts and supply store, and over the next ten years, I added a truck, a plumber, and a helper every year. Things were going well. I had twenty-five employees and construction was booming. I ended up having to close the store in time. Business fell off when they opened a large home improvement store not far away. It actually was a good thing because it gave me a lot more free time—more time to concentrate on the construction side of the business.

Difficult Changes

The year 2000 turned out to be a rough year for me. It started with a phone call from the daughter of my best friend, Lance, in Pennsylvania. Lance had been diagnosed with acute lymphoma cancer and was terminal. I flew up to spend twelve hours a day with him in the hospital for a week. It was very hard. He was only fifty years old. A couple weeks later, I flew back to be a pallbearer at his funeral. He had a full Marine funeral. I stuck one of my dog tags in his jacket pocket. I don't know why; it just seemed like the thing to do. *Semper Fi, my friend.*

A couple months later, I got another surprise. My wife and I were on our annual overnight canoe trip on the Suwanee River with three other couples. We had put in very early Saturday morning and canoed all day, stopping along the way to play and eat. That night we pitched our tents and had a big cookout. The next morning I woke up to my wife crying. I asked her what was wrong and she said she wanted a divorce. Wow! I didn't see that coming! We'd been together thirty years. Needless to say, the trip that day down the river to the pick-up point was pretty quiet for all of us.

I tried to talk her into maybe trying a separation or counseling, but she wouldn't have it. She told me she had hired a lawyer six years earlier, and had had plenty of time to think about it. A couple of months later, it was finalized.

It's one thing to fall out of love and want a divorce, but it's an entirely different thing to lie and steal. Without telling me, she cleaned out our savings, checking, all our bonds, and canceled all our credit cards.

She remarried. This time she got the naval officer she had been looking for thirty years earlier. My three children were all grown and gone at the time. They were more concerned about losing the log cabin than our divorce. After all, it seemed like everyone we knew was getting divorced or already had. Why not us too?

Moving On

Well, life continued, and life was short, so I knew I couldn't let this take me down. I thought it best to move on, and I did. Tippy, my border collie of ten years, and I moved onto my sailboat in St. Augustine. Kitty got the log cabin in the divorce, but hey, living on a sailboat was pretty nice. It was a thirty-eight-foot Endeavor that we had bought a few years earlier, and it was very comfortable. I spent a lot of my free time working on it.

About a mile up the road from my plumbing shop was a neighborhood tavern. I often had lunch there and invited my men there sometimes for drinks after work. I would also meet some of my sales reps there and conduct business. The barkeeper there knew me well and like everyone else around, knew I had just gone through a divorce. Well, she also knew that I was a diver. One day she told me she had a friend that liked to dive and take underwater pictures. She told me that she was always flying out to the islands to take pictures. She was also divorced like me. She thought I should meet her. I told her I wasn't interested in meeting anyone.

A few weeks later, I was in the tavern talking with a sales rep from Ferguson Enterprises, and the barkeep came over to our table and told me the diver was there. She had stopped in to drop something off for her. About that time the sales rep said they had to go. I looked across the room to the bar, and saw a young lady standing at the end of the bar. The barkeep urged me to let her introduce her. I thought, *What the hell! What do I have to lose?* She introduced us and after a few derogatory remarks back and forth, I bought her a drink. We made some small talk. I asked her if she was hungry and she said yes. I took her to dinner and ended up at her place. A whole new adventure began. Her name was Rachelle.

A Man Returns

She lived just down the road in Orangedale in a quaint little cottage on the St. Johns River. She and her ex had sold their house. I told her I was homeless and living on my sailboat in St. Augustine. To my surprise, she thought that was pretty cool. In fact, she had been looking to buy a sailboat. I thought *that* was pretty cool. She had a blue and gold macaw named Morgan that she had purchased about a year earlier. I thought that she would fit right in on a sailboat. *Arghh!!*

We started seeing each other regularly and the sting from the divorce slowly started to subside. On the following week on my way to St. Augustine to my sailboat, I stopped in to say hello to Rachelle. We were sitting in the living room talking, and all of a sudden, I had this terrible urge to go to the bathroom. I do all my business in the morning, so this was out of the ordinary. I sat down on the toilet to let loose and that's exactly what happened. I let loose, and oh, my God, blood everywhere. It splashed up under the seat, out onto the floor, and all over my clothes. *Holy shit! I just met this gal, and now I was having this terrible mess.* I didn't even think about what the hell was wrong with me. I was just so embarrassed. I knew she had to be wondering why I was taking so long. I finally got the mess mostly cleaned up except for my clothes, went out, and told her what had happened.

A few days before that I had surgery to remove a polyp they had found during a colonoscopy. My doctor recommended Dr. Healy, a butt doctor she said was the best in Jacksonville. I figured that this probably had something to do with that. Rachelle called his office, and the gal said she would have the doctor call me back. As we were waiting, it felt like my bowels were filling up. The doctor called me back, telling me to lie down and take it easy. A little bleeding was normal. I explained how much blood there had been and he told me to give it some time. I should be alright. Alright hell! About fifteen minutes later, I hit the bathroom again. This time I let it out easy—pure blood. Rachelle called the doctor again and again; he'd call us back. He called back right away. This time Rachelle jumped in his shit. He asked Rachelle if she could take me to the emergency room at Memorial Hospital; if she couldn't, he would send an ambulance. She assured him she could take me, and he said he would meet us there. I could feel it filling up again, so we needed to wait for me to discharge, and then drive like hell.

He was waiting when we got there and they rushed me into a room right away. He stuck a tube in my butt right away, and started working on me. The tube ran across me to a vacuum jar on the wall and I could see all this blood and nasty-looking stuff running though it! After quite some time and a lot of pain, he said he had it temporarily stopped, but I'd have to have surgery in the morning. I couldn't believe it. They put me in a room and told me that if I had any discharge during the night, I should not flush the toilet. The doctor wanted to see any discharge I might have during the night. My blood pressure had gotten pretty low, so they hooked me up to a machine and started an IV.

Rachelle called my kids to let them know what was going on. By that time it was getting late, and Rachelle decided to spend the night in the hospital with me.

Sometime in the early morning, I woke to that feeling of filling up again. Rachelle called the nurse and they got me to the bathroom where I unloaded. The nurse called Dr. Healy and he said he was on his way. By the time he got there, I had two more episodes, and they were talking about giving me blood. The bathroom was a mess; I felt bad for the clean-up crew.

They rolled me into surgery right away and put me out this time. Sometime later I woke in the recovery room, and Dr. Healy said he patched me up. It turned out that when he was using the laser to remove the polyp, he had nicked a blood vessel along the colon and had repaired it. Well, the repair job didn't hold, and that's where all the blood was coming from. I asked him if this one was going to hold, and he assured me that it would, but they were keeping me overnight again, just in case.

My kids came to see me and I had another surprise. My daughter had told my ex what had happened. Kitty had come to the hospital while I was in surgery and met Rachelle. I knew she hadn't come to see me; she knew Rachelle was there. She came to check out Rachelle. They had a little conversation about me and she told Rachelle, "Good luck."

Anyway, that's my colonoscopy story. They told me to get one again in five years and I'll tell ya, I wasn't looking forward to that.

Shortly after we met, Rachelle helped me move my sailboat from St. Augustine to Julington Creek right off the St. Johns River, about two blocks from my plumbing shop. About that same time, Rachelle and I decided to move in together. We rented a hundred-year-old cabin in Switzerland, Florida, on the St. Johns River. A friend of mine owned it and it had been in his family for those hundred years.

A couple months after we moved in, it was early evening and a thunderstorm rolled in. Morgan, our macaw, loved storms and rain. I took her out on the porch and had her on my arm, letting her feel the rain. Rachelle was in the back of the house making the bed. Suddenly, the weather got really weird. The wind really picked up. I yelled to Rachelle to come and check the weather out. Just as she reached the front door, we hear a roar and the wind slammed into us. At the same time, there came a huge crash in the house. Rachelle was standing in the doorway and a huge rush of air and small pieces of debris came rushing out around her from inside the house. Then it was over except for the intense rain. The house had gone dark, so I picked up the flashlight we had on the front porch, and went into the house. We couldn't believe it! A huge water oak about twenty inches in diameter, had fallen clear through the back of the house. The tree had crushed a dresser and lay across the bed and on out the back wall. Rain was pouring in and the clothes that had been in the dresser were getting soaked. We got everything we could pulled out of the rain and into the dry part of the house. Then we gathered up a few things and headed to the boat. We didn't know it at the time, but we would be spending the next few years living on that boat. I called my buddy to let him know what happened. At first, he thought I was kidding. He said, "That house has been there for a hundred years! What are the odds that this would happen with you living there?"

We met him at the cabin the next morning and wow, a twister had cut a swath through the woods, snapping some trees and knocking others down. If I hadn't called Rachelle from the bedroom, she might have ended up under the tree. We loaded up all our belongings and stored them in my warehouse.

The marina was not one you could live in, but I worked out a deal with the man who owned it. I would take care of all his plumbing problems at his house, restaurant, and the marina, and as long as no one complained, we could live there.

We decided to take a trip to Vegas. Rachelle had been there before, but I hadn't. We got to our hotel in the late afternoon, and I was ready to go and try my luck. Rachelle said, "Oh, no!" She wanted me to experience Vegas at night. She closed the drapes and said we were going to take a nap; when we woke up, she said, I'd be blown away. Wow, was she right! We opened the drapes, and it was a whole different world. We stayed up most of the night, moving from one casino to the next. I ended up hitting a $4,000 jackpot, and Rachelle did very well too. We ended with the trip paid for, and money in our pockets.

A couple months later, we got a letter from the Paris Casino where I had won the jackpot. They invited us out for a million dollar slot tournament, all expenses paid. We decided to go. I made it through three tournament eliminations, but came up short on the last one, which would have put me in the million dollar tournament. We had a blast and came away with money in our pockets again.

Rachelle worked for Johnson & Johnson. They were offering early retirement, buy-out packages to employees that had been there a while. Rachelle decided to take it, and went to work for me part time setting up my business on the computer. For the fun of it, she took another part time job just up the street from my shop at a chocolate shop where she learned how to make all kinds of chocolate candy. While she was there, she created six new chocolate candies for them.

We were becoming a regular thing. We took several dive trips to different islands and I even took an underwater photography class at one of the islands. One of our best trips was to Barbados, one of the islands I flew out of when I was in the Hurricane Hunters.

The marina I had my sailboat docked at was at the mouth of Julington Creek and the St. Johns River, which was about three miles wide. There was plenty of room to play with the sailboat. We started taking it out a lot on weekends. We would leave on Friday afternoon and return Sunday afternoon. I never had sailing lessons, so I was just sailing by the seat of my pants. We thought that since we were going to be sailing a lot, Rachelle needed to learn to sail as well, so we decided to take some sailing lessons. American Sailing Association in St. Augustine offered a complete sailing course. They had four different courses, starting with the basics course to the advanced course that certified you up to a fifty-foot sailboat. We took all four courses. It really made a huge difference in my sailing abilities, and it was nice to have Rachelle know what was going on so she could take the helm and give me a break.

Tippy's hip dysplasia had really slowed her down, so she spent most of her time lying around. Living on the sailboat was fine with her. She went with me everywhere, and on the boat, I took her to shore morning and evening.

Work was going well and Rachelle was a big help. I bought a computer, and she was busy working with my secretary to put my business on the computer.

Author's sailboat *The Seawolf*

THE SEAWOLF

S ince I was living on the boat and only two blocks from my shop, I started upgrading the sailboat. The first thing I did was have it pulled, and had the hull painted, including new bottom paint. I also had vinyl fire-breathing wolf heads put on each side of the bow. On the transom in vinyl, I had its name, *The Seawolf,* applied along with our homeport name: Fruit Cove, Florida.

I had a custom-built radar arch made for the stern. Within the arch, I had them build a support for two 110-watt solar panels. It also had two masts: one for a forty-mile radar transmitter and the other for a wind generator. They also made a support for a twenty-pound propane cylinder. I had two eight-pound cylinders on board already, but I didn't feel like that was enough. Also on the arch, I had them install a pulley and mount for my dinghy motor. I already had a dinghy davit on the stern, so I didn't have to worry about that. Then I mounted the VHF and GPS antennas on the arch, and installed a new helm which held the VHF radio, GPS, depth sounder, radarscope, along with a fold-up teak table. I bought all new cushions for the salon, and remodeled the galley with new countertops, sink, faucet, gas stove, and oven. The fridge and freezer were in good shape. I took out the three twelve-volt batteries and installed eight six-volt Trojan golf cart batteries. Along with the batteries, I installed a 3,000-watt inverter.

At the nav station, I installed a new control panel to handle all the new electronics, wind generator, and solar panels. I also installed a second VHF radio and an Icon ham radio. I used my backstay as the antenna, so I had a kickass antenna. I later took the written and the Morse code exam and received my ham license.

A Man Returns

I installed a new water heater that employed three different ways to heat up the water. I could use the engine through a heat exchanger in the water heater to heat the water, and I put in a dual element. One coil was 110-volts and the second coil was 24-volts. One of the things Rachelle said she had to have on the boat was hot water for showering. This water heater really did the job well. The hundred-gallon water tank was in bad shape. I took it out and put in a seventy-five-gallon poly tank which left me room to install a six-gallon-an-hour watermaker. When we were cruising out on the hook, we used the five gallons a day on average.

I also installed a stereo system and TV, along with several computer fans for circulation. This is just a partial list of the things we did on the sailboat. Part of the fun of living on the sailboat was making it our own.

My goal was to retire at fifty-five. I thought that at fifty-five, I was still young enough to do what I wanted and enjoy life. I'd seen too many of my friends and family retire so late that they were too broken down to do anything.

My business was really starting to get to me. Rachelle noticed that I was cussing a lot, mad at everybody, and didn't trust anyone. Between the government and the insurance companies, customers not paying you, and employees stealing from me, I was way too stressed out all the time. Age fifty-five was right around the corner, so we decided money wasn't everything and we started talking about selling the business and setting sail. We contacted an Edward Jones agent and told her what we wanted to do. Well, that started the ball rolling and things got very exciting, thinking that after all these years I had finally reached the point in my life that I was actually going to retire.

After several meetings with the agent and a lot of coaxing and persuading on Rachelle's part, we made the decision to do it. We sold the business, but kept the building, renting it to the new owners. I had an excellent reputation, so they also bought the name. To this day when I'm in Jacksonville, Florida, and I see a Sunshine State Plumbing truck on the road, I get a warm, fuzzy feeling.

Our agent took a lot of interest in what we were doing and set us up with a very good retirement program. They even took pictures of Rachelle and I and our macaw, Morgan, on our sailboat, and featured us in their magazine. She also pointed out something interesting. She told us that now that we'd sold the business, we were unemployed, so we could file for unemployment, which we did. Both our claims went through and we started collecting. In fact, because of 9/11 they extended the benefits and we were able to collect for an extra six months. It really felt good to get some of my money back from the government.

We took the next few months fine-tuning *The Seawolf* and stocking it with everything we thought we might need. We dehydrated a lot of food and vacuum-sealed it.

We took two more trips too: one back to Vegas, and believe it or not, we came back with money in our pockets again. Rachelle really hit some nice jackpots on that trip. We also went to Pennsylvania, so Rachelle could meet my mom and family and friends.

We set up a cruising homeport mailbox with a company in Green Cove Springs and had cruising cards made up.

A good friend of mine set up a Seawolf website, so that everyone could keep tabs on us. We could use it as a cruising log too. We used our cell phones for our computer connection.

We had to sell everything we owned—including Rachelle's new Trans Am. What we didn't sell, we gave away. We both had personal items we wanted to keep and we stored those with friends and family. We also both got in-depth medical and dental checkups.

A Man Returns

I stayed in communication with the new owners of the plumbing business because they had a lot of questions when they first took it over.

Finally, the time arrived for us to leave. The night before we slipped the dock lines, my daughter and her husband had a combination house warming/bon voyage party for us. On the way to the party, we stopped at a mall and I got my ear pierced and bought a diamond stud for it.

The next morning, we didn't leave as early as we had wanted, but ended up sleeping in. I think the party the night before had a lot to do with that. However, we did get off the dock and headed north up the St. Johns River. The Perkins 4.108 was purring like a kitten. We motorsailed with the jib until we reached Jacksonville and all the bridges. The current could be very strong going through Jacksonville because it got very narrow going through town. As we came through the last bridge, the engine started revving up and down. Then it would level off and then start revving again. I worked the throttle back and forth, and that seemed to stop it.

As we headed out, our radar picked up a huge thunderstorm coming straight at us. It slammed into us pretty hard and visibility went to almost zero. It was bad enough dodging the huge ships coming down the river when it was clear, but when visibility went to zip, it was not much fun. The rain finally let up and we made it to where the intracoastal waterway (ICW) crossed the river. It was getting late, and we needed to find a place to spend the night. I saw on the GPS that there was a small cove up the ICW, so we turned north and headed for it. We had gone about a mile when we ran hard aground onto a sandbar. We were in the middle of the channel, but that didn't necessarily mean we were in the deepest water. Shifting sand would create sandbars where they shouldn't be. Even with a depth sounder, they came up so fast it was nearly impossible to miss them. Not only were we hard aground, but another huge storm was moving in, and night was coming on. I tried rocking the boat with the engine but that didn't get us anywhere. I decided to try kedging.

I dropped the dinghy in the water and came around to the bow. Rachelle released the anchor to lower it down into the dink. She played the chain out, while I headed out in front of the boat about one hundred feet and we dropped the anchor. Our windlass was a very heavy-duty, two-speed mechanical windlass. I cranked down on the windlass in low gear, while Rachelle worked the engine. Slowly, we made some headway and got off the sandbar.

The wind had really picked up. I checked the radar and the storm was about twenty miles out. We finally made it to the cove and got the anchor set. I took Tippy to an oyster bed to potty; she didn't have a problem with that. The tide was going out and I wasn't sure how much water we would have left, but it was too late to worry about it now. The rain was coming in sideways and the wind was ripping at over 50 mph; this was a bad ass storm. Rachelle didn't skip a beat. She was busy cooking us a fine dinner. By the time we turned in, the wind had let up but the rain was still coming down. Wow! What a first day! We had truly started off on an adventure.

The next morning came early. About 5:30, we woke to what sounded like things falling on the floor, and Morgan's perch was hanging at a strange angle. Suddenly, we realized we were laying at a strange angle. It was exactly what I was worried about: the tide had gone out and we were laying on our side. It was not a big deal, but we were stuck here until the tide came in.

One of the upgrades I had done on the boat was I had screens made for all the portals, hatches, and the companionway. It was a good thing because they were all covered with all kinds of bugs, but mainly mosquitoes. After the sun came up, most of them left to find something else to suck on.

A Man Returns

It took a few hours, but we finally got enough water under us to get underway. The weather was still bad, and the wind was blowing pretty good. We had planned on taking the St. Johns River out to the ocean and then heading south to St. Augustine from there. With the weather like it was, we decided to take the ICW instead. We had plenty of time to get there. My motto, "Better to be lucky than good," was starting to let me down. The morning was going great and *The Seawolf* was running great. We were coming up on the JTB Bridge running along pretty fast with the current. The engine started doing the same thing it did when we were sailing through Jacksonville: revving up and dying out, revving up and dying out. Finally, it shut off. I tried restarting it to no avail. The bridge was coming up fast and I had very little steering without the engine. I told Rachelle to take the helm and take us hard to shore. I ran forward, unlocked the anchor, and waited for the boat to get as close as it could before the current started taking it, and I released the anchor. As the current took *The Seawolf* toward the bridge, I paid out the chain until I felt we had enough scope. Then, I locked the chain down and held my breath. The bow pulled around and the anchor held; we were good for now. We weren't in the channel. I went below and checked the engine, and decided it was the mechanical fuel pump. We had sea tow insurance, so I got on the radio and got a hold of them. They got to us pretty quickly, and towed us north to Beach Marina. We tied up to one of their docks and ordered a new fuel pump. I got the fuel pump off and the new one on. It took a while to get all of the air out of the system, but I finally got it. We spent two nights tied up and it cost us $110. The fuel pump wasn't too bad: $45.

Well, we'd had a hell of a start on our adventure. We just hoped that things would get better and they did. We reached St. Augustine City Marina without any problems. We took a slip for a month and then anchored out in front of the fort. We paid a small fee to use the marina's dinghy dock, shower, and laundry. There were several places to take Tippy to potty, which I did every morning and evening. She was not doing well, and I had her on several medications.

We stayed in St. Augustine for six months, enjoying everything it had to offer. We bought fold-up bikes in a bag and rode them everywhere. We also rollerbladed all over the place. We ate out a lot and enjoyed a lot of open air concerts.

While at anchor, we did have a couple close calls with other boats dragging anchor and bumping into us. One such incident involved a large catamaran. We were both below deck when Rachelle told me she heard someone on shore, yelling, "*Seawolf!*" I went topside and it was one of the homeless guys we had befriended. He was yelling and pointing. I looked where he was pointing, and holy shit, this large catamaran was drifting straight for our bow and anchor chain. I jumped in our dink and hauled ass around to intercept it, and see if anyone was on board. There wasn't. I got up against the stern to try and push it, but it was too big and the current too strong. Just then, I heard a police siren. I turned and looked, and a police boat was coming my way. With his help, I managed to get the cat re-anchored. I dinghied on into shore and thanked the homeless guy.

We weathered a couple tropical storms, and Hurricane Isabel gave a pretty rough ride. The *St. Augustine Record* wrote a story about what we did to weather storms.

We had a great time in St. Augustine and made a lot of new friends, but it was time to weigh anchor and head south for a new adventure. We still had my Tahoe. That was the last thing we needed to do before we headed out. It sold right away. It felt really strange not to have a vehicle. Everybody was kidding with us about being there so long that our anchor wouldn't come up, but on the morning we said our goodbyes, it came up fine.

A Man Returns

We set our sights on the Florida Keys, with lots of stops along the way. Eventually, we wanted to head for the islands and make our way to the San Blas Islands of Panama. As we headed south, we stayed only one day at some places.

One of the places we stopped was Titusville. The weather was really bad. When we dinghied in, so Tippy could potty, we noticed a Marine Patrol boat and a wildlife boat maneuvering around in the marina. When I docked, I asked a guy on the dock what they were doing. He said they were trying to catch a manatee that had got itself all wrapped up in a crab trap line; it was towing the trap around. When we started to head back to *The Seawolf*, I stopped and asked if we could help in any way. They said they had lost the manatee and it was getting late. They would look for it again tomorrow.

It was a very rough night. We were wide open to the elements. In the morning, I looked to see if there were any boats looking for the manatee yet and there were none. We weighed anchor and headed south. We made it to Melbourne and dropped anchor in the ICW in front of a public boat ramp. We spent the night there. In the morning, we noticed a small secluded marina (the Waterline Marina) on the GPS just south of us. It was about a quarter mile off the ICW connected by a small creek. We decided to go for it. It was tight, but then it opened up to a large bay, and the marina sat at the far end. We talked about it. If they didn't want an arm and a leg for dockage, we would get a slip. I hailed the marina on the radio; they were cheap enough and they had a slip. We decided to take it and spent the next month there. Everything was close and it was very protected.

As usual, everyone here was very nice. We had shore power here, so Rachelle decided it would be a good time to make a new Bimini top for the boat. We had three sewing machines on board and we had picked up a roll of Sunbrella in St. Augustine at Sailor's Exchange. I had visited this place many, many times when I had been doing all my upgrades. The only thing we needed to find was some clear vinyl and thread, which we did. Our present Bimini didn't have any sides or a back, so when she made the new one, she made those items. It turned out great and gave us a lot more protection from the elements. The sides and back rolled up when we didn't need them. She also made a large cover for above the cabin. This provided shade for the cabin and when we were topside.

While she was working on the Bimini top, I worked on a couple of other projects. One was an anchor wash-down pump at the bow. We used the pump not only for washing the chain and anchor, but also to rinse off a number of things, saving fresh water. We used an aluminum water heater pan for under Morgan's perch, and the wash-down pump worked great in washing it off. Rachelle made hatch covers, winch covers, a cover for the dinghy motor, as well as chaps for the dinghy.

The cushions in our salon were not waterproof, so if we didn't bring them in before a storm they got full of water. We bought all new closed-cell cushions. What a difference that made!

Over half the boats in this marina hadn't moved in years, and their bottoms had their own ecosystems growing on them.

One morning we were having breakfast in the salon and we noticed that a small school of pogies had come into the bay. I asked Rachelle if she wanted to go fishing today. She was always ready to go fishing. I jumped in the dink with my cast net and on my first throw, I got more than I needed. I went back and picked up Rachelle and our fishing gear, and we headed up this creek that ran off the bay.

Adventures of the Aquatic Kind

I call this story "Close Encounters of the Manatee Kind." We fished in a couple different places with no luck. Up ahead we saw an old railroad trestle and decided to try our luck around it. I tossed out our small dinghy anchor and we started fishing. We hadn't been fishing long when we both noticed a big swirl next to the dink. About that time, the dink lunged forward, nearly knocking Rachelle and I out of it! We took off down the creek, just missing some old pylons. Rachelle was on the bow, and she looked at me with a stunned look on her face. I yelled, "Hang on!" She already was doing that. Then, this huge manatee tail came out of the water and splashed down hard, sending a sheet of water on top of Rachelle, followed by a couple more. Then it turned and it was all over; we came to a sudden stop. Apparently the flukes from our Danforth anchor had gotten caught on its flippers, and when it turned, it slipped off. We both looked at each other and started laughing. Wow! That didn't happen every day. Rachelle was soaking wet and it was chilly. On top of that, the fishing wasn't good so we called it a day.

The best fishing we had was right there in the marina. We had caught glimpses of some big fish that looked like they were feeding off the pylons. We picked up some fiddlers and tried our luck. The people in the marina couldn't believe it. We pulled in some huge sheepshead which we shared with everyone. While we were there, anytime we wanted fish, we'd just catch another sheepshead. We had a great time at Waterline Marina, but it was time to head south. Next stop, Ft. Pierce.

We only spent a couple days in Ft. Pierce. We anchored out in front of the Harbortown Marina. When I took Tippy in to potty, I saw a boat tied up to the dock that belonged to some friends we met in St. Augustine. We all got together that evening for drinks, dinner, and more drinks.

The next day, we went in to see the SEAL Museum. Wow, did we get a warm welcome when they found out I had been a Seawolf! We had a great time there: lots of stories and our own private tour guide, a retired Navy SEAL.

The next morning we headed to Stuart. Stuart lies up the St. Lucia River, and as we were making our way, we noticed we were in high dollar country. Huge mansions and just-as-huge yachts were on both sides of the river. It took longer than we thought, and we didn't quite make it to Stuart. We dropped anchor in the river just in front of the Pelican Nest Marina. The water was gorgeous. At night, if you swished your hands through the water, it lit up the phosphorus. When you flushed the commode at night, the whole bowl lit up!

Stuart was a lot like St. Augustine: laid back. Lots of things to do, lots of shops and restaurants. You could get to the west coast of Florida by taking the St. Lucie Canal to Lake Okeechobee, and then to the Caloosahatchee Waterway. It came out at Ft. Myers.

We called the city marina (Southpoint Anchorage), but they had no mooring balls available. We put our name on a waiting list. Rachelle called over ten marinas, and they were all full. Finally, Stuart Harbor Marina had a slip available. It belonged to someone that would be gone for a couple months, so we could have it, and we took it. We spent about a month there until we got a mooring ball at Southpoint. What a nice marina. It was eight dollars a day. We were moored in front of a large park, and it was perfect for Tippy. Every Sunday evening, they had what they called "Night of the Drums." Lots of people showed up drumming and playing different kinds of instruments. We sat and listened sometimes.

We did a lot of fishing and exploring in Stuart. We ate out a lot and rented a car once in a while to travel the area.

The marina had a great café, and we became very good friends with the gal that operated it. She had a very nice sailboat moored next to us. She sometimes got real busy, and Rachelle would give her a hand and make a couple dollars, while I drank for free.

A Man Returns

Latitudes and Attitudes magazine did a two-page story on the café. We helped the gal host a huge "Lats and Ats" party to celebrate. Morgan and I took care of the bar. Morgan was an instant hit.

Our insurance came due and we had to do an out-of-water survey. What a pain in the ass. It turned out it was a good thing in the end though. I found out my cutlass bearing was worn, so I replaced it. I also cleaned the bottom and thru hulls, along with the prop and replaced the zinc. Insurance was $2,081!

The dinghy bottom was getting pretty bad, so I asked the dockmaster where I could find a good place to take it out. He told me that an area the city owned would be a good place. After cleaning the dink, I was on my way back when a police boat pulled me over. The officer was an asshole from the start. He asked me where I was coming from and I told him. He asked what I was doing there and again, I told him. He claimed I was trespassing on private property. I told him that the city owned the property and the city dockmaster had given me permission. He said, "It's private property and I'm the one wearing the gun." I couldn't believe it. He went on to tell me that he didn't like sailboats, and that we were nothing but trouble and "shit in the water." I couldn't stand anymore and told him what I thought about that. He told me he was two seconds away from arresting me if I didn't get out of there. I pushed off and headed for the marina. He stayed right on my ass being a smart ass all the way. I told the dockmaster about it, including his name. He told me he harassed a lot of boaters out here, and that he was going to take it up with the police chief.

One morning, I awoke to Morgan growling. I sat up, and looking out the portal, we were floating down the St. Lucia River, trailing the mooring ball. It had come loose from the shackle that holds it to the anchor cable. I fired up the engine and called the marina on the radio. We had to anchor out until they made the mooring repair. How we didn't run into anything, I don't know. I guess it's like I always say, better to be lucky than good. We found out later that this had happened to an elderly couple, and they had come out unscathed too. It took us coming loose for them to go around and safety wire all the shackles.

While we were in Stuart, we sold the building we had been renting to the new plumbing business owners. A realtor bought it for a real estate office. One less thing that we had to worry about.

The café gal had a car, and let us use it whenever we needed. That was really nice.

I took the written part of the ham radio license test and only missed one question. Now I needed to work on the Morse code part.

Rachelle made a sort of sling to put under Tippy's back end to help support her when I took her in to potty. It really helped her get around. The only problem was that she didn't like me looking at her when she went, so I had to turn my head.

Everywhere we'd been I had been able to pick up a few dollars. We figured every dollar we could make kept us from dipping into our retirement money. I'd climbed the mast to do a number of things, replaced zinc, and cleaned bottoms. I had a fifty-foot air hose adapted to connect my regulator and scuba tank. This enabled me to dive under a boat without carrying a heavy tank.

People always asked us what we did on our sailboat all day. For one thing, we spent most of our daytime topside: cleaning, polishing, doing repairs, reading, playing the guitar, or just plain relaxing and enjoying the outdoors. We paid a lot of attention to the weather. The weather really dictated what we were going to do that day.

The dockmaster and the café gal were having problems, and it got pretty nasty. She finally closed the café, which everyone was sad to see. We had all really enjoyed the Wednesday night cruiser parties and having someplace close to eat.

A Man Returns

The elderly guy in the sailboat next to us dropped his dinghy outboard in the water. I felt bad for him, until he told me he did it on purpose. He said it had been giving him nothing but trouble, and he wanted to buy a new one, but his wife would not let him. Now he was getting a new outboard. Problem solved.

We had so much fun in Stuart and made so many new friends, but we were both getting antsy. We were ready for a new adventure; it was time to leave. We partied the night before and said our goodbyes and headed south on the ICW. We made good time and dropped our anchor just south of Peanut Island. Hundreds of boats were there; it was very busy. The inlet was close, so there was lots of current. I had to keep an eye on my anchor and set the anchor watch on my GPS.

We weighed anchor early the next morning. The weather was good, so we headed out the inlet, put up the sails, and headed for Ft. Lauderdale. We made good time, thank goodness, because the weather turned nasty. We turned into an inlet and tried to hail the A1A bridge tender with no luck. I had to keep circling. It was a real bitch: lots of current and boat traffic. I kept calling the bridge with no luck. Then a police boat came alongside us and told me I was getting too close to a docked cruise ship. Well, excuse me! Finally, the bridge tender answered me and opened the bridge. We headed north on the ICW. We were headed to Lake Sylvia to spend the night. It was tight—lots of boats and huge houses on both sides. We found the canal that let us into Lake Sylvia and turned into it. Bam! Hard aground. We radioed BoatUS and he got to us pretty quickly. He said this sandbar kept him busy. He told me that I had to stay tight against the north shore of the canal all the way in.

Lake Sylvia was a tiny lake surrounded by huge houses and boats, the land of the wealthy. We no more than got the anchor set, and a police boat pulled alongside and told us this was a twenty-four-hour anchorage. I told him we were pulling out in the morning.

In the morning, the weather was still bad, so we stayed on the ICW right through Miami. It was very stressful with lots of rude boaters, bridges, and wall-to-wall concrete. Once we got through Miami, Biscayne Bay lay ahead. The wind was in our favor and our sails stayed full. We made it to Tarpon Basin just southwest of Key Largo. It was completely surrounded by mangroves, so we dropped our anchor. I was ready for a cold one. After we got settled, we happened to notice a boat up ahead that looked familiar. Sure enough, it was friends from Stuart. We ended up having dinner with them.

We stayed there a couple of days, and then moved south to Sunset Cove in front of the Upper Keys Sail Club. We dinghied in to the sail club, and what a bunch of nice people! For a dollar, we became honorary members. We spent some time at the bar, talking with people and swapping boat stories. Since we were members, we could use the dumpster, and water was only ten cents a gallon.

We spent about a week there, exploring Key Largo, and ran into more friends we had met along the way. They had a slip at Del Ray Marina, which cost $1,000 a month! Yikes! We did some shopping and checked out some of the tourist spots.

Morgan loved the boat. When we were underway, we kept her in a collapsible cage, either down below or topside. When we were at anchor, she liked to run around on the life lines or up and down the mast. She sometimes sat on top of the mast and screeched at all the birds. Her perch down below was right next to the mast and under the hatches. It was also at the level of the portals to give her the perfect view. She was an excellent watch bird; whenever a boat approached, she let us know. One of the big problems you had at anchor was when you left the boat. Ospreys liked to catch fish and sit on top of your spreaders and tear the fish apart and eat it. All that blood and guts would fall down on top of your canvas and boat. Then the sun just baked it on and it was very hard to remove. Cormorants also

A Man Returns

liked to sit on your boat and watch for fish or dry their wings. While sitting there, they often took a dump. Have you ever seen a cormorant dump? Yikes, it was a real gully washer, and the sun baked it so hard on your deck that you almost needed a chipping hammer to get it up. This was where Morgan really earned her keep. If any birds tried to land on our boat, she let out an extremely loud screech, scaring them away. Sometimes we took Morgan ashore with us. We had a harness we put on her, and we placed her on our handlebars. She just loved riding the bikes. We took her into all the restaurants and tiki bars we frequented, and everyone just loved her. She had a large vocabulary from living so close to us all time. If there was music playing, she loved to dance.

One morning, we awoke after a hellacious storm and our dink was gone. I could see where the painter had worn through on a loose piece of metal trim. The wind was still blowing at thirty mph straight out of the east, so I knew which direction it had gone. I looked on our chart and there was a line of mangroves west of us and north of the channel. I got on the radio every fifteen minutes and asked if any boaters in that area or heading west in the channel would keep an eye out. In the meantime, Rachelle made breakfast and we crossed our fingers. After breakfast, I decided to weigh the anchor and head in that direction. Lo and behold! About that time we had two different boats call out on the radio that they had spotted our dink. It was in the mangroves that I had spotted on the chart. They gave me the coordinates and we headed in that direction. About thirty minutes later, we spotted it; it was quite a way from the channel. Once I left the channel, the water got real skinny so I took it real slow. The wind had not let up and the water was really rough. Our keel was four and a half feet and our depth sounder kept sounding at five to six feet deep. Then *crunch*, we went aground. The wind kicked us around; it was blowing so hard it had us partly laid over. It was a bad situation

194

and the dink, looking at our GPS, was still about a quarter mile away. I shut the engine down and dropped anchor. We couldn't see the bottom because of the waves, so I put on my fins and mask, and jumped overboard to take a look. It wasn't good and the wind was making it worse. I decided to call sea tow, and boy, did I get a surprise. In all that was going on, I didn't even realize that we had ventured into the Everglades National Park. He told us that we needed to get in touch with the park rangers. When they got our location, they would call them. He told me I was in for a hefty fine, and that once they got us off the bottom, the rangers would assess the damage we did to the seagrass. We would be charged by the square foot. He told me that was also a hefty fee. He gave me the ranger's phone number and with real reluctance, I called. I told them what had happened. He said it would be two to three hours before they could get to us. That wasn't good news. When they did get out here, we were going to have to wait for sea tow and hope they weren't busy too.

I was worried that the wind was going to rock us deeper into the sand. I decided to do the quarter-mile swim. In this wind and rough sea, it was going to be a rough one. I put my mask, snorkel, and fins on and headed out. If the dink was damaged or the motor wouldn't start, there would be no way I could get it back to *The Seawolf* in this wind, and I would have to swim back. As I got closer, I could see that all the tubes were still inflated. Now if it would only start. When I reached the dink and climbed aboard, I had to take a second to catch up with myself. I squeezed the primer bulb a couple of times and gave the rope a pull, and she fired right off. I headed back to *The Seawolf*. On the way back, I decided to try kedging it off the sandbar. It worked, but it took us over an hour. I had to keep relocating the anchor. By the time we got off the sandbar, I was a whipped pup. Our CQR anchor weighed forty-five pounds plus the ⅜-inch chain. We made it back to the channel without a problem. Next, I had to call the rangers and tell them that I was off the sandbar. I called them. He asked me how we got off, and I told him that the wind had finally blown us free and that we were underway. He said that it sounded like there was probably not much damage, and that today was my lucky day. They were on a serious call and couldn't make it out anyway. Then he chewed my ass for being in park waters, and that was the end of it. Like I said before, better to be lucky than good.

After I got off the phone, I happened to notice the engine temperature. It wasn't pegged, but it showed hot. I checked the exhaust at the stern, and it wasn't discharging as much water as it should. I shut the engine down and Rachelle took the helm while I unfurled the jib. I knew what it was. I figured we had probably picked up seagrass with all that rocking of the boat on the sandbar. Sure enough, the strainer was almost packed full of grass. I cleaned it out and we were back in business.

We dropped anchor in several different places and checked out the areas, but we finally settled on Islamorada. Everything was close by, and the bay there was fairly protected. Lots of restaurants were close by and we ate a lot of fish and lobsters.

Tippy had taken a turn for the worse, and it was time to let her go. There was an animal hospital about three miles up the road. Another three miles further was a VA representative's office, and he was back from vacation. I needed to talk to him about getting tested for Agent Orange. One of the boaters in the Anchorage had told me the VA was testing everyone that had been to Vietnam. I decided I could do both on the same ride. I rode my bike up to the animal hospital, and before I got there, I started crying. I went in and told the vet what needed to be done, all the while crying. I paid him and told him I would bring Tippy by in a few days.

I headed up the road on my bike and hoped that I would calm down by the time I got to the VA office. I had pretty much regained my composure and went in to see the rep. I walked into his office and sat down. He introduced himself as Bear; he was an ex-Marine. I asked him how his vacation was and he told me it wasn't really a vacation. He had put his dog down and had flown him up to Pennsylvania to bury him in the family cemetery. Holy cow! I started to tell him what I had just done and started crying which started him crying too. About that time, his secretary come into the room. She took one look at us and turned around. I finally told him my story and we both got our composure back. He was going to get me into the VA system, and make an appointment for me for my Agent Orange test. He did get me into the system and I tested negative for Agent Orange. I also got a complete physical; they found I had a hearing problem and tendonitis.

A few days later, we called the car rental place for a compact car to be delivered to our boat ramp. When they got there, we couldn't believe it. They did not have a compact, so they sent a huge black GMC Envoy. It looked like a hearse. I gave the guy a ride back to the rental place and came back and picked Tippy up. I carried her into the vet's and laid her down on the table. I gave her a hug and a kiss, said goodbye, and walked out. That was thirty years ago and it still brings tears to my eyes just to write about it. I had her for thirteen years. She went to work with me every day and everywhere else I went. She was small for a border collie and so smart.

What a life! We spent our days fishing, diving, and exploring the waterways and all of the Florida Keys. We met many people and made so many friends. The Lor-e-lei Restaurant and Cabana Bar was located on the same cove we were on, and we became regular customers. Our sailboat lay between the restaurant and the sunset. The place was always packed, and at sundown, I bet we had our picture taken a thousand times.

A Man Returns

New Ventures

About a block from where we dinghied in, was a small strip center and it had a T-shirt shop that we visited off and on. One day we were in there and the girl asked Rachelle if she would be interested in a job. She hadn't really thought about working. After all, we were retired. We talked about it, and Rachelle thought it might be fun and it was only part time. We had a lot of time on our hands and a little extra money never hurt. She met with the owner a few days later and took the job. It turned out that the owner owned the entire strip center, plus a couple sandal shops, a sunglass store, and a couple of restaurants.

Rachelle was really liking the change: meeting people and staying busy. I would hang around a lot of days, folding T-shirts and doing odds and ends. Rachelle got to talking to the owner one day and found out her boyfriend had been an Army door gunner in Vietnam. Later, when I met him, I found out he was with the Gunslingers and we had done several operations together. And what a coincidence! He had also sailed into the Keys and that's where he had met the owner of all these properties. You might say he really fell into it. Well, that started a real friendship that lasted for years.

They were millionaires and had a huge mansion on the ocean, complete with a large marina. They owned about ten acres on the ocean and had built these beautiful high-dollar rentals. Like I said, we had become friends, and had many drinks, dinners, parties, and the whole nine yards. One day he asked me if I would be interested in working part time, cash money. I took the job and had nothing but fun. We worked part time for them until we left the Keys. They didn't want us to leave and made us all kinds of offers.

When we sold the plumbing shop, I made three times the money I paid for it. We needed to send a lot of paperwork back and forth, and there was a little office supply place within bicycle range that we used. Next door to the office place was a plumbing shop, and I stopped in and said hello. Of course the guy offered me a job right away, working in the office, doing take-offs and bidding. I turned him down. His secretary stopped me on my way out and gave me a card. She told me that if my girlfriend and I decided to get married, she did that on the side.

I told her that Rachelle and I had been talking about doing just that. A few weeks later, I gave her a call and we set it all up. We got married at MM88 on the beach at sunset; it was very nice. We had a few friends attend and we all had dinner and drinks at the restaurant there. The next morning I rented a large pontoon boat and took everyone out snorkeling on some of the popular reefs.

What a bad time to be in the Keys as far as the weather went! Four hurricanes—yes, I said four hurricanes: Charley, Frances, Ivan, and Jeanne. We evacuated for all but Jeanne.

I had a two hundred feet of ⅜-inch chain for anchoring with the CQR (a pivoting shank). I had two hundred feet of ¾-inch line out with a Danforth anchor, and two more ¾-inch lines out with three hundred pounds of concrete on each one. It was a job, but I hauled the concrete into *The Seawolf*, mixed it with salt water, and filled two garbage cans with three hundred pounds of concrete each, with a piece of ⅜-inch chain sticking out to tie them. It worked well and we held through all the storms. I did have a bit of a tangled mess, but not a big problem.

I received a letter from my uncle, my mother's brother. He informed me that my mom's place was in really bad shape, and with her bad health, she couldn't do anything about it. I bought the place for my mom and dad in the early 80s. My father passed away in 1989, so not much had been done to keep it up since then. I had a brother and three sisters that lived near Mom, but they wouldn't do anything because they felt that it was my place, and I should take care of any of the problems. I called and talked to my mom. Yes, there were things that really needed to be done, but she didn't want to bother me.

Rachelle and I talked about it and decided we really needed to go up there. Hurricane season wasn't over yet, so we would be taking a real chance since the season had been so active.

The Seawolves, my old Vietnam outfit, were having a reunion and a memorial dedication the first week in November in Charleston, South Carolina. I really wanted to go to that as it was a chance to meet all my brothers and see how they were doing.

We decided to go three weeks before the reunion, and then catch the reunion on the way back to the Keys.

We secured everything on *The Seawolf* the best we could; I still had the four anchors out. We had made a lot of friends in the anchorage, and everyone said they would keep an eye on her while we were gone.

We rented a car and loaded it up with our personal belongings: four dinghy loads and the weather was terrible. Not only was the wind howling which made the seas very rough, but it was also pouring down rain. We had to cover each load with a tarp. Finally loaded up, we headed to Pennsylvania in a storm.

We stopped in Stuart and checked out the terrible damage Hurricane Jeanne had left behind. The City Marina where we had hung out on a mooring ball was destroyed. We saw lots of masts sticking out of the water. The mooring balls were rated for 100 mph winds and Jeanne had come in packing winds of 120 mph. We were so glad we had left there when we did. Again, better to be lucky than good.

We headed on up to St. Augustine and stopped there for three days, visiting with family and friends.

When we got to Pennsylvania, they were already having frost in the morning. It was 27 degrees. Yikes! The leaves were in full color and I breathed in that wonderful fall air. Mom's house sat 3,000 feet up in the Pocono Mountains, so winter came early and stayed late.

My mom was so happy to see us and us, her. We visited a while, and then went next door to my aunt's trailer to see what kind of condition it was in, and to see if I could get the furnace going. My aunt, my mother's sister, had moved a trailer onto my property several years ago. Her husband died, so she had sold her big house and bought a trailer. I let her move onto the property, so she and my mom could be closer and help take care of each other. My aunt had passed away a few months ago, and the trailer had just been sitting there. It was a nice trailer, but she had kind of let it go. I got the furnace going and we did a quick clean up—enough so we could crash for the night.

The next day I got busy. There was so much to do on my mom's house. The first thing was to replace the bathroom floor. It was rotted, and in places you could see the basement. Then we replaced the back porch and steps. I moved the washer and dryer upstairs, so she would not have to go down the steps to the basement. I had to run all new plumbing and gas lines along with a dryer vent. I also moved the two propane cylinders from the back of the house to the side. In the winter, the gas people would not deliver the gas unless a path was shoveled. I installed a new fuel oil furnace along with a couple of ceiling fans. I repaired or replaced all of the plumbing fixtures. I changed the rise on all the steps too, so it would be a smaller step up and installed grab rails where needed.

As I did this, Rachelle cleaned and took care of Mom's medical and health needs. My brother and sisters did come by a few times to lend a hand. I also replaced some carpeting and vinyl where needed, resealed the windows and doors, and replaced and patched duct work.

We took a break and went to Atlantic City with Lance's wife and mom and dad whom I called Mom #2 and Dad #2. We stayed two

days at Caesar's Palace and had a great time, but didn't do as well as
we had in Vegas.

Then it was back to work, but this time it was on my aunt's trailer.
We decided to rent it out. That way the elements wouldn't claim it
and it would supply some small income. It would also give my mom
a close neighbor to possibly call on if she needed help. We ran an ad
in the local paper.

My mom was so pleased with the new furnace. She had been
dreading winter's arrival, remembering all the problems she had the
year before. She was afraid of freezing to death. This one was so quiet
and so much more efficient, especially with the ducts replaced and
repaired.

The day before we were to leave, we had a call about the trailer for
rent. It was a young couple and they seemed nice. I introduced them
to my mom, and that seemed to go well. They wanted to move in
right after we left which was great, and they paid me in cash.

Like I always say, better to be lucky than good.

The next day we headed for Charleston and the Seawolf reunion.

Wow! It was so surreal seeing the guys I flew with and had become best friends with after over thirty years. The voices were all the
same, but the faces had changed. Morgan was a big hit and we took
her most everywhere. We had several days of events. Business meetings, tours of Charleston, and a banquet. The hotel found me an old
slide projector, and I was able to show my Vietnam slides—over three
hundred of them.

The memorial dedication was beautiful. They read the names of
my forty-four fallen brothers. The memorial was a large granite mon-
ument with the forty-four names on one side and the Seawolf logo
on the other. They also had a ship's store set up and we bought several
items.

It was good to see all the guys again. Everyone was telling stories—some you remembered, some you didn't. It was a real memory rush.

We got lucky again. There were no more storms while we were gone and hurricane season was almost over.

Back to life on *The Seawolf.* We were really enjoying the good life. Two of the biggest problems you had living on the hook was garbage and water. I had a watermaker but it was a real pain in the ass, and water was expensive in the Keys. By luck, I met a guy who turned out to be a Vietnam vet who managed a marina not far away. He let me get all the water I needed and I could dispose of all of our garbage in their dumpster.

There was a laundromat within bicycle range so we had that problem solved too. The first time we went there I saw a large UA[1] decal on the front door. I found out that the guy who owned the place was a retired UA member who had moved down here from up north. It was the same union I belonged to, which made us brothers. We became good friends.

The car rental place that we used had a special deal on the weekends. For $19.95, you could rent a compact car from Friday evening until 8 a.m. Monday morning. We took advantage of that off and on, and it allowed us to enjoy a lot more of the Keys.

I found out from Bear (my VA rep) that the VA was going to start sending me a 10 percent disability check for my tendonitis. It wasn't much money, but then again, we didn't need much, and it was a nice surprise.

---

1 UA stood for the United Association of Journeymen and Apprentices of the Plumbing and Pipefitting Industry of the United States and Canada, of which I was a member.

A Man Returns

As mentioned before, we did a lot of fishing. We often took out the dinghy and explored all the mangrove areas for the best fishing. Sometimes I put my mask and fins on, grabbed my pole and spear, and jumped overboard. I would sit on the bottom under the boat and wait for the fish to return after the initial scare and then spear the biggest ones.

Tarpon fishing was great, and we caught our share of monsters. If it was clear and calm, I could climb to the top of the mast and look for them. They usually traveled in pairs and were easy to spot. I would also put a line out with the reel on clicker; if we got a strike, I would jump in the dink and Rachelle would hand me the rod. Once I set the hook, I would just let them pull me around the bay to wear them out. Once we got them up to the dink, we would release them.

Looking across the bay one morning, I spotted something floating that looked like more than seaweed. I motored out to it with the dink and found a teak dink that was completely covered in barnacles and sea growth. It was barely sticking out of the water; it was so heavy. It had been in the water a long time. I towed it back to *The Seawolf* and called the Coast Guard, the police, and the Marine Patrol to see if I could claim it and they all said I could. It became a nice project. Once I got it cleaned up, I could tell this was a quality boat. After completely redoing it, I sold it for $700.

I was working at my part time job one day when my phone rang. It was one of the guys in our anchorage. A very strong storm had rolled in during the day and the anchorage was taking a beating. A large trimaran had come loose from its anchor and was hung on *The Seawolf's* anchor chain. They were bow to bow and both boats were slamming up and down with the rough waves. Our anchor was sawing through the bow of the trimaran. My anchor was essentially holding both boats. I stopped by and picked up Rachelle at the T-shirt shop. We rode our bikes in the blinding rain and wind to where we kept our dinghy. It was one of the roughest dink rides out to *The Seawolf* we had ever been on. The chain had sawed a big gash in the trimaran, and the weather showed no signs of letting up any time soon. Heavy lightning was busting all around. The Coast Guard station was only about five miles north, so I radioed them. They told me that the weather was too bad to launch. It had to be a life-or-death situation. I told them that it just might turn into that, but they still wouldn't come. The guy that called me came over with a large anchor, and we carried it out a ways, dropped it, and then tied it off to the trimaran. Then he and Rachelle and I got on the bow of the trimaran, still in our dinks. As the waves raised the trimaran's bow, we all tried lifting at the same time. It was very dangerous and we were getting beat up pretty bad. After several tries, a big enough wave hit us and we were able to heave it off the chain. When it came off the chain, it took off down the side of *The Seawolf.* Then the anchor we had put out grabbed it. We had to get back on *The Seawolf* and put fenders out right away. It was a job, but we finally got the trimaran anchored away from *The Seawolf.* About an hour later, the weather finally let up and guess who called us on the radio? Yeah, the Coast Guard. They wanted to know if we still needed their assistance.

The man who owned the trimaran finally showed up and I had a little talk with him. People would come into an anchorage, drop anchor, then haul ass into the shore, not taking the time to make sure their anchor was holding.

Challenges

One of the aggravating problems we encountered living on the water was the law enforcement people. There were several different organizations and one was as bad as the other. Nothing like waking up in the middle of the night with a large spotlight on you and someone yelling that you were being boarded! You would tell them you lived on the boat, and they would answer with, "Sorry about that," and walk to the bow. Then came the usual two questions: Do you have drugs on board (as if anyone says yes to that question!) and do you have guns on board? Does a one-legged duck swim in circles? Are they loaded? They wouldn't do me much good if they weren't, would they? Then they wanted to know where they were. I would tell them, "Rachelle's pistol is in her panty drawer. Knock yourself out. I also have a pistol, a Mossberg riot shotgun, and two canisters of mace." They would always take all the bullets out of the guns and invite us into the cabin. Next, they would do a quick search, ask a whole bunch of questions, and then they'd be gone. We had been harassed several times since we set out on our cruise. They also liked to pull you over when you were in your dinghy to make sure you had your safety gear and to check your paperwork. One of the things that really burned my ass was *their* failure to comply with the no wake zones in an anchorage. I guess they felt like they were above that. I saw this mainly in the Keys.

I want to share the following story because it really pissed me off when I heard about it. We had friends with a large Sea Ray, and they were cruising up the St. Johns River through Jacksonville. As they went under the Main Street Bridge, two black kids dropped a brick on them and shattered their windshield. They turned around and headed back to their marina. En route they picked up the big pieces of glass, but they didn't have a vacuum cleaner to get the small pieces that were in the cracks around the engine hatch. A Marine patrol boat spotted the smashed windshield and pulled them over. They told the officers what had happened, but they decided to board them anyway, check their paperwork, and do a search. They asked them to please not pull the hatch on the engine because of all the glass. The police said that wasn't their problem and pulled it anyway.

All the glass went into the engine compartment and it was a real mess to clean up. Needless to say, I don't have much respect for water law enforcement. Their attitude is my biggest problem.

My mom's health had taken a turn for the worse, and we had just been talking about going to the Bahamas and starting a new adventure. Instead, we left the boat in the Keys to go and take care of Mom. (Leaving *The Seawolf* somewhere in the Bahamas didn't seem like a good idea.) We decided to stay with Mom and see how things went.

The café gal from Stuart showed up in our anchorage. We had been doing the Keys with her. She had a friend drive her car down from Stuart.

We'd been running into quite a few people that we'd met during our journeys. When we did, it was nothing but party, party, party.

The renter in my aunt's trailer had been paying hit-and-miss. He knew I was far away, and there was not much I could do about it. Even so, it was okay, as he was keeping the trailer alive through the winter, and when the time came, I'd have a good reason for throwing him out.

I'd been studying Morse code regularly, and driving Rachelle batty. It turned out to be a good thing I did because my time to take the code part of the test was almost up. I made a run to Marathon Key to take the code test. You had to be able to receive at least five words a minute. I did not study my numbers much, but I was out of time. I took the test and did fine except for the numbers. It took three signatures to pass you, and one of the guys didn't want to pass me. When I got to talking with him about being a radio operator with the Hurricane Hunters, that pushed him over the top and he gave it to me. A few years later, they did away with the code part.

Preparing for a Move

My mom called 911 again. On top of her congestive heart failure, high blood pressure, diabetes, and lupus, she now had pneumonia. She was not doing well. She had a couple of big problems, primarily her diet and heavy smoking habit. She had never really taken care of herself.

We talked it over, and we had some real hard decisions to make. If things didn't get any worse, we were going to head up there in the spring. The really difficult decision we had to make was to sell *The Seawolf.* We had no idea how long we were going to be up there, and if we decided on continuing the journey, we could buy another sailboat, so up for sale it went. Lots of people saw it and said they might buy it. It was ridiculous. We spent the rest of the winter enjoying adventures every day in the Keys.

One evening while we were talking about the big transition we would have when we moved to Pennsylvania, we suddenly wondered what the hell we were going to do up there while we took care of Mom. We weren't the type to just sit around and watch TV with Mom. We talked about a few things, and Rachelle suggested building a log home and selling it. Well, that started the ball rolling. We spent weeks looking at log homes and land for sale in Newfoundland. We bought a Toyota 4Runner which gave us the flexibility to go to a couple log home shows and look at model homes.

We ended up going with a cypress log company. I decided on cypress because you didn't have to worry about rot, bugs, or shrinkage. We also bought three two-acre lots on the side of the mountain overlooking Newfoundland. They were located on the mountain opposite the mountains where my mom lives.

We took a trip to St. Augustine to see my first grandbaby and spent a few days there. We stopped at the casino in Hollywood for a couple of days, and gave them some of our money.

Rachelle was busy with lots of paperwork going back and forth between the realtor, the log home company, our broker, and a loan company. She found out I didn't need a contractor's license where we were going to build. We formed a new company called Pocono Cypress Log Homes.

A local newspaper took Rachelle's picture and did a story about her living on a sailboat and working part time. Right after that she had to give up her job. We were just too busy trying to get all our ducks in a row.

We got a storage unit not far away, and slowly started moving things off the boat, so it would be easier when we decided to head out. And if the boat sold, we would be ahead of the game.

I did some running back and forth to the Miami VA. Security was tight there. You had to show an ID just to get into the parking lot. Once you got to the building, you showed your ID again and they did a facial recognition. I got checked out by the dermatologist for having too much tan. She burned some things off and told me I needed to get checked every six months.

We took a trip to Marathon. About a hundred dolphins had beached themselves and were dying. A lot of people were helping get them back in the water; it was really bad. We decided to get a place on shore for our last month in the Keys. That way we could get everything we needed off *The Seawolf*. I'll tell you, we had a lot of mixed emotions. We had been living on *The Seawolf* for almost four years and in the Keys for almost a year. It was going to be a tough transition. Pennsylvania was a far cry from the Keys and winter in the mountains was going to be something to deal with.

Like I said, we got lots of calls about buying *The Seawolf,* but none of them have panned out. We checked with a couple dozen marinas, but they were either booked up or way too expensive. It looked like we were going to have to leave it anchored there. It had done well through several storms and hurricanes, but I was worried about vandalism and theft. We made a deal with one of the boaters in the anchorage that was going to be there for a while. He said he would check on it and also show it for us when we had a potential buyer for a small monthly fee. That made us feel a little better about leaving it.

We took a trip to Key West for a couple days to unwind and kind of get our last Florida Keys fix.

We spent our last week visiting all the friends we had made and saying our goodbyes. We also had a yard sale. What we didn't sell, we gave away. I collected ten hermit crabs and some shells to take with us for my mom. I knew she would really enjoy watching them and painting their shells.

A pair of bald eagles had been bringing their two babies to the two birdbaths in front of our apartment. Morgan went crazy every time she saw them. All the wild birds were doing the same. Mom and Dad Eagle both keep a sharp eye out while their kids were in the birdbaths. It was pretty cool, so I took a video of it.

A few weeks before, I got a hold of my renter in Pennsylvania, who was behind on his rent. I told him he needed to be out of the place in thirty days because we would be moving in and he agreed.

A couple days before we were to leave, I picked up a six-by-twelve U-Haul trailer so we could start loading it. We finally were on our way to start our next adventure. We stopped to take one last look at *The Seawolf* sitting in the bay. It looked lonely.

On the way to Pennsylvania, we stopped in St. Augustine and spent a few days with family.

The Poconos

Newfoundland was a very small town, with only about 1,500 people. It still looked about the same as when I was a kid growing up there. About the only thing it had going for it was that it was located in the Pocono Mountains. Therefore there were a lot of summer homes there.

Mom was overjoyed to see us, and she loved the hermit crabs. We bought her a crab habitat enclosure for them.

We spent the first week unpacking, shopping, checking out the property we bought, and finding out where everything was.

We started off the second week by calling 911, and Mom spent a week in the hospital. We had a lot to get done in a short amount of time. We had already ordered the cabin. We only ordered the shell—no doors or windows, just walls and the roof. We had to clear the lot and get the basement in, the floor trusses made and in, and the floor sheeted before the cabin arrived. We elected to have a log company erect the cabin, so we could have it dried before winter.

Seeing that we were the new kids on the block, it was hard to find contractors. We couldn't find anyone available to clear the lot. We found a guy with a backhoe that would remove the stumps if they were four to five feet. I bought a chainsaw, and Rachelle and I took down and cut up nearly one hundred trees. We had to clear room for the house, driveway, septic tank, well, road to the drain field, and the drain field. We cut up all the trees for firewood and stacked it between trees, burning all the branches. The guy with the backhoe pulled out all the stumps and hauled them all off.

Yikes! What a start! We were into it now, but you know what? This was fun.

A Man Returns

There was lots of paperwork: we needed permits, septic approval, and a power pole. All of this was new to the area. They had never had permits and inspectors before, so I was a little ahead of the game.

I drew the interior of the cabin and that got approved. We also got the basement going. The block mason had to lay the basement, a well had to be drilled, and the septic tank, lift station, drain field, and power pole put in.

In between all of this we were getting Mom's place in shape and making our place livable. The renter had left it in bad shape.

We had our real estate agent run our cabin with an artist's rendition of the cabin for $299,000. We sold it before we set the first log to a doctor and his wife in Philadelphia. When we met with them, they wanted about $25,000 in upgrades. No problem.

Everything was coming along fine. The logs made it on time, along with the crew to place them. I rented a Sky Lift Forklift to unload and set the logs.

I got all the windows and doors ordered, and as soon as the crew was done with the roof, Rachelle and I got all of them in.

We traded the 4Runner in for a Subaru. The 4Runner did not have four-wheel drive and we needed something that could handle the mountain snow and ice. We also bought a four-wheel drive extended-bed Dodge Ram pickup truck to haul building materials.

I was all set to put a wood-burning fireplace in, but the new owners wanted a remote-controlled gas fireplace instead. I found out from the realtor that very few people wanted a wood-burning fireplace.

We visited Mom every morning and evening. We always took Morgan with us. She had Pecan Sandies and coffee with Mom. All her cats were very curious about Morgan, but they found out right away not to mess with her. Mom's English sheepdog was a mess. Its' fur was matted and dirty; it looked nasty. I had asked my siblings time and again to get the dog bathed and groomed, and I would pay for it, but it never got done. We paid the groomer triple her fee to get the job done, and what a different dog!

We had been slowly getting rid of all the unwanted cats. What a job! Rachelle was overseeing Mom's diet for diabetes, and making sure she was taking all her meds. We also got the cataracts removed from both her eyes. She was really excited about that. She said that Judge Judy never looked so clear.

Rachelle and I were going balls to the walls on the interior cabin. The only things we subbed out was the heating system and a little bit of sheetrock work. We had the stairs to the loft custom made from cedar, and they turned out gorgeous. I hauled rock in from the property for the fireplace, and Rachelle and I installed it. I picked up a nice cedar beam from a local sawmill for the mantle. We got the well and septic put in, along with a five-hundred-gallon propane tank. I got the propane line run to the heater, stove, and fireplace, so we could work in comfort.

I got things rolling on the second cabin, and it was going a lot easier than the first. This one sat higher on the mountain and there was a lot of rock to contend with.

Hurricanes Katrina and Rita came through the Keys and really tore the place up. *The Seawolf* stayed put, but suffered some canvas damage, and the two ¾-inch anchor lines broke, but the ⅜-inch chain and the forty-five-pound CQR held. I had to fly down to the Keys and take care of it. I borrowed scuba gear, found my two anchors and rope, and got her re-anchored. The canvas damage was minimal. I met with a young fellow who was interested in buying *The Seawolf*. We had been going back and forth on the price. As luck would have it, he decided to buy it and gave me a deposit. It sure would be nice to not have to worry about *The Seawolf*.

As it turned out, the gal we met at the café in Stuart (and later hooked up with in the Keys) wanted me to build this second cabin for her as an investment. I liked the idea of guaranteed money. We worked out a deal that we would build it for cost plus 10 percent.

Rachelle and I took a break and went to Atlantic City with some friends for two days. We did better this time, and came back $800 ahead. We caught the free bus, and that made it nice.

When they delivered the block for the basement on the second cabin, the mason found five newborn kittens in the web of one of the blocks. We called the block company to see if they had a mama cat running around the place, and they assured us there were no cats on the property. In fact, they had two Rottweilers that patrolled the yard. Against my better judgment, Rachelle brought them home. I told her we didn't have the time to take care of five kittens, and she told me that we'd make time. We called my daughter who was a vet. She told us what we needed to feed them and we got them started. Long story short, we found homes for three of them and kept two. One that we kept was small and gray and so spastic that we named her Spaz after the mason who found them: Joe Spazeone. It has been sixteen years and we still have those cats.

The Seawolf's Demise

Hurricane Wilma came straight through the Keys, and we got a call we didn't want: *The Seawolf* was gone along with *all the boats* in the anchorage. Some of them were sunk and the rest were missing. Two days later I got a call: they had found *The Seawolf*. It was thirteen miles north at MM-95 laying on its side on shore in someone's backyard. The Coast Guard told me that for the boat to get that far up the coast through all the mangroves and small islands, they thought someone may have tried to steal it during the storm. They said it wouldn't be the first time someone tried that. I had to wait my turn for a recovery outfit. My insurance company needed an estimate on repairs. My youngest son and his partner went to the Keys and worked up an estimate. It would cost $40,000 to repair it. I had to make a decision. We ended up putting the insurance money in our pocket and sold *The Seawolf* as it was for $11,000. We actually got $1,000 more than I was originally asking for it. I had put a lot of money in it, but it was twenty-six years old. It was time to let it go.

Just before we started working on the cabins, Harbor Freight showed up at the fairgrounds with a couple of tractor trailers full of tools. I bought just about everything I needed to build a log cabin. Like I always say, better to be lucky than good.

I needed a lot of scaffolding, and renting that would be very expensive. I got lucky again. I found an ad in the paper. A man was selling a ton of scaffolding. He told me that most of his work was with the Catholic churches and schools, and that with the big shakeup over the Catholic priests, his business had dropped off by fifty percent. He had a huge warehouse full of scaffolding and I got a truck full of it for a great price.

I had never owned a nail gun until I built the cabins. Oh my God, what a freaking time- and arm-saver! Not only with all the framing, but I also covered all the interior walls of both cabins with one-by-six tongue-and-groove cedar. I can't even imagine doing it with a hammer now.

I had a little setback on the first cabin. We put ¾-inch oak flooring in both cabins. I was just about done with the flooring when I had a sciatic nerve attack in my right leg. I had to crawl down the steps, and over to the truck, and get in while in excruciating pain. I stayed on the couch for almost two weeks. It was unbelievable.

We finished out half the basements in both cabins and put lofts in both cabins.

We had cleared the third lot and had a perk test done, but didn't do anything else, pending my mother's health.

A Man Returns

The Seawolf Reunion

I had been communicating back and forth with the Seawolf Association for several months. They had notified me that I qualified for induction into the Combat Aircrew Roll of Honor. I was so honored and humbled that I would be chosen to be a part of something like this—something that would be part of history. I was proud to be a part of an organization like the Seawolves—an outfit I had volunteered for because I believed in the cause, even though a lot of my friends had told me I was crazy.

It was time to head to South Carolina and the Patriots Point Naval and Maritime Museum. They asked if we could wear our uniforms, so I dug out the old uniform I wore in 1969, and it still fit!

It was such a flashback to see some of the guys I had flown with. On the first day, there was a reception on the USS Yorktown Aircraft Carrier. There were lots of people. I found out that twenty-six men were to be inducted that day. I was really surprised to find out that several of them were from WWII. The next day was the induction ceremony, and we all met on the Yorktown again. I was excited to see that they already put up the brass plaque with the 2005 inductees' names on it. It really does something to you when you see your name in bronze alongside a long list of heroes. The ceremony was very moving. Richard C. Knott was the guest speaker. He was the author of *Fire from the Sky*, a very good book on the history of the Seawolves. They gave all of us a plaque, and we said our goodbyes and headed for Newfoundland.

Back Home

Despite bouts with my sciatic nerve and heel spurs, we managed to close on the first home on December 14. The new owners wanted to spend Christmas in their new cabin and we had just made it. Now to concentrate on the second cabin.

One evening when we got back to the house, I reached for our five-gallon bucket of birdseed, and it wasn't there. I asked Rachelle where it was, and she said she had not touched it. I looked around and found bear tracks running right up to the front door. I followed the tracks across the road and over the stone wall fence, and into the woods. There it was in the snow, birdseed everywhere.

We decided to take a few days and celebrate the closing on the cabin. We spent Christmas in Atlantic City and they comped our room. The city looked great, all decorated for Christmas. We had a good time but came out $200 down.

It was really strange to be working in the ice, snow, and cold. It had been a long time since I had to deal with snow. At times it was beautiful and I would go for hikes with the snow falling around me, but it was a challenge to work in it.

We worked on the second cabin every day, but not at the pace we did on the first one. We were getting lots of tire-kickers about the cabin, but nothing definite yet.

We had been talking about what we were going to do when we left the mountain. We had originally planned on sailing to Panama in Central America. Now we were tossing around the idea of flying down and taking a look. We'd been doing a lot of research.

We got all the doors and windows for the second cabin in, and decided to take a break from the cold and head to the Keys for a month. Rachelle found us a nice place on the water. It was big enough to have friends and family visit while we're there. A friend of ours had our dinghy there too, and we'd be able to use it while we were there. We ended up selling it before we left.

It was so great to be in the Keys again. We did a lot of fishing, visiting friends, and taking it easy.

A Man Returns

My mom's health was up and down. The problem was that she was not getting any better. She was just hanging in there.

The second cabin was coming right along, and this one was a lot easier now that we'd become familiar with where everything was.

We had one potential buyer, but so far, no one had been able to get financing.

PANAMA

The Vacation of the Decade

We found an international real estate agent in Florida. She was raised in Panama and had a home in Panama. She set the whole trip up for us: we were going to spend a week down there and have a look around. We flew out of Philly to Atlanta, and Atlanta to Panama, and landed at 10 p.m. She flew us in VIP which was very nice. The VIP gal met us as we disembarked and took us directly to the VIP lounge. It was very nice—with drinks and hors d'oeuvres. We bypassed check-in, customs, and baggage, which they brought to the VIP lounge. They got us a taxi, and it was a twenty-minute ride to Panama City and the Radisson Hotel which overlooked Panama Bay. The hotel was connected to a casino and mall via a glass walkway over the highway.

The room turned out to be a great suite, complete with a large basket of flowers and fruit.

The next morning, we had breakfast at the hotel and decided to take a walk along the bay front to take in the city. What a surprise we got. The tide was out, and the smell was so bad that Rachelle was getting sick to her stomach. We went back to the hotel.

Panama City was nothing like the postcards. It did have a hell of a skyline and there were lots of condos along the shore, but there were no sandy beaches in Panama City. Several large rivers made their way from the mountains through villages and the city, picking up raw sewage and garbage along the way and dumping it into the bay. Not only did you have polluted rivers, but also hundreds of ships anchored in the bay, waiting to go through the canal. They just added to the problem. We spent the rest of the day at the casino and mall.

A Man Returns

Early the next day, we caught a cab to Old Panama City and checked out the old ruins and the Kuna Indian shops where we bought several items. They used the American greenback there so that made it easy.

We spent the afternoon with our real estate gal and the ReMax gang. We made plans for the next day to look at properties. We had dinner at the mall, and returned to the hotel lounge for drinks. While we were having drinks, one of the vice presidents of Panama came in and introduced himself and sat down. We had a nice talk with him, and he gave us a card with his private number, and told us if we ever had a problem to give him a call. Now that was something that didn't happen every day!

The next day, we drove all over the place with them, looking at beach property a couple hours out of town. We found out right away that beach property was not going to work out unless you wanted a condo, and we didn't want that. You could get a nice house on the beach for $100,000, but the roads were just dirt and very bad. There was also garbage everywhere and it was very dangerous, unless you hired twenty-four-hour security. We heard many terrible stories. Rachelle and I were thinking that these people were wasting our time. On the way back, they took us on a sightseeing tour.

The next day, we met at the ReMax office to discuss our options. They told us about a community up in the mountains, 3,000 feet up on top of the Continental Divide. Instead of the sweltering hundred-plus degree heat, it stayed between 68 and 80 degrees all year round. It was a gated community called Latos De Cerro Azul, and was located about an hour straight up the mountain. We decided to take a look. What a scenic drive! It was the only road up and went through several small villages. About three quarters of the way there, we came across dozens and dozens of chicken houses. Mr. Melo, one of the ten wealthiest men in Panama, owned 40,000 acres there in the rainforest. After he had removed all the good timber, he put in the infrastructure for 2,000 home sites, and then added all these chicken houses for his poultry business. It was too hot for the chickens down the hill, but up here, it was just perfect. The Panamanian government took control of the 40,000 acres and made it part of the Chagres National Park, grandfathering everything that was already in place.

Upon reaching the entrance to the community, we were met by two uniformed guards carrying machine guns. We stated our business, and they opened the gate and let us through. This community had been developed for the rich and famous as a vacation getaway far from the city and the sweltering heat. No A/C or heat was required up here. There were about five hundred homes scattered throughout the mountains with very few people living there full time. A lot of the street signs were missing, and we got lost several times, but we finally found the house we were looking for. It took another hour for someone to bring us a key to unlock the gate to the property. We absolutely loved it! It was a two-story concrete, glass, tile, stone, and cedar structure with a metal roof. Three bedrooms and three baths with a small basement. Sitting on two and a half acres at the end of a ridge and completely private, overlooking the national park with Panama City and the Pacific Ocean to the south, and the Caribbean to the north. You couldn't get a better view. We could see the ships in the bay and the entrance to the canal. To top it all off, it was fully furnished. It had been built by Mr. Melo's son as his vacation home. He sold it years later to the couple that owned it now. He was an architect and she was a lawyer.

We took a tour of the house, and it was just as nice inside and had a beautiful stone fireplace for those chilly rainy season nights. Rachelle and I stepped out on the back porch overlooking the city. We looked at each other and both said, "I want it," at the same time. We put in an offer, they accepted it, and that started the ball rolling. We

A Man Returns

didn't know it at the time, but this was the start of a ten-year adventure. What an adventure it would be!

We spent the next morning taking care of all the paperwork necessary to purchase a home in Panama. Then we had lunch overlooking the canal. We got to see two ships raised and lowered; it was quite the operation. Then we drove out to the Gamboa Rainforest Resort, passing the famous Gamboan El Renacer Prison, and checked it out. It was situated along the canal.

Rachelle and I wanted to see the house again in more detail and look at the area again. Just outside the gate was a small store, also owned by Melo that carried groceries, hardware, and a small amount of building supplies.

We stopped in at the Melo's office, located within the community and got a whole bunch of information. Water was about seven dollars a month. Electricity averaged about fifty dollars a month. I was surprised to find out that all the houses were only 60 amp. Later on, I changed that to 100 amp. (Anything over that was considered commercial.)

The community had a neat clubhouse, huge pool, tennis courts, and lots of picnic areas and trails.

The houses were all shapes and sizes and very colorful. We saw very few people, and they told us that there were more people up here on the weekends.

The road up the mountain could be a little treacherous—there was lots of erosion, potholes, sharp turns, and dropoffs, but they assured us that Mr. Melo kept it halfway repaired because of his chicken farms.

The next day was a combination of paper signing and sightseeing.

Traffic in third-world countries is always pretty bad, and Panama was no different. Forget about the rules of the road. You had to drive aggressively all the time. We had dinner with the gang at a dinner theater. This was so different than what we were used to. It was just what we were looking for.

Departure day came, and our heads were spinning. It was so exciting. We owned a home in a foreign country. Wow!

When we landed in Atlanta, our plane to Philly was overbooked, so Rachelle and I gave up our seats, and they gave each of us $400 toward our next flight, first class tickets to Philly, and a food voucher. All that for a two-hour delay in our flight!

Getting Ready

Back to 20 degrees and two feet of snow. We spent the day with Mom, telling her about our trip. We had only been gone a week, but our kittens seemed twice as big as when we left. I checked in at the Wilkes-Barre VA hospital for a complete physical and tests for my sciatic nerve problem.

When I got home, we stayed busy working on the cabin. This one was a lot more fun—no pressure. I was able to spend more time with Mom too; she hadn't been feeling well.

We also had visits from a couple of our sailboat friends: a couple from Nova Scotia and Canada as well as our café gal had flown in a couple times.

Mom took a turn for the worse, and we had to call an ambulance to transport her to the hospital. She spent the next few weeks in the hospital trying to get better. The day they moved her into ICU, we got a call from Rachelle's mom. Rachelle's dad had passed away. She had found him in the garden; he had had a heart attack.

Her mom called the rescue, but when they got there, they pronounced him dead and called the coroner. When the coroner got there, he couldn't move the body because there was a shotgun near him. Joe kept a shotgun handy because of gopher problems. The coroner called for a state trooper and stayed with Mom until the trooper arrived, which was several hours. Mom was very upset that Joe had to lay out there all that time. When the trooper finally got there, he looked at the shotgun, determined it hadn't been fired, and allowed the coroner to move Joe. I guess it's a good thing Joe hadn't shot a gopher. Who knows how long he might have had to lay there?

Rachelle needed to fly to Missouri to be with her mother. Since flying out of Scranton was way too expensive, I drove her to Philly.

She had a real experience there with the TSA—you know, the people who take the fun out of flying, also known as the Transportation Security Administration. She had purchased her ticket, and was going through security when she was approached by a TSA agent and told to follow her. They took her to a small room where they checked her bag. Rachelle asked them what was going on, but they wouldn't talk to her. They went through her suitcase and carry-on, and then did a body search. Then Rachelle went off on them, telling them that her father had just passed away. She was only trying to get to Missouri to be with her mom. They finally let up, and told her she had been flagged because she was flying on the same day she bought the ticket. Wow! They finally let her go, but she was pretty upset and angry at the same time.

Mom's condition worsened. Only the machines she was hooked up to kept her alive. Mom had made me promise that if she was ever being kept alive by machines, she wanted the machines turned off. I had a meeting with my siblings and the three doctors that were taking care of her, and we made the decision to turn off the machines and move her to hospice. That's what we did. Mom rested in hospice, completely sedated. We knew it wouldn't be long.

Rachelle called and I went to pick her up at the airport, leaving my sisters at the hospital. On the way back, I got the call—Mom had passed on. As we drove along the mountain overlooking the valley, fireworks were still going off all over the place. My mom's favorite holiday was the Fourth of July. To this day, I think about the sendoff Mom had that night and it makes me smile.

My mother was a woman of nature. She loved all God's creatures, and even though she had very little, she made sure the deer, turkeys, and birds had something to eat. She even had a black bear that would stand up in front of her picture window, looking for the hot dogs she fed it by hand.

She requested that her ashes be spread on an active deer trail.

We had a small memorial for her attended by friends and family. I was unable to say anything, but my son-in-law did a fine job. He also read Mom's poem titled "Country Lane" that I had picked out. She had written a couple hundred poems, but this one was the only one that was published, and it was my favorite.

Country Lane

Walking down a country lane, dirt road beneath my feet.

I pass through todays and nows 'til yesterday I meet.

And dreams unfold of seasons dear—Sun rising until dark,

The days spent in adventure my youth to leave a mark.

I pick the berries, warm and sweet; the briars hold no fear,

So gently hold the daisies and feel the touch so near.

The flowers of my youth are gone but the fragrance still remains,

And sometimes in a quiet time the scent returns again

To unlock a rusty lock with a forgotten rusty key.

Then down a memory country lane a youth again I'll be.

The memorial was at Mom's house. After the reading of the poem, I picked up Mom's ashes and we all walked down in the woods where there was a gap in a stone fence where the deer came through on their way to Mom's feeders. I started sprinkling ashes on the trail followed by my siblings, then other relatives and friends.

The next morning, I got a thermos of coffee and went down by the deer trail and climbed up on a boulder and watched the deer parade by, their hooves working my mom's white ashes into the black dirt. It was an awesome feeling, and I continued to do this for quite a few mornings.

One of the hardest things I had to do was put Mom's dog down. Sassy was an old dog and not in good health. I could not find anyone to take him in. I had flashbacks of when we took Tippy in. We found homes for some of Mom's cats, but we had to put the rest of them down.

For the next month, we stayed busy working on the cabin and cleaning out Mom's place. We did get a little help from my siblings, but not much. Again, I think they figured it was my house and I should take care of it. They were more interested in what they could take.

A Second Trip

We moved on and went back to Panama, this time for three weeks. We found out that everyone called the house below us the Audubon House. The owner was the president of the Panama Audubon Society, and there was an Audubon trail that ran from their house and alongside our property on into the rain forest. Incidentally, the area we were in was called the Cloud Forest for obvious reasons. The Audubon House was their vacation house, and they had another small house on their property where their caretaker and his family lived. His name was Nando. He spoke pretty good English and would take care of our property too. The gardeners and housekeepers charged eight dollars a day, and any type of construction was ten dollars a day.

We spent a lot of time up and down the mountain, shopping for everything to make the house our own. It was the rainy season, so we had been dealing with some heavy-duty thunderstorms. Our house gave us a spectacular view of the storms in an almost 360-degree span. The clouds floated right through our house. The rain forest was incredibly beautiful. We'd already seen so many different kinds of birds and insects.

We found a place called the Do-It Center, and it's like a home improvement store. We spent several hours buying all kinds of appliances: a dryer, washer, and gas stove, along with other household products for a total of $1,800. They had a promo set up that day. It was a dartboard with circles marked on it giving you 2 percent, 5 percent, or 10 percent off your next purchase. They gave me three darts. I gave them to Rachelle, and she gave them back to me. All the store personnel gathered around to see the Americano throw the darts. I walked up to the dartboard, stuck a dart in the center and pointed to it. They all laughed. I walked back to the line they had on the floor and threw the first dart. It stuck exactly dead center. They all went crazy cheering. We got a certificate for $180 off our next purchase, and every time we went into that store, everyone remembered us.

Some things were cheaper here, but you had to learn where to shop. Gasoline was not cheap. They did not have 87-octane, only 91; and in 2006, it was three dollars and fifteen cents a gallon. A case of Panama beer was seven dollars and if you went to a Ma & Pa bodega, you could get a heaping plate of either chicken, pork, or beef with rice, beans, and a small salad for a dollar and fifty cents. All their fast food places like McDonald's and Burger King were just a little cheaper than the U.S.

A Man Returns

Reba Smith was the grocery store for the upper class. They had a lot of American products which their prices reflected. Ray's prices were just a little below Reba Smith, and then you had the three Panamanian stores: El Super Xtra, Super 99, and El Machetazo. These stores were a real experience. Anytime we had people visit us from the States we always took them to one of them jut for the experience. You were not allowed to take a shopping cart out of the store; a bag boy has to do it. Security guards were everywhere which we liked. They were inside and outside all stores. They were in the parking lots, and all delivery trucks had a guard riding shotgun. If you entered a store with a package, you had to check it. There were also fruit and vegetable stands everywhere, and they sold some pretty crazy stuff.

Nando found us a hundred-pound propane tank full for fifty dollars. It was normally fifty dollars for the tank and seventy-five dollars to fill it. Most everyone had a twenty-five-pound tank, and they only cost four dollars and fifty cents to fill them because the government subsidized them.

We were so glad we didn't buy a home when we were down the mountain, just because of the heat and humidity. As you came up the mountain, you could really feel the change in the air. The fog on the mountain could get really thick.

My daughter, son-in-law, and their baby flew in, and we got to spend a few days showing them around and doing some exploring ourselves.

We all went down and visited Nando at his home, and we were surprised he had a wife and three children. Their home was concrete block with no windows or doors, and they all slept in hammocks. They did their cooking on an open fire outside. His father was there with his horse; he had been in the interior getting provisions. He lived a two-hour ride on horseback from there. Nando took us for our first trip down the Audubon trail. He took a lot of bird-watchers from all over down this trail. What an interesting trip that was. Over the next ten years, I'd be going down it a lot.

I had Nando and his dad take down two large eucalyptus trees in our front yard that had been hit by lightning. They did it all with machetes until the very last, when they finally used a chainsaw to cut the big trunk. They hauled all the debris into the forest. He charged us ten dollars and I gave him twenty dollars. We'd been warned about overpaying; everyone there had a tendency to do that.

We gave Nando a bunch of household stuff we didn't need too: chairs, a small table, bunkbeds, and a bunch of other stuff. We also gave him a large playground, which we found out later he sold.

We took my daughter and her husband to the canal and had lunch. In the future, we would be making a lot of these trips. We also visited the Smithsonian Institute, which had some very nice displays about Panama. We bought some bird and insect identification books, and stopped by the Kuna Indian artisan building and picked up some souvenirs.

Our poor grandbaby had a rough time on the mountain road. Her little stomach could not handle it. I took it real easy on the way to the airport to drop them off, and she did real good, I thought. We later found out that she threw up all over her mama while standing at the ticket counter. Thank goodness, she hadn't given them their bags yet, and was able to do a quick change.

We checked on a couple container shippers but didn't settle on any.

We spent the last couple of days working on the house, exploring, and taking a lot of pictures. So far we had seen a lot of different birds including hummingbirds, toucans, tanagers, and chachalacas on the property. We also had a three-toed sloth hanging from one of our trees.

A Man Returns

We paid Nando for five months to take care of the yard, keep an eye on the place, and pay our electric bill, which, when we were not there, would only be about three dollars a month.

When we got to Miami, we had a nice surprise—our flight to Philly was canceled. We had to wait nine hours for the next flight. Once we got on the plane, we had to wait for over an hour for two children. It wasn't over yet either. When we got to our car on arrival, the battery was dead and it was 1 a.m. Thank goodness, a security guard was there to jump-start us. We got home at 5 a.m., pretty well bushed.

Rachelle had been suffering with allergies for months. We were hoping she would get a break in Panama, but she didn't.

We picked up Morgan at a friend's house and gave them a couple Kuna souvenirs. My sister had fed our two cats, Mable and Spaz, while we were gone.

We had 290 emails to answer when we got back. We stayed busy the next couple months working on the cabin and getting Mom's place cleaned out, as winter was coming on. We put her place up for sale.

We got three quotes for a forty-foot container from New York harbor to Panama: $10,000, $8,000, and $3,300. We locked into the quote for $3,300. We also had to renew Morgan's passport and get all her paperwork done, which was a real ordeal. They first said we couldn't bring Morgan into Panama. It took several months of back and forth, three different Panamanian consultants, and our lawyer to finally get her approved. We also did a lot of research on what kind of car to ship to Panama, as cars were very expensive there. We finally settled on a Toyota FJ Cruiser. It was the first year they made them but everything we read about them looked like what we needed in Panama. It proved to be the perfect vehicle—ten years in the rainforest without a problem. Tires in Panama only lasted between 10,000 and 12,000 miles, no matter what kind they were.

We got our official Construction Document (CD) on the cabin, but I still had a lot to do to be completely finished. We decided to move into the cabin to cut down on all the back and forth. We had a lot on our plate at this time. We were working to finish the cabin, clean out Mom's and my aunt's places, do a lot of repairs on both, and start packing for Panama. We also had a lot of paperwork going back and forth with our lawyer in Panama. We had several garage sales and got rid of a lot of household stuff and construction equipment. What we didn't sell, we either gave away or burned.

To our surprise, we sold our third property. We had put a high price on it, figuring we would be sitting on it for a while. We paid $10,000 for it and sold it for $40,000. The only thing we did to the property was clear it and get a perk test. That was a pleasant surprise. (Our realtor had told us we would never sell it for that price.)

We took a road trip with our new FJ to Missouri to visit Rachelle's mom for a month. While we were there, she kept me busy doing all kinds of work. Her house was located next to railroad tracks, and the backside of her house had settled about four inches. So while I was there, I went under the house and got it all jacked back up into place.

The Golden Seal

While we were at Mom's, we had to fly to Panama to get what they call the Golden Seal, which was our Pensionado Visa, which was almost like a citizenship. It took us several months to get all of the necessary paperwork, and the total cost was about $2,000 each. There were several ways you could be approved to stay in Panama. We chose the route in which you had to prove you had a certain amount of guaranteed retirement coming in monthly. We met our lawyer and she led us through the whole process. We had to go to several government buildings to get all of this done. Panama was no different than the U.S.: it was how much money you had or who you knew. The only difference was that it was more wide open.

Nando had our grounds looking great and his wife had our house spotless.

We stopped by the Cerro Azul real estate office and got squared away with them on our property fees. We also got set up on cell phones. Then, we did a little more exploring the community and some more shopping for the house. We also picked up Christmas gifts for Nando and his family.

Then it was back to Missouri and Mom's for a week. Again, the airlines lost our bags and had to bring them out to us the next day. While we were there, we had a brush guard and fog lights mounted on the front of the FJ cruiser. We spent a week working on Mom's house and her yard.

On the way back to Pennsylvania, we stopped in Ashville, North Carolina, and visited our friend whom we were building the log cabin for. We got back into Pennsylvania on Christmas Day. It was 20 degrees and snowing. We spent Christmas afternoon with friends and family.

Our realtor had an open house for the cabin and we had several people come by. I got talking to one of the guys about Panama. He told me he was in the Army (special forces) and had participated in the invasion of Panama called Just Cause. He said their outfit took out Noriega's radio house in Cerro Azul. I told him he probably wouldn't believe it, but we had just bought the house at the end of the street that the radio house was on. We had walked down there and checked it out. There were still a few big antennas remaining and lots of racks where radios were kept. The place was torn up pretty bad though: all the windows were broken out and the doors were gone.

They once had telescopes set up, but they were gone too. He told me he remembered the spectacular view from there.

At one of the log shows we attended, we saw this gorgeous cedar log furniture, and long story short, became dealers. We were able to buy about twelve pieces of furniture for a 50 percent discount! We put them on display in our sales office. Well, they were too expensive for most, and we only sold a couple pieces. We decided they would be perfect in our new house, so I had to break all that down and wrap it in cardboard and shrink-wrap it. We bought quite a few items that were either very expensive or not available in Panama: a big screen TV, a five-burner gas grill, and kitchen appliances. We packed over one hundred boxes and plastic tubs for the container.

The animals were a problem, especially Morgan. Trying to get all their shots and paperwork to satisfy Panama, and then carriers to satisfy airlines, whew! Morgan's shots were the biggest problem because a couple of the shots were only good for a certain number of days. Another major problem was that two of the shots that Panama wanted were for chickens and the vet told us that if he was to give Morgan those shots it would kill her, so we had to get our lawyer involved again and it was a battle. You would think that no one had ever brought a parrot into Panama.

The weather was also a big problem—very cold and windy with lots of snow.

I had bought a guitar in the early 80s, but never had a case for it, even on the sailboat. A friend gave me an old guitar case for my guitar's trip to Panama.

Better to be lucky than good. We sold the cabin, were leaving in two weeks, and I really didn't want the hassle back-and-forth in Panama. We got the asking price of $305,000 and sold it to another doctor and his wife. They too were only using it for a vacation home.

A Man Returns

We rented a twenty-four-foot box truck and started loading it until we were down to a mattress and what would fit in a couple of suitcases. Then we packed the FJ full of personal and fragile stuff. The high for the past few days had been 18 degrees; we were ready for Panama. We'd had a lot of bullshit back-and-forth with Panama about bringing the FJ into the country. Then again, this was not the first time someone had brought a car into Panama. Our real estate agent got us a customs broker (her cousin), and that was a really big help.

We picked up a rental car, a Mercury Mountaineer. Rachelle drove the FJ and I drove the box truck, and we headed for New York harbor, a two-hour trip, in the freezing cold and snow coming down. When we arrived at the warehouse, we could see the Statue of Liberty in the distance. The area looked pretty rough, and we were both concerned about leaving all of our worldly possessions there. I backed the truck up to the warehouse, and about four guys started unloading, stacking everything in a chain-link cage that didn't look very secure. They assured me they had never lost any merchandise yet. We had to leave the FJ running in the parking lot to run out as much gas as possible. We got insurance on the FJ, but they wouldn't insure the cargo because they didn't box it! What bullshit! It was rough driving off and not feeling very confident in the people in charge. It was supposed to take two weeks to get to Panama if everything went okay. Customs had to give their approval.

We still had paperwork going back and forth, and lots of documents to get authenticated by a Panamanian consulate.

Finally, all our ducks were aligned and we spent our last night with family over diner.

Getting There

The next morning before we headed to the New York airport, we called the airlines to confirm our flight and our animals. We had a terrible surprise: they had bumped Morgan! The cats were okay, as they were going under our seats. We made a half dozen calls and found out that whoever confirmed Morgan's flight didn't have that authority. She was bumped because of cargo and they couldn't give us a guaranteed date. After a bunch of bullshit, we ended up losing the money we paid for our tickets. We tried fighting it later, but didn't get anywhere. After a bunch of phone calls, Rachelle found us a flight out of Miami in two days that would guarantee a spot for Morgan. Florida, here we come. We first had to do a side trip to Avoca Airport in Wilkes-Barre, Pennsylvania, to change the contract on our rental car. On the way, we stopped in Philly at the Panamanian Consulate just for reassurance that our paperwork was all okay, and it was.

We stopped in Jacksonville and visited my daughter who was in the hospital getting ready to have her second baby which she did the next day: a baby boy named Gavin, eight pounds, fourteen ounces. We made it to Miami in plenty of time, which was a good thing because cargo was backed up with flower trucks for Valentine's Day. They told us to get in the back of the line and wait our turn. After we sat in line for half an hour, and had only moved two car spaces, Rachelle jumped out in search of someone who could help us. She did, and the gal told her to drive our vehicle to the head of the line and take a chance that nobody would raise hell. I eased around everyone and pulled up to the unloading dock, getting Morgan out of the car right away. I think all the drivers saw that it was an animal, so no one said a thing or blew their horn. It took quite a while for them to do the paperwork. We still had to drop off the rental car and we were quite a way from the terminal. Time was running out and traffic was backed up. I had to drive like a madman and use the median all the way to the car rental. I threw the keys to the rental gal, grabbed our luggage, and we jumped on a shuttle that was just pulling out. When we got to the terminal, Rachelle ran to the ticket counter, while I grabbed the bags and the cats and followed the best I could. Rachelle made it with three minutes to spare. When we got to the gate, everyone had already boarded. Rachelle told the stewardess that we weren't leaving unless she could tell us that Morgan was on board. It took a while, but she finally confirmed that Morgan had made it. We were wiped out. When we landed at the Tocumen Airport in Panama, everyone had their hand out: agriculture, two vets, and customs. We paid everyone and were on our way. They did show us a chopping block along with a big cleaver that they used to chop the heads off of birds who didn't have all the proper paperwork. Our lawyer really came through for us. She was also one of the lawyers for the Panama Canal and had an office in England.

When we got up the mountain to our house, we found they had pulled our electric meter and Nando had put jumper wires across the terminals, so we would have power. We found out later that the electric company had pulled the wrong meter. Welcome to Panama.

Our container arrived three weeks later in Colón. We got with our custom broker and she arranged to get our container to a warehouse in Panama City. She also got us a box truck, a driver, and three helpers. The total cost for all of this was $850. At the warehouse we paid the custom agent $250 which they called a warehouse storage fee, but was really a payment to look the other way when we unloaded the container. We met everyone at the warehouse the next morning and right away there was a problem, as we were surprised that the lock was already off the container. The problem was that the container was not backed up to the loading dock, so we couldn't get the FJ out of the container and they didn't have a rig to move it. The FJ was in the back of the container so we couldn't start unloading. Better to be lucky than good! Another rig pulled in with a container, and I was able to get him to move our container for a small fee. Getting the FJ out of the container turned out to be an ordeal. They had it tied down to the deck with heavy rope and blocking on all four wheels. I had my knife and was able to cut the rope, which the guys on the dock wanted to save, so they weren't very happy about that. They had nothing to remove the blocking with, but I found a six-foot piece of two-inch pipe, and with a lot of banging, I was able to get most of it out. You have to remember we had just come from 15 degree temperatures. It was probably 125 degrees inside that container, and 100 outside. One of the windows was down, and I was able to squeeze in through there because you couldn't get in through the door. Once in, I tried to start it, but the battery was dead. I was able to borrow tools and took the battery out of one of the helper's cars to put in the FJ. No one had jumper cables. Once I got it started, I saw the battery problem—the dome light had been left on. I backed the FJ out of the container and drove it down and off the dock. While it was still running, I changed the batteries back. The FJ was filthy, just covered in rock salt from the snow-covered roads back home.

Rachelle stayed in the customs shack with two agents eating watermelon. That was a good thing because we had a lot of new stuff still in their boxes which you were supposed to pay duty on (not to mention two pistols and a shotgun along with ammo which is a real no-no). The car and the household goods were separated by a plywood wall. I used my pipe to tear it down. Finally, we were able to move the boxes to the box truck. The trip up the mountain was not good. They almost burned their truck up coming up all the steep hills, and the driver was not very happy. In the end though, it was unloaded and we could relax a minute. What a stressful day.

A Man Returns

Alterations and Money

One of the first things we did was have a twenty-five-foot by twenty-five-foot garage built attached to the house. We didn't use it as a garage; it became a workshop and laundry space. Most of the houses there did not have an inside laundry. They usually had a cement sink on the outside of the house for washing and a clothesline for drying.

We also had a huge covered back porch built, and I built a summer kitchen area with tile countertops, sink, refrigerator, and the grill we bought. I had the ceiling on the porch done in cedar keeping with the rest of the house. I had a big surprise buying the cedar. I bought the cedar by the cubic inch and it came from the Darién Gap in huge square logs. They cut the boards with chainsaws and then planed them right there on the job site. You had to have a permit to own a chainsaw; it was fifteen dollars a year. I bought a chainsaw, but never bought the permit.

We also bought seventeen palm trees for $300—six different species. In ten years some of those trees grew to be thirty feet tall.

One of our big problems was that we didn't speak a lick of Spanish. We started studying a Rosetta Stone language course and that helped. Later, we took classes and that really helped. We never got fluent, but we learned enough to get by.

Our car was a major problem. Customs did not know how much import fee to charge us. For six months, we had to ride around with stateside plates. Having stateside plates and driving a new car that no one had ever seen made us a target for the police. It was bad enough being American. The first time we got pulled over was scary. We had already been warned to just pay them off, but as Americans that was just something you didn't do. All you had to do was hand them your driver's license with a couple dollars wrapped around it, and they handed your license back and you went on your way. I can't tell you how many times we had to do that. The only time you had a problem was when they wanted more money, and sometimes that could get a little stressful. One time we got pulled over by a police truck, and the next thing we knew, we were surrounded by five men with automatic weapons wanting $300. I acted like a crazy American and went off on them. People started gathering, and they finally got back in their truck and drove off.

When customs finally got around to registering the FJ, we ran into another snag. I swear every time we turned around, you would think it was the first time this had ever been done in Panama. Instead of the VIN number on all the paperwork, they wanted the "motor number." We had to go back to customs with the motor number and pay them yet another fee and redo all the paperwork. We also had to go to motor vehicles, and one of the guys there had to get under the car and do a pencil and paper rub of the motor number. How ridiculous! After all was said and done, they charged us a $4,000 import fee. To get our driver's licenses, we had to give them a police report from our last state side address and take a hearing and eye test.

You hear a lot about retiring in Panama, Costa Rica, and Mexico. They all say the same thing: you can live there on $800 a month! I'm here to tell you that's bullshit. You might be able to do that if you live like the locals, but if you're from the United States, I'm telling you there is no way you're going to live like the locals. You need to figure on $2,000 to $3,000, not counting a mortgage or rental cost. Health insurance is not a problem up to a certain age and doctor and dental is very reasonable.

Before we moved, we had a mail service set up in Texas. They only kept our first class mail and only sent what we requested. We also set up an account with FedEx in Panama. We usually requested our mail every month or two and they sent it to us by FedEx. FedEx would call us to let you know when it arrived.

A Man Returns

When Mr. Melo had bought the 40,000 acres, he had taken out all the big trees and replanted pines. As a result, I had about forty pines partially blocking our view. Nando got a couple guys and they cut them down for three dollars apiece, and we got rid of them farther down our hill.

We lost power fairly often, so we bought a whole house gasoline and propane generator. We also bought six one-hundred-pound propane tanks, just in case we had a problem getting propane, like if the road were washed out. They had a twenty-gallon 110-volt water heater, so I changed it out to a forty-gallon propane one.

Nando had a friend named Omar who had lost his job at a gas station. The owner shut it down because he was robbed one too many times. He wanted to know if we could put him to work for a while until he found something. He had three kids and lived in a dirt floor shack with no doors or windows, and only an outside toilet and a hose for water. He wanted ten dollars a day, so we put him to work for twelve dollars a day. Then we found out he lived quite far away, and was taking three buses to get here at a cost of three dollars a day. We upped his wage to fifteen dollars a day. He turned out to be a really hard worker and spoke a little English. Sometimes we took him downtown with us as a translator and he helped me a lot in learning Spanish. We gave him a lot of stuff for his home, and when his wife had their fourth baby, we had him get a list from his wife of things she needed. We took him downtown and bought a shopping cart full of stuff. Whenever we gave him too much to carry on the buses, we took him home. He worked for us for nearly a year before he found something closer to home.

The Jungle

We met a gal who worked for the Smithsonian Institute as a scientist and we became very good friends. I loved hiking in the jungle with her; she knew so much about the insects and plants, so I learned a lot. We called her the bird whisperer because she had such a way with birds. In her spare time, she rescued parrots and had a large aviary at her home. Rachelle got involved with doing the same thing and I built an aviary at our house. Of course, we started taking in parrots. We adopted two parrots ourselves and what a joy! Ceaser and Pokiata. Ceaser was a fast learner. I taught him quite a few tunes to whistle like the Navy and Marine Corps hymns, "Pop Goes the Weasel," "Old Macdonald," and more. Sometimes he would mix them all up, so you never knew what he was going to whistle.

After many years, our friend with the Smithsonian took a job with the U.S. Agriculture Department and became the director of fly sterilization in Panama. They sterilized millions of flies a week and flew out over the agricultural areas and released them. They did this in Mexico and Guatemala.

We planted lots of trees and plants. I planted over one hundred banana plants, seventy-five pineapple, thirty mango, and grew lots of papaya and avocado from seed. From the forest, I dug up one hundred coffee plants birds had helped start, and transplanted them to our property. I also transplanted countless palms and Heliconia from the forest. We also hunted orchids in the forest, especially after a bad storm which often knocked down trees that had orchids attached.

We had a large fountain in the front yard. It was about ten feet tall and had three tiers. I redid it and put in a new pump. During the dry season especially, the birds just flocked to it. We took much pleasure in watching all the different kinds of birds (and sometimes animals) that came for a bath or just a drink. When I remodeled the kitchen, I put the sink in front of the window so it looked out on the fountain. Morgan just loved the fountain. She would go absolutely crazy, flipping and flapping in the water.

We hadn't sold Mom's property yet, and I received a letter from the county, telling me I had thirty days to move my Aunt Maddie's mobile home or there would be fines. They said it was too close to the road and needed to be moved back. I thought, *That's bullshit! The place has been there long enough that it must be grandfathered in.* I got a hold of my lawyer and he said the same thing. It was grandfathered, but (and there's always that but!), they could tie up the sale of the property for quite a while if I decided to fight it.

After I got over being pissed off, I decided to give it away. Rachelle and I had fixed it up real nice inside; in fact, it had a lot of new stuff inside that we had just bought. I got with the real estate agent that I had used for the log cabins and told him to find a needy family for it. He told me he already had one in mind, and would talk to them. He got back with me right away, and yes, they would accept it. It turned out that the family was on Robinson Road. That was so unique because I had spent the first five years of my life on Robinson Road. My father had worked the dairy farm for Franklin Robinson who owned hundreds of acres on both sides of that road. We had lived directly across from the dairy barn in a converted chicken coop with tar paper sides and cardboard on the inside walls. We had no running water, but we had a well, and an outhouse. There were two light bulbs hung from the ceiling and a wire stretched across the room with sheets hanging down that separated the beds from the rest of the coop. My mom had three more children while we lived in that coop and another one after we moved to a shack in Newfoundland, so Robinson Road had a special place in my heart. It was ironic that I was able to donate a home to a needy family in that same place.

A pickup pulled in the driveway and four locals jumped out of the truck headed for the house. I met them halfway. They were all excited about something they wanted me to see. In the back of the truck was a seven-foot Fer-de-lance snake with its head missing. They had been clearing a lot down the street when they found it. The word had gotten around that I was the crazy American snake guy. The snake looked like it might have babies, so I pulled it out of the truck and cut it open. The heart was still beating. The men couldn't believe it; they had never seen anything like that. When I cut a little farther, I pulled fourteen live babies out of it. Then they were really taken aback.

People and Wildlife

When we first moved to Cerro Azul, there were very few people. Rachelle and I often rode around trying to find other Americans; we did, but very few. There were a lot more Europeans than Americans, and we found out right away that Americans were the only people that spoke only one language. Everyone else spoke five or six or more languages. Canadians started showing up too, and over the years, we had a lot of them, but only during their winter. Because of their six-month rule, that was as long as they could stay. The first few years were pretty quiet, but when people started moving in more, the place became a lot more fun. There were always dinners or parties or BBQs going on somewhere. Rachelle and I got involved in some of the local Panamanian things going on, especially at Christmas. At Christmas, a group of us collected donations, went into town (usually at the Chinese stores), and bought hundreds of gifts. Then we had a big gift-wrapping party. On the day before Christmas, we drove all over the mountain in a caravan, handing out gifts to all the local children.

A Man Returns

An American couple we met at a dinner party (and with whom we later became best friends) played Santa Claus. He had the Santa suit and the whole nine yards.

He came here from Nebraska where he had a heavy equipment training academy. Through the United Nations, he certified heavy equipment operators for the canal expansion. He found out pretty quickly that anybody connected with the canal was crooked. He was told right away that he was not to fail anyone. Not too long after he started certifying trainees, the payoffs started. If that wasn't bad enough, when his contract came up for renewal they wanted part of that. He had finally had enough and went back to the States. It was a shame because he was making really good money. I used to wonder why in the world the U.S. just gave the canal to Panama, but the longer we lived in Panama and the more corruption we found, the more I realized it was probably the best thing to do. By the time the wealthy people took their share of the canal money, there wasn't much left over for the people who really needed it.

The forest around us had many trails and roads. Most roads required four-wheel drive. We spent a lot of our time driving these roads, which our FJ cruiser was well adapted for, or hiking the trails. One of our favorite places to see was Romeo and Juliet, twin waterfalls about an hour's hike into the forest. It was where two rivers came together to form one river. There was a large pool there for swimming, and you could jump off the top of the falls into this pool. It seemed to be a favorite place for different kinds of monkeys. They could be seen jumping across the rivers in the treetops. I discovered that the butterflies used the rivers as highways so they could fly through the forest unobstructed. It was really cool to see them navigate the falls by flying either up them or down them. The Menelaus Blue Morpho butterfly was seen here a lot; they were so gorgeous with wingspans from five to eight inches. When snorkeling below the falls, I discovered large bright red, white, and blue crabs. I couldn't believe it. The rivers were a big adventure; the wildlife and plant life were awesome, and the trees that grew along the river were gigantic.

During the dry season when the rivers weren't raging, two of my friends and I would go what we called rock-hopping, which was getting in the middle of the river and following it for hours into the jungle, either hopping from rock to rock or just wading. All the different rivers in the mountains were full of rocks, and I mean, gigantic ones and lots of them. I really loved doing this. We were always looking for different rivers to explore, or a road to a different part of a river we had already done. Panama had gold mines here and there; on occasion, I would pan for gold in some of the rivers. I never found any, but it was sure fun trying.

We had to go to the airport one day to pick up our sailboat friend (the one we met running the café in Stuart and later built a log cabin for). Well, that's what Rachelle told me anyway. As I was standing in the waiting area waiting for our friend to get through the lines, I spotted a guy that looked just like my son. I said, "Hey babe, doesn't that guy look just like my son, Chris?" I looked again, and this time the guy broke into a big smile. I turned toward Rachelle and she was smiling too. *Holy shit*, I thought, *it is Chris!* She had pulled off a big surprise, but that wasn't all there was to it. There was another surprise: he had an Australian Shepherd puppy with him that he had brought from Florida. My daughter, Kathleen, the vet, had taken care of all the paperwork. I turned to Rachelle, still smiling, and she said, "Happy early birthday, sweetheart." Oh, my goodness, the cutest little puppy; she was a tricolor with one blue eye. We named her Cash or *Efectivo* in Spanish. We named her Cash because of how much money it took to buy her and get her there.

A few months later, Rachelle travelled to Missouri to see her mother. She timed it so that she could pick up another Australian

A Man Returns

Shepherd she had picked out on the internet. It was a male this time: a blue merle, and he was just as gorgeous as Cash. I had never owned two dogs at the same time before, and I wasn't sure how I was going to love them both at the same time, but I found out that it was not a problem. We named him Tango. With Cash being Cash, we had to name him Tango after the movie, *Tango and Cash*. We waited two years before we let them mate, and at 9 a.m. on Easter morning, Cash walked across the living room and started dropping puppies, five of them. Instead of Easter bunnies, we had Easter puppies—three females and two males. The two males didn't make it, which was pretty upsetting. I buried them on El Cerro Jefe under a large eucalyptus tree.

I can't even begin to tell you how much fun we had with five shepherds running around. We found good homes for two of them, and kept the one that was mostly white with two blue eyes. We named her Kayro, and what an awesome addition to our family. Everyone told

Cash, Tango, and Kayro in Panama

us we would probably lose them to snakes, but that never happened. Tango and Cash both got torn up by a coatimundis, a tropical member of the raccoon family, and that was a bad ordeal.

Chris stayed a month and we had a great time. We did the tourist thing—the canal, shopping, the Indians, and sightseeing, but mostly, we explored the forest. We did a dive trip on the Caribbean side to Isla Grande. A friend of ours owned a very nice place on the island, and they let us stay there. On the way out, we stopped at a dive shop and picked up a couple of tanks, but had the rest of the dive gear already as I had brought it from the States. We found a secure gated place to park the FJ, and then found a local to take us to the island, about a forty-five-minute trip. We found the path to our friend's place. It was on top of a hill with a gorgeous view. We had dinner along the beach at one of the local restaurants followed by a few beers on the water. The area is a real tropical paradise. My friend had given me the number of a local guide and set up the dive trip. We contacted him, set a time for the morning, and turned in.

I woke early the next morning to a downpour and my cell phone ringing. It was Rachelle Skyping me. She had been struck by a snake late yesterday evening, and wasn't able to get a hold of me because the power was out. I had the car, so she couldn't go anywhere and couldn't contact anyone. She was a little scared and had had a rough night. She put her foot in ice off and on, and she could see the two puncture holes on the side of her foot. Her foot had turned black overnight, she was nauseous, and had slept off and on. Nando had come and checked on her, but there was nothing he could do. He felt bad because I had asked him to keep an eye on her. I told her we were headed home, but we were a long way from there, about six hours. She told me she thought she was okay, but I told her I was headed home. Chris and I packed in a hurry and headed down the hill to the docks in a heavy rain. There was not a soul around, and it was another

A Man Returns

hour before my dive guide would be there. I tried calling with no answer. The rain was not letting up. About a half hour went by and a fisherman showed up. I made him an offer he couldn't refuse, and he took us to the mainland in his panga, a small boat, in the downpour.

We headed home and the rain was relentless. We dropped off the two full dive tanks and thanked them anyway. There was only one highway that ran from Colón to Panama City and we ran into a huge backup. We finally found out it was a roadblock. They were checking cars. Somebody had robbed a tourist in Colón, which was a common occurrence. People came from all over to shop the duty-free shop in Colón. They liked to rob tourists on the way to Colón because they knew they usually had large amounts of cash. One of the ways they robbed them was to dress up like police, put a couple blue lights in their car, and then just pull them over.

We finally made it home, and Rachelle was doing fine. Even with icing, her foot still swelled up. It was pretty scary for her: home alone, no car, no electricity, no phone, and no one close by except for Nando, and he felt bad because there was nothing he could do.

On one of our hikes into the forest, we found a huge, I think, mahogany tree. It was only about forty feet tall. It had probably been hit by lightning a number of times, and then finally died. It had a large hole in it next to the ground, like a doghouse. We shined a light in there, and it was huge inside. It was so big that Chris was able to climb inside and stand up and move around. I climbed partway in. Shining our lights around, we found bats hanging from the ceiling, all kinds of spiders, one snake, several scorpions, and all kinds of bugs. There was a root that ran off from it along the ground that was three feet in diameter and hollow, large enough to crawl through. It ran out about thirty feet from the trunk, tapering as it went. It also had a large hole at the end like an escape hole. I pulled a vine down and we wrapped it around the tree, head high, and broke the vine to mark the diameter, and put the vine in my backpack. When we got back, I laid the vine out on the back porch and measured it. It was twelve and a half feet in diameter. I have a picture of Chris standing up inside the tree.

Chris's time with us came to an end and I hated to see him leave. We had such a great time exploring the forest. Rachelle liked to hike the forest but she didn't enjoy *leaving* the trails, and I cared nothing for staying *on* the trails.

More Changes

I gutted our kitchen and took out the wall between the kitchen and dining room. I put in a new tile floor and built all new cabinets out of cedar. Rachelle wanted drawers, so I built half of the cabinets with large pullout drawers. I made the backsplash and most of the trim with bamboo I harvested from the jungle. The countertops were made from the *corotú* tree, also known as the Elephant Ear and other names. Its wood is very dense and water resistant. I relocated the sink in front of the window where it should have been in the first place.

I had several vegetable gardens growing year round. I also grew Panama Red cannabis year round.

I got involved with Panama University's herpetology department and captured venomous snakes for their antivenom program. Whenever I captured a snake, I called the professor and he and the snake handler came up the mountain and picked it up. I caught several very rare snakes, one of which was a Panama coral snake. When I called the professor, he didn't believe me. He told me the only Panama coral snakes they'd ever seen were dead on the road. Two professors came up the next day; they were so excited. That snake threw up a snake almost as long as it was.

A Man Returns

I took the herpetology class out to the forest at night a couple of times and we hunted venomous snakes and scorpions. We only found non-venomous snakes, but lots of scorpions which we hunted with black lights.

I kept aquariums around, containing snakes, scorpions, lizards, and tarantulas, including the huge Goliath birdeater spider, the largest of the tarantulas, just so people could see them.

I also captured hundreds of insects and butterflies, and mounted them in glass cases for people to see.

Over the years, I studied a lot of insects. A few of my favorite were the zebra butterfly, one of the longest living butterflies, the golden orb weaver, the tarantula wasp, and the hooded mantis; but by far, my favorite was the moss mimic stick insect. When I first spotted one, I couldn't believe my eyes. The tree it was hanging on was covered in moss just like the bug, and it was also covered in orchids, the bug's favorite food. It became a challenge every day to find it again. Sometimes the only way I could spot it was by its gentle swaying back and forth. I ended up studying the stick bug for three years. I never saw one mate, but they did and the female laid eggs. The way they mated was fascinating. In the fall when they started popping out their eggs, I kept a close eye on them to watch them launch them. The egg would ease out into a cradle, and just above the cradle, was a small opening that oozed out a liquid that coated the egg. The egg reminded me of a micro pineapple. It would lie there for a short while and the liquid would dry. Then the cradle would slowly drop for a short distance, as if cocking your arm to throw, and that's exactly what it would do. It would release the cradle and sling the egg several feet away from the tree onto the ground. Every year I would place a tarp on the ground and catch several of the eggs, but I never had any luck in getting them to hatch. I found out later that the eggs needed a little help from the ants. When the eggs hatched, the little ones make their way back to the tree; they looked like they were made from white threads. I had three trees in the yard that had plenty of moss and orchids on them, so when I'd see the little ones, I would catch them, and put them on the different trees because they would kill each other off until there was only one left. I didn't have any luck doing that because each year I would still end up with only one stick insect on the original tree. Over the years I found lots of different kinds of stick bugs, some of them measuring over a foot long but none of them as cool as the moss mimic stick insect.

Every now and again, I would have what I called "Black Light Night." I would invite a bunch of friends over and hang a white sheet on the party patio with a black light in the middle of it and turn out all the lights. It wouldn't take long before all kinds of insects began showing up—mostly moths, but you never knew what you were going to attract. It was a lot of fun. Rachelle took dozens and dozens of macro pictures; they were awesome. Most of the moths looked like little jewels, like something you would pin on your blouse. I framed a lot of insects and brought them back to the States.

We made a few dollars taking care of the homes of snowbirds when they were gone. We also picked them up or took them to the airport. We also took care of any work that needed to be done on their homes.

I developed a very bad skin rash and spent a lot of money on different doctors and treatments. All kinds of treatments, and when I say all kinds, I mean all kinds. One of the guys I knew told me about a medicine man that lived in the forest. We took an all-day hike to his village and I showed him my problem, which by now was pretty bad. He thought he could help me. We spent the night in the village, and he gathered all kinds of stuff to make up a concoction. In the morning, he gave me two large soda bottles full of this black liquid which didn't smell very good. He told me to drink a glassful in the morning and evening. We hiked back out of the forest and that evening I took a drink of the stuff. It was terrible, and I had to pour it all out.

Finally after years of suffering, a doctor in downtown Panama put me on steroids. After taking the first pill, my body started settling down, and by the second day, I was a new man. Little did I know what the steroids were going to do in the long haul.

After years of feeding the animals and birds we became quite popular. We were going through a lot of bread, seed, and bananas. The hummingbird population grew until it was almost out of hand. Hundreds of them and all kinds. We were going through, without exaggerating, three gallons of sugar water a day, and in November when the migrants came through, we went through four gallons a day. I had to bag the feeders at night because the fruit bats would come in, smother the feeders, and leave bat shit everywhere.

We had lots of Audubon people there, taking pictures. We also had the Discovery Channel people to our house several times. *The New York Times* did a full-page story on us, complete with pictures. There were not too many homes where you could see the Pacific Ocean and the Caribbean Ocean from your porch. We had a two-million-dollar view. On the Fourth of July and New Year's, we would have as many as sixty to seventy people, partying and watching Panama City come alive with fireworks. One year people brought nearly $2,000 worth of fireworks to set off. We ended up having to move the fireworks to another location because of our dogs.

A Caterpillar Sting?

One morning Rachelle asked me to check the back of her neck; she had some burning and itching going on. I took a look at it and it looked just like a caterpillar sting; not much we could do about it. I told her it should go away by morning.

You always hear people talk about the dangers in the forest: the snakes, ants, scorpions, and bees, but you never hear anything about caterpillars. Well, I'm here to tell you that I've been stung and bitten by a lot of different creatures, and the caterpillar sting ranks way up there on the pain chart. The bad thing about a caterpillar sting is that it stays with you. The puss caterpillar is very bad. I've been stung by them several times. One time I got stung on both hands multiple times. The poison travels up your lymph glands to the inside of your elbow, stopping in your armpit, so you not only have the pain where the caterpillar contacted you, but also in the inside of your elbow and your armpit. I've tried all the different things that are supposed to help for it, but they don't. You will go to bed with it, and if you're lucky, when you wake up the pain will have subsided and all you will have is the cat tracks.

Unfortunately, Rachelle did not have a caterpillar sting. When she got up the next morning, the rash had spread and the burning and the itching were more intense. We went down the mountain to Panama City to an ER. They told us it was a caterpillar sting. We argued that a caterpillar sting did not spread, but they wouldn't listen. The next day it had spread even farther and she made an appointment with a doctor she had seen before. He took one look at it, and said she had the shingles. He gave her a Vitamin B12 shot and a Vitamin C IV drip. It spread over her shoulder and partway down her chest before it stopped. She went to see him for one more Vitamin C drip. It took a while, but it finally cleared up.

Rachelle and I loved to fish in salt and fresh water. Since we'd been together, we had fished a lot and Panama was no different. There was a small lake in the community that we fished quite often. We caught tilapia and a fish that looked just like brim. There was a large fish that we caught called a "paca"; it was a fruit eater and had molars like a human to grind the fruit. Our most popular fishing by far was for peacock bass in Gatun Lake. We knew an American that had two pontoon boats, and for $110, he supplied the boat, the guide, and the shiners, and you were good for the whole day. Usually four or five of us went, and we would catch a couple hundred bass for the day. In one trip, we caught 350 bass. We only kept the bass, but we also caught mojarras, snook tarpon, and tilapia. The scenery was gorgeous; and if we fished close enough to the channel, we could see the huge ships traversing the lake.

After a long day of fishing who wanted to clean a couple hundred fish? The guide and usually one of his buddies would fillet the fish for ten cents each! Who could turn that down? Sometimes we would split the fish up amongst us, but most of the time, we had a huge fish fry and invited everyone.

Driving and Ninja Cops

Driving in Panama was always an adventure and I have plenty of stories, but one trip really sticks out in my mind. We had taken Cash down the mountain to get fixed and that all went well. On our way back, we were in line at a toll booth to get on the Corridor Sur when a car full of young Panamanians tried to get in front of us. I was in the back of the FJ with Cash, and Rachelle was driving. They kept trying to inch forward and we were up against a wall on our left, so we couldn't move over. They couldn't see me, and they started to get aggressive. A couple of them got out of their car and started pounding on our hood for us to let them in. I climbed into the front seat and rolled the window down and yelled at them. I couldn't open the door because they were tight against us. They got back in their car and Rachelle eased forward. Our brush guard put a nice crease in their fender and they backed off and we went through the toll booth.

Once through the toll booth, Rachelle put the pedal to the metal to 90 mph. I was watching out the back and they hadn't got through right away so I couldn't see them coming. Then I saw them. They were driving crazy, even driving on the median, trying to catch us. We knew there was a large toll plaza just ahead and there were always ninja cops there. We called all the motorcycle cops "ninja cops" because of the way they looked: two cops to a bike all in black, wearing thick bulletproof vests, carrying automatic weapons. We could see the plaza; Rachelle started blowing the horn and flashing our lights.

About that time, they came across traffic and slammed on their brakes in front of us. Cars went flying everywhere and Rachelle slammed on the brakes and slid sideways. I looked out at the plaza and the ninja cops arrived with lights and sirens. All the traffic had come to a stop. The boys in the car took off with one of the motorcycle cops in pursuit. The other bike pulled alongside of us and told us to pull over to the side of the road. About that time it started to pour, so the cops told us to pull through the plaza to the overpass just ahead, and we did so. We figured we were toast, but there wasn't much we could do right now. The other cops had caught the other car and they were also pulling to the overpass. We got out and fortunately one of the cops spoke some English. Two other cars pulled up, and the people in them got out, and to our surprise, told the officers what had happened. Wow! Like I always say, better to be lucky than good.

The boys got out of their car. There were five of them, and one was waving an American flag, yelling that he loved Americans. They were all drunk. The officer who had chased them saw them throwing beer cans out of the car. The ninja cops took all our info and told us we would have to wait for a traffic cop, since they didn't handle traffic problems. So we waited. The rain finally stopped and it got hot as hell again. One of our friends from the mountain pulled up and we told them what had happened. They ended up taking Cash to our house, where it was a little less hectic. It turned out that one of the boys worked at the American embassy and his father was some important guy. After about an hour, a big black Cadillac pulled up and a well-dressed man got out and walked over to the police officer.

At the same time, a well-dressed woman got out, walked over to the boy who was waving the flag, and took him with her, yelling and shaking him. Then, the officer came over to us and wanted to know if we were going to press charges against these guys. I asked him if he was kidding. We were just trying to go home. He walked to the Cadillac people and talked to them. Then, *all* the boys came over and offered us their sincere apologies. They made all five boys apologize. We got in our car, breathed a sigh of relief, and headed home.

The one ninja cop was very nice and we talked a bit. He gave us his personal cell phone number and told us he patrolled from the plaza to the city. If we ever had a problem, we could call him. Every once in a while, we saw him at the plaza and we blew our horn. He would always wave and smile.

Arthritis was taking over both my hands. Three fingers were affected on each hand. It was not a big problem except that I had to give up my guitar, which was kind of a blow. The doctor told me that as we age, things start to surface like the arthritis and that damn skin condition. I liked to think of myself as getting older, but not getting old. It sounded better. The major problem with getting older is that you start losing things like friends, family, hair, eyesight, hearing, balance, and let's not forget that bad one—memory. Hey, they say age is just a number, and I was going to try and live by that.

The Monkeys and Other Animals

The most popular monkeys at one of our feeders were the Geoffroy's tamarin; they came most every day, and usually in a group. They liked the bananas. Off and on, we would be visited by the white-throated capuchin. Very seldom did we see the mantled howler monkey, but we heard them most every day, especially when it rained. It always sounded like they were playing in the rain. The white-nosed coatis were regular visitors. The tayras came around off and on. They were mistaken a lot for jaguars. If they looked straight at you, you could see a white diamond on their chest. I mentioned the three- and two-toed sloths. They came by quite regularly. We also had capybara, agouti, paca, anteaters, olingo, rabbits, and deer. We never did get to see any of the cats, not even on our hikes. If you went for a hike in the forest, even regularly, you would be hard-pressed to see any of these animals. The reason we saw a lot of them was because we put food out.

The squirrel population would sometimes get out of control. Usually when that happened we could count on our resident boa to take care of them. We ate most of our meals on the deck, and one morning we were having breakfast and noticed that the squirrels were very loud. I looked to see what all the fuss was about, and found a large, nine-foot boa coiled up on a pine branch just off our deck. A squirrel would run up the tree and onto the branch the boa was on, and chatter at him. We sat there eating breakfast and watched the show. The squirrel ran out on the branch again, but this time the boa nailed it. All in one move, it wrapped it up and squeezed it to death with the squirrel screaming. Then the boa hung his head down with the squirrel in its mouth and slowly swallowed it. While we sat there, he did it two more times, ending with three large lumps in its belly. That took care of the squirrel overpopulation for a while.

One day we had a small boa, about five feet long, hanging from the roof of the bird and animal feeder. I watched it grab a squirrel and crush it between the tree and its body. He then let it drop to the ground and slithered down to it. He got the head of the squirrel in its mouth, but it was too big for him to swallow. Not a problem.

A Man Returns

It braced itself against a small tree, put the squirrel against the big tree, and then kind of forced the squirrel down its throat by pushing against the small tree.

We had lots and lots of birds of all kind. The most popular of course were the hummingbirds. Some of my favorites were the toucans, crested guan, chachalaca, kite, roadside hawk, squirrel cuckoo, potoo, motmot, masked tityra, ornate hawk-eagle, and last but not least, the Montezuma oropendola. I brought one of their nests back with me. They lived in colonies and their nests hung from the trees. The nest was made of sticks, leaves, and pine needles all woven together. It was about two feet long and six to eight inches in diameter at the bottom. They entered the nest from the top. Legend had it that the oropendola wais attracted to shiny objects and would pick them up and take them back to its nest. Well, Panama had gold here and there. It was said that the Indians used to knock the nests down to check them for gold. I thought the oropendolas were very cool. They also made a couple cool sounds, one of which sounded like water dropping into a bucket.

The Panama Canal expansion was going on while we lived there and they built a visitor's center overlooking the expansion. It was quite a project. The visitor's center didn't open until the expansion was almost complete. They had so many problems that kept delaying the opening, but they did finally let the first mega ship through in 2016, just before we left.

The cecropia tree was a very important tree in Panama with over sixty species. It was the go-to food for the three- and two-toed sloths. One of the species had huge leaves. I found one in the forest and cut one of the leaves down. It was almost six feet in diameter. I took it to one of the houses we took care of that had dehumidifiers and laid it on the floor with plywood on top to keep it flat. I left it there for a month to dry out; it shrunk almost a foot. I sprayed it with two cans of clear coat and it turned out nice. I decided I was going to take it to the States whenever we headed back. I sandwiched it between two sheets of plywood in a bed of newspapers. I thought it would look really cool hanging on a wall. I found out later from our mover that it might put our shipment in quarantine and hold everything up, so I gave it to a friend who was very excited to get it.

Changing Course Abruptly

I started having all kinds of problems with my body. I had a lot of swelling going on. My hair started falling out, my nails started disintegrating, and my eyes were doing strange things. I bruised very easily and my skin would just peel off if a dog scratched me or I scraped something. I went to see my doctor and he freaked out, telling me he didn't realize I was still on steroids. They were causing all the problems. He started me on a decrease in steroids schedule and said I should start to get better. Well, things got a lot worse. If I put a bandage on and then removed it, it took my skin with it. After several weeks, my rash and itching came back and I felt terrible.

We started talking about moving back to the States. We had been in Panama for nearly ten years. Our families were putting pressure on us to move back. We had gone back to the States several times. We would rent a house on the beach in Florida and tell our friends and family to come and visit us there. The problem with that was that we had family all over the States. We had sixteen grandchildren and hadn't seen half of them.

Then one night, our whole world got turned upside down. I woke about midnight and my stomach was killing me. I got up and walked around and tried to get in positions that would help with the pain, but it kept getting worse and I could tell my stomach was swelling. I woke Rachelle and told her what was going on; she offered to make

A Man Returns

me some tea. I told her I was putting my pajamas on and getting in the car. We needed to go to the emergency room right now. She called a friend to let her know what was going on, and that she may have to take care of our animals in the morning. We headed down the mountain and the rough road was killing me. It was about an hour down the mountain if you didn't run into a problem, and then another hour into the city. Rachelle was headed to the city (to the John Hopkins-affiliated hospital) or what everyone called the "rich man's hospital."

One the way, there was another hospital, the social security hospital or the "poor man's hospital." It did not have a very good reputation. Well, I was in so much pain, I asked Rachelle to stop there, which she did not want to do. We went into the ER, and I'm sure I looked like a crazy gringo. What hair I had left was sticking up like Einstein, and I was wearing a torn T-shirt and pirate pajamas. She told them what was going on and they handed her a clipboard with papers to fill out, all in Spanish and told her to take a number. She told them that I needed to see someone now and they told her all the people sitting over there were ahead of us. She looked at me and said it was my call. I said let's go. I could barely walk. When we got to the John Hopkins hospital, she ran in to get someone, and they came right out with a gurney and loaded me up. They started running all kinds of tests and decided to do an MRI of my stomach. They stripped me down, put me in a gown, laid me on the MRI table, covered me with a sheet, and we waited for the machine to get warmed up. They also gave me some nasty stuff to drink. Well, it was freezing in there and my whole body started shaking, so they brought a blanket out. I still kept shaking, and then all of a sudden, I threw up all that nasty stuff they gave me. I continued to shake and they couldn't put me in the machine until I stopped shaking. They brought more blankets out and wrapped me like a cocoon. It was quite some time before they could put me in the machine, but they finally got it done. They rolled me into the hallway and there I lay for what felt like forever. I was in so much pain, I just knew I was dying. I don't know how much time went by, and I wondered where Rachelle was. I found out later she was in their office, trying to convince them we were good for the $10,000 they wanted before they would do the surgery needed. They wanted cash and she told them in the morning when our broker got in her office, she would wire the money. They went ahead and called the surgeon in and the surgical team, but if she didn't come up with the money they were sending me to the social security hospital. I was lying in the hallway, thinking they had forgotten about me when a pretty young woman came up to me, took my hand, and told me that they were taking me to surgery and that she was the lead surgeon in charge. She then told me my colon had ruptured. They were going to do a colostomy. She further explained that they were going to cut me open, take a section of my colon out, sew one end closed, pull the other end out of my belly, and attach a bag to it, and that I would be pooping in a bag! Then she left! My head was just spinning. I was thinking, *Are you kidding me? Is this for real? After all, I am in a third world country. This can't be happening! Just yesterday, I was doing fine, except for the itching and steroid side effects.* A short time later, a couple of guys rolled my bed into a brightly lit room full of people and I remember seeing a clock; it was 8:30.

Rachelle reached our broker and she had wired the money.

I don't remember the recovery room at all. I remember waking up in the ICU to bright lights hooked up to all kinds of machines. My surgeon who looked to be about twenty years old explained what I had just gone through. I had spent five hours in surgery. They had split my belly wide open and had to remove all my guts to clean everything. The colon had leaked all throughout my stomach. They had removed a tumor the size of a baseball that was attached to my colon.

A Man Returns

They had also removed a section of colon. I didn't know at the time but they had sent the tumor out to be checked for cancer.

Rachelle had to wait three days before she found out it was benign. They believed that the combination of the tumor and the thinning of my tissues due to overuse of steroids may have caused the rupture. She told me that I wasn't out of the woods yet though. Infection was going to be a key factor in me making it. She also told me that there was a chance that I might be able to be reconnected in six months.

My arms were a bloody mess. They had used tape everywhere to hold tubes and needles and when they had removed the tape, it took my skin. I'm here to tell you that both my arms are scarred to this day. They also had to remove the circulation boots from my legs because they had bruised my legs so badly.

In the meantime Rachelle had to come up with another $10,000 for me to remain in the ICU.

It was touch and go, and I stayed in the ICU for nine days until they finally let me have a regular room. I never cried so much from the outpouring of support from all my friends. One of our friends set up a to-go fund and raised several thousand dollars toward my hospital bills.

I never spent a night alone. There was always a friend staying with me. My best friends, Jim and Sally, flew in from New Mexico and stayed three weeks helping out and they were a big help. You know you have a good friend when he helps you change out your poop bag.

I spent another four days in the hospital and we had to pay another $13,000 before they would release me.

I felt so bad for Rachelle. She had a lot on her shoulders while I was down. But even with all that going on, she managed to sell our house while I was in the hospital. She sold it to a Spanish guy who was living in China setting up an import-export business. The good thing was that he didn't want to move in for six months, so that gave us a lot of time to get all our ducks in a row.

They had told Rachelle I had a 30 percent chance of making it. Well, they must have done a good job because I was coming along very well. I had forty-five staples up the front of me from near my Johnson to just below the bottom of my sternum, and I was a happy camper when they finally pulled all them out. I lost over twenty pounds. It was slow going to get my strength back and I tired easily.

Rachelle stayed busy up and down the mountain, taking care of all the paperwork involved in selling a house in Panama and closing out everything else. I did as much packing as I could. We had several offers on the cruiser and decided to sell instead of taking it back; after all, it was ten years old.

We secured a shipper and it was going to cost us $2,200 to ship our stuff to Florida, and it would take two to three weeks. We were also busy trying to find a house. After months of looking, we finally found a four-bedroom, two-bath house on two and a half acres in North Central Florida. We had friends look at several places for us and they really liked this one. We also had deeded lake rights with this house. Our friends put a deposit down for us. We also had to get all the paperwork for our three dogs and two cats along with airline-approved carriers. We decided to leave Morgan, our macaw, with our diplomat friend. She would bring her back to the States later.

In the meantime I got myself re-registered with the Veterans Administration and tried to find out if they would do my reconnect.

I have to say that it was a life-changing situation, learning to deal with a bag attached to you and taking care of it.

My battle with the skin rash and the steroids was not getting any better, and coupled with my fight to recover from the surgery, I wasn't doing very well. A very good friend of ours from New York who had a very nice place on the mountain asked Rachelle one day why we hadn't gone back to the States yet and put me in a VA hospital. Rachelle told him we couldn't buy our new place yet until we got the money for this place. He asked how much it was and she told him. He wrote out a check for the full amount and said, "Now, let's get Smitty back to the States where he can get the proper care." Well, that was a real surprise, and again, I still can't believe all the support I received from friends. That same friend bought my entire workshop, right down to the last nut and bolt.

In the middle of all the chaos, Rachelle got a call that her mom was not doing well. A few days later, she was told her mom had passed away. She flew back to the States for a week to take care of all of that. Upon her return, the first thing we had to do was get a closing date on our new home; everything would revolve around that date. Then there were the shippers and the airlines. We also had to renew our passports because we had less than six months left on them. It took a while to get all those ducks in a row.

Back to the USA

We decided I would fly out first with one of the cats. When I got to the first TSA check, they told me I had to take the cat out of the carrier and run the carrier through without the cat. I pleaded with them that with all the noise and everything, the cat might get loose, and with my skin the way it was, I was afraid she might tear me up. They didn't care. It wasn't their problem. So I took Spaz out of the carrier and held her close to me as tightly as possible. She wanted to squirm, but I was able to get her back into the carrier without a problem. When I finally got to my gate, they were already boarding, and I couldn't believe it, there was another TSA checkpoint. This guy told me the same thing: take the cat out of the carrier. I told him that I had already been through this and I didn't want to have to do it again. Well, again, take the cat out of the carrier. This time I wasn't so lucky. Spaz decided to make a break for it. I held her by the scruff of her neck, but she reached out and got me on the chest and arm. It was all I could do to get her back into the carrier. My chest and arms and shirt were a bloody mess. Everyone had already boarded the plane and I had no choice but to get on the plane like that. The stewardess gave me some paper towels to clean up. I flew into Tampa and my brother-in-law picked me up, and I spent the night there. The next day he dropped me off at the Orlando airport and I rented a large van.

We needed something big enough to hold the luggage and all the carriers. The dog carriers were huge. I met up with Rachelle and she had Mable, our other cat, and we headed to cargo to pick up our dogs. It was so good to see them, knowing that they had made it safe and sound. We spent the night in Orlando. It was fun in the hotel with all the animals. The next morning we headed to Palatka to meet the sellers and close on our new home, one we had just purchased sight unseen. When we pulled into the driveway, we both looked at each other and said, "We love it!" (without having seen the inside yet). It was only thirteen years old and they had only occasionally used it, so it was like new. It had a huge fenced area for the dogs and we let them go right away. Inside was also like new and we really liked it. We were lucky: they had left us a bed, couch, dresser, and a table with four chairs, plus some kitchenware.

It was a good thing they left us a few items because that two to three weeks our shipper had predicted turned into fourteen weeks. Yes, fourteen weeks. We started believing that our stuff was simply stolen, so when it finally did arrive and everything was there, we forgot about the fourteen weeks. We went to garage sales and thrift stores to get by because we didn't want to buy new, knowing we had our stuff, hopefully, coming. We settled right in and started making the place our own. The VA agreed to do the reconnect, thank goodness, so I had to do a lot of back and forth to the hospital for different tests, and then they put me on the schedule.

They also put me on a different steroid and told me that I should never have been on the one they gave me in Panama. They were also working on getting my skin problem resolved. I was still very miserable that the steroids really messed up my whole body. My hair got so thin that Rachelle had to cut my ponytail off.

Rachelle had to fly back to Panama to close on the sale of our house and to sign the papers on the sale of the FJ cruiser. She was only going to be gone a couple of days. But no, in Panama nothing is easy, and you have to pay everyone off to get anything done. What should have taken her two days took over two weeks and she had to get a lawyer involved to get it done.

A couple weeks before my surgery, Rachelle took a nasty fall and broke her leg, foot, and ankle on the right side, and broke her foot and leg on the left side. Yikes! Talk about doing it up right. That put her out of commission for a while. Lots and lots of trips to the doctor and therapy. I should have rescheduled my surgery, but I had been wearing the bag for a year and I was ready to get rid of it, and besides, I didn't know when the VA would be able to put me back on the schedule.

Rachelle was in a lot of pain and could barely get around. This was when friends and family came to the rescue again. Our friends from New Mexico flew in and stayed six weeks with us, and another friend from Panama came and stayed a week with us.

Rachelle's daughter took me to the VA hospital for my surgery. They put us up in a motel the night before. The surgery was only supposed to last a couple hours but they ran into a problem and it lasted five hours. I woke up in the recovery room, and I remember reaching down to where the bag used to be and it was gone. I thought alright, but then I felt something on my right side. *Holy shit, I had a bag on that side. What in the hell did they do?* I lay there remembering the stories of people getting the wrong operation while in a VA hospital. I was almost in a panic by the time someone came in and told me what had happened. I was now wearing a bag on my intestines. There was a problem with the surgery they had done in Panama. The surgeon explained that if she hadn't put a bag on my intestines I would have had to wear a bag on my colon for the rest of my life. Not only did I have a new bag, but I also had two large weep holes in my stomach to allow for drainage. She told me they would be able to reconnect me in about six months. I spent eleven days in the hospital, and my son, Chris, stayed with me the whole time. The VA had a nurse come by every day for two weeks to clean and repack my holes and then every other day for two weeks, and they healed up nicely. I was up and getting around fine the second day out of the hospital. I tired real fast though, and had to take it easy. My itching bothered me more than before the surgery.

Rachelle was getting around very carefully but she was in a lot of pain. She had to go to therapy for months. We couldn't have gotten through all that without our friends helping out.

Six months later, I was back in the VA hospital and again they put us up in a hotel the night before. The surgery only took two hours and I stayed in the hospital for less than three days. Wow! At this writing, I'm now bagless after a year and a half, and it feels great.

The VA finally got me off steroids and got my itching under control. It took many months for my body to finally bounce back from the steroid reaction. Funny thing is that when my hair grew back it came in curly and stayed that way for over a year.

Finally, after well over a year, we were both well enough to set out on another adventure. We found a housesitter on the internet, rented a Volvo, and headed out on the road for a five-week trip around the

USA. We visited friends and family, staying with them most of the trip. We also did a little sightseeing along the way. All and all, we put 6,500 miles on that Volvo and had one hell of a good time.

After the trip, we settled back into our house. We made a lot of changes to the place and I got back into my gardening. I also built a greenhouse and started doing hydroponics; that was a lot of fun. We bought a boat and did a lot of fishing. I got into metal detecting and bought an Excalibur II detector and put Grey Ghost headphones and an ultimate double-D coil on it. That made it a bad ass detector. Rachelle can attest to that. She has diamond rings on most of her fingers. I also got back into hiking and did all the trails in the area. Rachelle got back into sewing, making really nice quilts and embroidery. She also made purses and sold them on the internet.

Old age, hip issues, and several other problems got the best of Tango, and we had to put him down. It's never an easy thing. It takes a lot of time to get over the passing of your pet.

We did take in a new kitten that had been hanging around. Spaz and Mable weren't too happy about it, and we weren't too sure for a while if it was going to work out, but it did. We named him Motor because he purred so loudly all the time.

I stayed in touch with several of my Seawolf brothers on the phone and by visiting. It's kind of crazy, but even after all these years you still had a bond with these guys, one you can't explain. I received a newsletter from the Seawolf Association, and it was sad to see how many brothers we were starting to lose in every letter.

Finding One Last Home

After five years, we both started to get a little antsy, but it wasn't only that. We were tired of the county not maintaining our dirt road and having everything so far away. I hated to say it, but at our age we saw doctors more often and they were all a bit of a drive. I also wanted to move a little farther south where my plants wouldn't get frostbitten every winter. So, we started looking. After several months we found a very nice place that fit all the things we were looking for: one and a quarter acres on a lake, room between the neighbors, fenced backyard for the dogs, screened-in swimming pool, all tile floors, two fireplaces, open concept, and best of all, just ten minutes from everything. It wasn't quite as quiet as the other place, but the tradeoff was worth it. We were a little over an hour further south, so hopefully my plants would do better in the winter.

We had no trouble selling our place. The second people that looked at it bought it with cash.

On a sad note, shortly after we moved in, old age along with a few other problems got the best of our girl, Cash, and we had to put her down; she was almost fifteen years old. Today, Spaz and Mable are starting to show their age: they are both seventeen years old. Morgan is twenty-four, but she's just a youngster. And then there's Motor, our latest addition, and he is doing great. He is now going on four years old. Kayro is getting lots of love; she is thirteen, and so far so good.

We are settling into our new place just fine and having fun making it our own. Who knows how long we'll live here, but we are always ready for another adventure.

The journey is over for now, and I hope you enjoyed the ride. I know I did.

As they say, you only go around once, and it's only when you get older that you realize what that actually means. As we go through life, we make choices and hope that most of them are the right ones, but right or wrong, we made them and we have to live with them. Looking back over my shoulder, I've made some risky choices in my life, but I'm still living by my motto: Better to be lucky than good. That has always carried me through life. You can go through life playing

A Man Returns

it safe and taking the easy road, but for me, that just wasn't enough. I was always looking for the adventure, and getting a little more of something out of life.

I've already started my next book-writing adventure and the book is titled *Country Lane: Dirt Road beneath My Feet.*

IF YOU ENJOYED THIS BOOK, THERE ARE MANY WAYS TO HELP ME GET THE WORD OUT.

- Post a 5-Star review on Amazon, Goodreads and other places.
- Write about the book on your Facebook, Twitter, Instagram, Google+, any social media sites you regularly use, and use the entire title.
- If you blog, consider referencing the book, or publishing an excerpt from the book with a link back to my website: SeawolfAdventurer.com.
- Recommend the book to friends—word of mouth is still the more effective form of advertising.
- When you're in a bookstore, ask them if they carry the book. The book is available through all major distributors, so any bookstore that does not have it in stock can easily order it.
- Do you know a journalist or media personality who might be willing to interview me or write an article based on the book? If you will email mail me your contact, I will gladly follow up.
- Purchase additional copies to give away as gifts.

You can order additional copies of the book from my website, SeawolfAdventurer.com, as well as bookstores. To inquire about special bulk discounts, use the contact form there.

Ten percent of profits from the sale of the book will go to the Sunny Memorial animal relief fund.

If you would like to know more about the Seawolves go to: seawolf.org

If you are interested in the documentary of the Seawolves go to: scrambletheseawolves.com